TEED OFF
IN THE
U.S.A.

BY
JUSTIN BROWN

iPicturebooks
Habent Sua Fata Libelli

iPicturebooks
1230 Park Avenue
New York, New York 10128
Tel: 212-427-7139
bricktower@aol.com • www.BrickTowerPress.com

Library of Congress Cataloging-in-Publication Data

Brown, Justin.
Teed Off in the U.S.A.
p. cm.
1. Sports & Recreation. 2. Golf—General
I. Title.

978-1-876963-15-6, Trade Paper

Copyright © 2006 by Justin Brown

November 2012

For Amy

To all those wonderful Americans who could see the point
in a pointless adventure, thank you for your spirit and generosity.

Special thanks also to www.heybarn.com.
The Golf House and Telecom Mobile.

CONTENTS

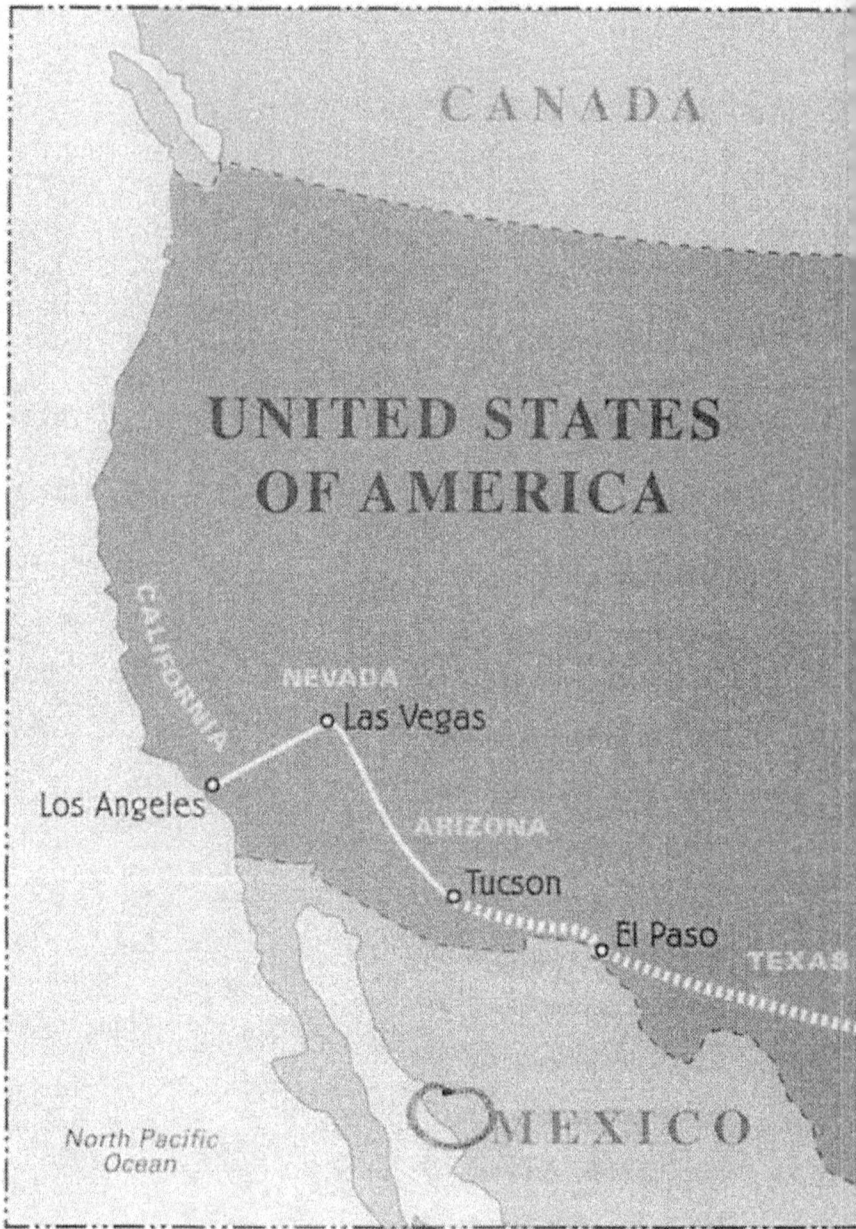

Justin's route around the USA

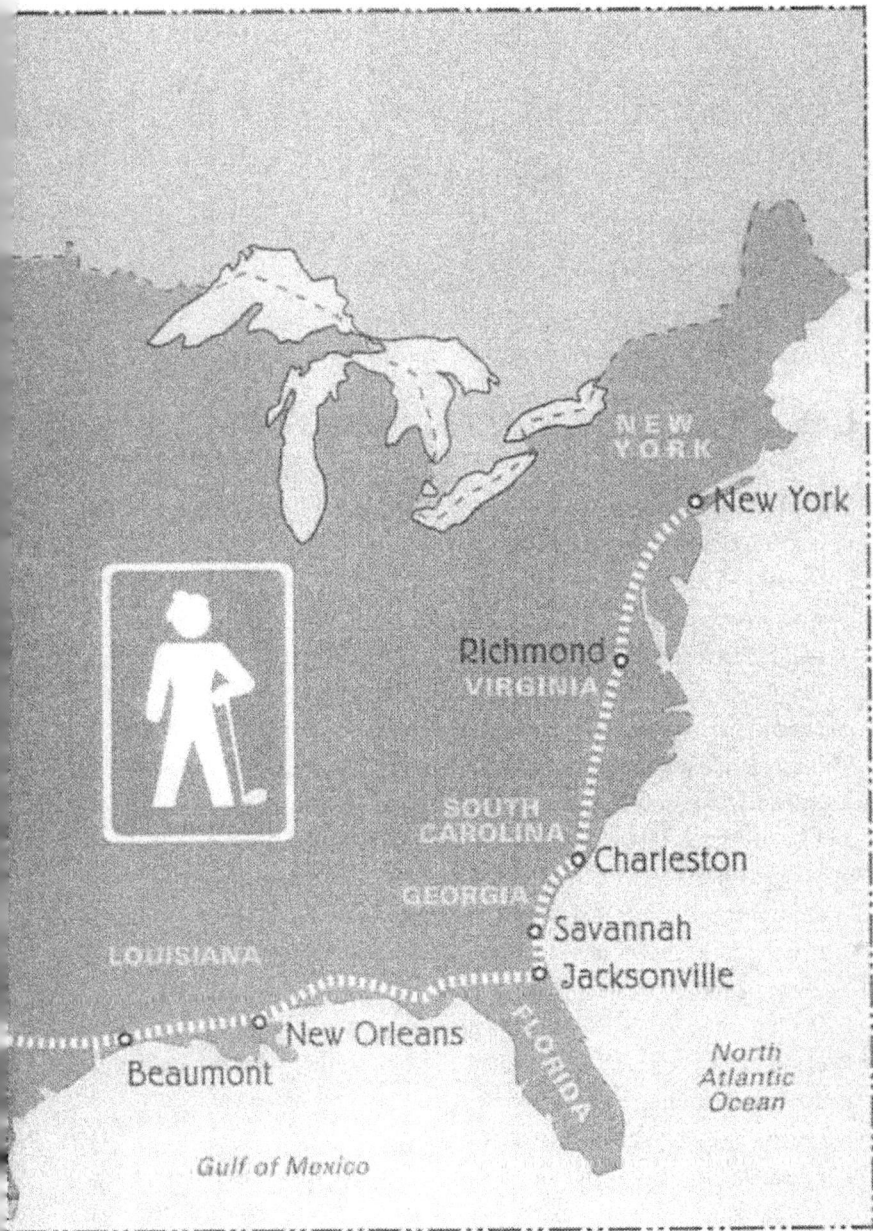

DAY 1: LAX, LOS ANGELES, CALIFORNIA

THREE PEOPLE I would have had to play golf with had I been staying in Los Angeles:

Donald Rumsfeld

André Agassi

Buddy Hackett.

Thankfully, I was only in transit on the way to the Big Apple. I say *thankfully* because it may have been slightly difficult getting hold of any one of these gentlemen from the front page of the *Los Angeles Times*. Donald Rumsfeld was in Washington, André Agassi had just lost at Wimbledon and Buddy Hackett (while there's no dispute he would have made a great playing partner) had died 10 hours earlier in his Miami home.

God, some people will do anything to get out of a game.

It was Mark Twain who once said, 'Golf is a good walk spoiled by a small white ball.'

Well, my good walk had indeed been a long one, all the way from New Zealand to Los Angeles. As for small white balls, they were not nearly as important as finding the nearest newspaper, tracking down someone from the front page and taking them out for a round.

I do realise this is not your typical vacation; others may prefer to sunbathe in the Bahamas or ski in Austria. Me, I chose to embarrass myself for an entire month, meet strangers and spoil their walks.

But, then again, I do love a challenge.

I should make it clear at this stage (before you see the disasters that later unfold) that I had it on good authority from a number of American friends that the States was 'absolutely teeming with golfers' and 'you will have no trouble finding someone to play with.'

I left New Zealand a confident man, with plenty of balls.

Golf is a popular game, no doubt about that. Due to someone like Tiger Woods' success, more and more parents are urging their kids to swing a club so they can swing into early retirement. But money and fame aside (something the average weekend hacker will never have), there are other reasons men and women spend their Sundays bashing around (and losing) little white balls. It's a game where you don't have to be fit, you don't have to be good and, if all else fails, there's always a bar at the conclusion of the round.

It's also one of the only games where young and old can bowl up to a course, by themselves, and not feel like a loner; then approach someone on the putting green and ask if they'd care to spend the next three hours of their life with a complete stranger.

One of my favourite strangers was an Englishman called Frank. A short man in his sixties, he announced on the first hole that he had only a few months to live. Being on a golf course is a bit like an open-air taxi of sorts: you'll often find out more than you really need to know. Deep down, though, I was touched that Frank decided to confide in me.

'I've only got nine months to live,' he told me. 'I want to get as much golf in as I can. I want to prove the doctor wrong. He's such a prick.'

Before I could ask any questions, or play a shot, Frank was off again.

'I only started playing at Christmas, now I'm addicted. To hell with spending money on women, this is much more fun. I've got my handicap down to 22, it should be under 10 by this Christmas.'

With that sort of blind optimism, Frank *obviously* hadn't played for long.

'Just worked out a new swing, Justin,' he said, as I was attempting one myself. 'My aim is to get to the 1000-hour mark. At the moment I'm up to 400.'

And just as I was about to putt:

'Since I found out I have this disease I couldn't give a damn. I haven't got a care in the world. I've got my own little apartment. Got my own keys and everything.'

And just as I was about to hit from the woods:

'Used to work for the government, Justin. Only retired last year. Was supposed to get $60,000 off them, they paid me $12,000. I'm taking them to court — pricks.'

'What did you do for the government, Frank?'

'I could tell you but then I'd have to shoot you,' he winked. 'That's confidential.'

At least it *was* confidential until we reached the seventh. Frank was obviously bursting at the seams to tell someone. During the 402nd hour of his new swing he informed me he used to work for the civil service in England and at the age of 16 was sent to Saudi Arabia, where he dressed up as a Muslim woman for three years in search of terrorists.

So, there it was. This man, my new friend, in the bunker for seven, was a cross-dresser in 1952. When I asked whether it was worth working for the civil service all those years he said that although the travel was amazing, he lost a wife and many friends because he could never tell them what he did for a living. Needless to say, Frank, if your wife found out how you *really* spent your days (i.e. wearing a dress in the desert) she may have left far sooner.

As Agassi and Rumsfeld had failed to return my calls, I figured now was as good a time as any to check my bags for appropriate summer golfing attire. Having left New Zealand in the throes of winter, the last things I had thought to pack were dress shorts and collared shirts.

'Dress shorts and collared shirts?' I hear you say; 'It's only a game of golf, surely you can just bowl up wearing surf shorts and a T-shirt?' This, too, is what I used to think, until I discovered that golf is also a game for the very badly dressed. Along with finding American news-makers, the serious lack of collars in my bag was potentially a problem of epic proportions. You see, on most courses around the world, if you're not wearing a collar you can forget about playing — surely one of the more bizarre laws of the game. I mean, what other sport behaves in such a senseless fashion? Do you ever get asked to leave the football field because your shoes don't match your shorts? (You should see Frank; he's wearing a dress.)

Don't get me wrong, I have no problem *wearing* a collar, it's just that I possess a number of smart shirts without one. Does that make me a criminal?

Some courses would rather turn you away if it meant they didn't have some uncollared maniac stalking their well-manicured fairways. It does make you wonder, what *is* it about an uncollared shirt that is so unattractive to a golf course anyway? Do collarless men and women have a history of starting something untoward? I would have thought it was the complete opposite. It's the well-dressed ones you've got to look out for: the Mafia, Hitler, Saddam Hussein — all very well dressed. Most collarless men don't even have the sense to buy a fashionable shirt; they're hardly going to have the brains to start World War III on the 13th green. Unless, of course, they're playing very badly, then anything's possible.

I finished reading my newspaper and walked around LAX in a daze. The flight from New Zealand had been 12 hours; I still had a connecting flight to Phoenix, then another one to Newark, New Jersey. I wouldn't actually be in New York until some time tomorrow. Or was that yesterday? Damn time zones.

An intercom announcement told us not to give money to 'solicitors' (those who solicit, rather than lawyers), though this didn't stop them trying to sell everything from Bibles to time-shares. Between that and constant security checks, the only peaceful place in the whole airport seemed to be the toilets. And even they provided a curve ball a weary traveller didn't need.

It all started innocently enough; me marvelling at how wonderful it is that the water spins the other way when you flush in America. (Anticlockwise southern hemisphere, clockwise northern, in case you're wondering.) To me, this may as well be the eighth wonder of the world. It's fascinating! This little experiment all ended in tears, however, when the entire contents of the bowl decided to leap onto the floor and towards my travel bag. 'Jesus Christ,' I yelled. The roar from the next-door cubicle suggested this was a daily occurrence, and I was the mug who took the middle door.

I departed rather quickly and headed for the domestic terminal. Having told a man standing in line what I was doing in his country, he clogged my already jaded mind with recycled and reworked travel tips. I know this gesture is normally made in good faith, but 'Refrain from walking down unlit, seedy streets' and 'Make sure you have enough money for the *whole* trip' aren't exactly gems I will take to the grave. The best advice I ever received was from an old aunt: 'When overseas, don't talk to strangers.'

Now that *would* make for an interesting trip.

ANOTHER AIRPORT, this time Phoenix, Arizona. I was beginning to wonder whether I wasn't taking the longest possible route to the Big Apple. With three hours to kill before my next plane/plain meal, I headed to a bar where I met a robust, cheery-looking man called Jeff. An avid golfer, he was delighted to hear of my impending adventure ('You're mad but you'll have a great time'), but was disappointed he wouldn't be able to take me out for my first round. Instead, he handed me a copy of the local paper, hoping he might at least be able to help find my first news-maker.

Unfortunately, it wasn't going to come from *The Arizona Republic*. A picture on the front page showed four bearded locals attacking a barren hillside. 'Gobbling Goats on Cleanup Duty' was a story about 600 goats being used to chew through 30 acres of dry underbrush in Prescott National Forest, all in an effort to reduce fire risk.

'You'd have a hard time getting hold of those guys,' Jeff said. Jeff lived an hour south of Detroit and was on business in Phoenix. 'I suppose they'd keep the greens in good nick though.'

'Would definitely make for an amusing round,' I agreed.

'I had to buy a goat for my wife once,' he said.

'Pardon me?'

'My wife, she wanted one when we first started going out.'

'Okay. Why?'

'I don't know why, she loved goats. It was a little cozy there for a while; we lived in a one-bedroom apartment. We kept it till it was a full adult.'

'I noticed, flying into Phoenix,' I said, 'that everyone seems to own a pool.'

This was an obvious thing to say, given that it was well over 100 degrees outside, but the sheer number of blue, sparkling oases, resembling thousands of tightly packed Italian tiles, literally blew me away.

'You should come to where I live,' Jeff said, downing his drink and ordering another. 'Everyone owns a lake!'

'A lake?'

'Yep, we dug our own, it's an acre big. Took three days; we hired these big diggers.'

'A lake . . . where do you get the water?'

'The hose.'

'The hose!'

'Yep, took 44 and a half days. I know that 'cos I promised my boys a swim. I was told it shoulda taken longer but I was in a hurry.'

He paused while I laughed.

'So, golf huh?' Jeff asked. We had demolished a plate of nachos, knowing our next meal would be a mile up and taste of cardboard. 'I'm envious of you; I wish I could do what you're doing.'

'You should come for the ride, mate. Bring your goat.'

Jeff laughed. 'Goat's long gone. Although, you *do* know you've come at the wrong time of year, don't you?'

It was easy to see why. For the past hour we had been watching weary, hot and bothered travellers unload bags from taxis and literally run inside the terminal to escape the heat. Once inside, a complete reversal would take place. Air conditioning cranked up to maximum, they would then have to put on a sweater.

Still, better to wear one than *be* one, I suppose.

In the meantime, Sally, a friendly Phoenix local, had joined us. In a bid to kill time, Jeff told his goat story, I told my golf story and she told us her life story. Which wasn't that long: she was 22 and had never left Phoenix. She, too, was off to the Big Apple.

'I sure hope New York's not as bad as they say. I read once that a woman is mugged every two minutes.'

'Poor woman,' Jeff said.

A bewildered, blank stare crossed Sally's face while I tried to explain what I would be attempting over the next month. When I finished my spiel she looked across to Jeff, needing confirmation that the man who spoke funny wasn't taking her for a ride.

'He's from New Zealand,' Jeff shrugged, as if this were somehow an excuse.

This was obviously all too much for Sally, who then launched into a barrage of questions.

'But where will . . . how will . . . what will you do for . . . why golf?'

Seeing that her line of questioning was of no use to anyone, she then tried to put a positive spin on things, although all she could muster was, 'Haven't you come at the wrong time of year?'

'That's what I keep telling him,' Jeff said. 'I told him to stay up north, it's cooler up there. He's even going to Augusta — that's gonna be hot.'

'Well, all I can say is I'm sure glad he's not going to Louisiana.'

'Oh, he's going there too!'

'Goddamn!' she howled.

'So, have you always lived in the States?' I asked Jeff, ever thankful I had someone to clock-watch with. After all, the only thing that *doesn't* seem to fly in airports is time.

'As far as I know,' he said. 'I wouldn't live anywhere else. Everywhere else is too crappy. I mean, look at your country.'

'What about it?' I asked, thinking maybe he knew something I didn't. Compared to other nations, I had always thought New Zealand enjoyed one of the more peaceful existences.

'With the bombs and all,' he continued.

'Bombs?' I asked. 'Where?'

'Bali. That's in your country isn't it?'

'Um, no, Jeff. Bali is about as far away from New Zealand as Greenland is from Phoenix.'

'Oh.'

'To be honest, I was a bit worried about even getting into your country,' I confessed. 'It's not exactly a normal vacation, hunting down news-makers and subjecting them to 18 holes of golf. I thought I'd fly into LA and they'd tell me to bugger off.'

'Security is tough, but once you're in, that's it. You could drive around America for years and no one would notice. And that's what people do.'

Surely in this day and age, the powers that be would catch anyone who attempted the above, I thought. Jeff could read my mind:

'Serious,' he concluded.

Back in LA I had queued behind a well-travelled, elderly gentleman who passed the time peppering his speech with one-liners and pithy comments. One such observation was something he called the 'supermarket philosophy'. Three immigration officers sat in front of us at three different cubicles, stamping passports and doing their best to look glum. After 40 minutes of waiting, we finally reached the front of the line, whereby the officer slapped a 'Closed' sign on the counter, slammed shut the plastic window and unpacked his sandwiches.

'That's exactly what I mean!' he shrieked. 'Happens to me in the supermarket as well.'

The supermarket philosophy reared its ugly head again as I queued for my connecting flight to Newark. A family, who appeared to be shifting house and home, held up 50 irritable punters by packing and unpacking teddy bears, pillows and board games at the front of the line. Having decided what to throw away and what to keep (hence saving on a baggage fee), we were thankful to see the line moving again, only to find a uniformed woman waving around boarding passes and yelling, 'Can we have a show of hands of people on Flight 232 to Las Vegas?'

A dozen hands went up. All behind me.

'This flight is early. Everyone on Flight 232 must come to the front of the line!'

Would I ever make it to New York?

TWO MONTHS EARLIER . . .

World Ice Golf Tournament Put On Ice

Unseasonably warm weather has forced one of the world's most challenging golf tournaments to be called off just days before competitors, including a New Zealand player, were set to leave for Greenland. The Drambuie World Ice Golf Championship was due to take place from March 28 to 30. However, the committee announced this morning it had cancelled the event because unseasonably warm weather over the last month had created poor ice conditions.

IT WOULD BE FAIR to say this news had a big say in why I had started this adventure in the first place. Two months earlier I had been chosen to represent New Zealand in surely the most bizarre golf competition on earth, but now, quicker than you could say 'No ice in Greenland — are you nuts!', my chance to bring back the coveted trophy (and a case of Drambuie) had been washed down the sink along with my jet-lag pills. It would now be another year before 36 golfers from around the world would meet 400 miles north of the Arctic Circle and compete in sub-zero temperatures on a course where the greens are white, the balls are orange and the risks of exposure to sun blindness, polar bears and seal holes are very real indeed. So like a racehorse with an injury, like an Olympic athlete with a drug problem, there I sat in my kitchen, midsummer in New Zealand, caressing my passport, golf clubs at the ready and equipped with clothing fit for the coldest place on earth.

All dressed up and no place to go.

I have to say that the reason for my representing my country at ice golf had nothing to do with skill. I am a very average golfer. It's not as if I was born and bred on an ice-golf farm and later became champion of my village. Basically, being in the right place at the right time meant I could now at least say I represented my country at *something* (defending oneself from a polar bear with a three wood). Since hearing the good news I had embraced the opportunity and done everything in my power to win that booze.

Such as: going to the driving range in the middle of summer dressed in long johns, ski jacket, gloves, beanie and ski boots. Sneaking my golf balls into the nearest ice rink and practising my putting while kids skated (and fell) around me. I even went as far as putting water into an oven tray, putting the oven tray in the freezer, waiting 24 hours, then playing off a nicely formed chunk of ice, which was housed next to the frozen peas.

> Course designer, Henrick Bergqvist, was quoted as saying, 'The ice is simply not stable enough for an event of this calibre to proceed safely. As this is an extreme sporting event the safety of our representatives is a major concern.' New Zealand's ice golf representative, Justin Brown, says the setback has made him even more determined to take out the tournament next year.

Take out the tournament? Thanks for your confidence, Henrick, but I would have been happy just to make it around a full 18 with my ears intact. I know for a fact I wouldn't have troubled the scorers but I had entertained the thought of meeting a bizarre range of people and competing on icebergs. For now, at least, I had to take comfort in the fact that elsewhere in the world, 35 other golfers were moping around blaming global warming and thirsty polar bears.

Even though the Ice Golf Champs had been cancelled, the thought of a life-changing event like this had put me in a rather adventurous mood. What *could* I do over the next year to brush up on my skills that was a little different? I needed something as ridiculous as Greenland. Having lived in New Zealand where, some say, extreme sports are part of the diet, it is often hard to avoid attempting a few yourself:

Bungee jumping (hated it).

White-water rafting (fell out).

Skydiving (lost car keys).

Okay, that's not entirely true. I did enjoy all of the above, but mostly because along with milking a poisonous snake and learning to fold maps, they're the sorts of things you'd like to do before you die. Sometimes two birds can be killed with one stone; sometimes you die *doing* them. Of course, much of the adrenalin rush comes afterwards when you can look back at the video from the safety of your sofa, wondering if that was really you jumping off a bridge with nothing more than dental floss attached to your legs. Was that really *me* who free fell 12,000 feet in 45 seconds? you ask. What if the guy I was attached to had had a heart attack mid-jump? What cord would I have had to pull? Why can't I hear myself screaming? More importantly, has anyone seen my car keys?

Golf, though, is nothing like that. Not an extreme bone in its body. At least that's what I *thought* until I discovered the ice variety. Add a few polar bears, seals and snow blindness to your round and you have an interesting Sunday afternoon.

Ordinary golf may not be extreme but that's not to say it's not dangerous. Just ask my mother; here she was standing in the gallery at the New Zealand Open, generally minding her own business, quickly tiring of other gallery members yelling out 'Get in the hole!', when a fly ball from a very amateur professional smacked her in the head. A rescue helicopter turned up and took her via the hospital to home where Dad, the ever-keen and committed golfer, gave her a cup of tea and an aspirin and returned to the tournament.

So, after hearing the news I would now have to wait another 364 days, 11 hours, 10 minutes and 15 seconds (hey, I was looking forward to this!), I guess I should have then headed to the nearest golf course to vent my frustration. Yet, somehow, a bar seemed a far more attractive option. There I met my friend Jon, another fellow average golfer. We talked missed putts, best drives and reasons why we never seem to play any more.

'But you're still going next year, aren't you?' Jon asked, placing a beer in front of me.

'Yeah, but that's next year, isn't it?'

'So? It's something to look forward to.'

'But it's a year away.'

'Well, you'll be getting lots of practice in, won't you?'

Even though I had been playing since the age of seven, when my father had sliced a five iron in half so I could swing the thing, I had never really got used to the fact that golf is a game about practice, patience and . . . practice. As I wasn't patient and didn't practise much, I was confined to the group of golfers who complain when they can't get on the course wearing a T-shirt, complain when they don't shoot under 100 even though they haven't played for years, and never replace their divots. Okay, that's not entirely true either — I do make a point of replacing my divots.

'Well, it just sounds like you just need a new challenge,' Jon offered, placing fresh drinks on the table. 'Like playing somewhere as equally bizarre as Greenland, to brush up on your skills for next year's tournament.'

'Like where?' I asked.

'How about the Sahara?'

'Too many bunkers.'

'The Amazon?'

'Too many trees.'

'Okay, how about the Middle East?'

'Very funny.'

'No, I think I may have the answer,' I said, placing the newspaper that bore the Greenland cancellation on the table. The article featuring my ugly mug stared up at us.

'Shoot,' Jon said, resigned to the fact that the Middle East obviously wasn't it.

'Well, I'll be travelling by myself, right?'

'Right.'

'And I won't have anyone to play with?'

'*Right.*'

'What better place to find potential partners than on the front page of the newspaper?'

Jon obviously didn't follow. I continued: 'How about I challenge to a game of golf anyone who happens to feature on the front page of the newspaper, on that day, in that town?' I said proudly.

'Why?'

'Why not! For a start, they're bound to be interesting, otherwise they wouldn't be on the front page. And they've obviously got a story to tell *and* they'd be great company.'

Jon looked confused, then slightly pensive. A small, wriggly smile formed.

'The front page, you say?' he asked.

'The front page.'

'Of any paper?'

'Any paper.'

I could hear his brain ticking.

'In the Middle East?'

'No, Jon, not the Middle East. The States,' I smiled.

'Okay, wise guy,' he said, looking pleased with himself. 'What if that person happens to be George Bush?'

'Problem.'

'Or Marilyn Monroe?'

'Bigger problem.'

'You're mad.'

'Thank you.'

And so it came to be: I would travel to the USA (the Sahara and the Amazon being out of budget range, not to mention limited newspaper print runs) and traverse it, east to west, on a train. I would get off at smaller places, and play golf with whoever happened to feature on the front page of the newspaper in whatever town I happened to be staying in that day. Why? I hear you ask. Why would you put yourself through such trauma? How will you get hold of all these people? How on earth will you convince them to play golf?

It's quite simple. In a world full of anger, confusion and unrest here is a pointless challenge by a pointless man who could at least see the point in a pointless game.

'And what's that point again?' Jon asked.

'That point, my dear friend, is to meet news-makers and thrash them at golf.'

'That sounds as ridiculous as Greenland.'

'Thank you.'

DAY 3: NEW YORK, NEW YORK

THE FIRST THING I DID in New York was step into a yellow cab. I didn't plan it that way, it just happened. Before I knew it I was standing outside Penn Street Station where a well-dressed, very polite young man had opened the cab door. And I was in, just like that. I found this a little bewildering. I was confused. I mean, I had always been led to believe New York cabs were impossible to get hold of. I thought they were the proverbial black jellybean. That's what happens in the movies. And that's what *I* had planned.

I wanted to stand in the pouring rain with my golf clubs and yell, 'Taxi!' I then wanted the first seven to drive right by. I wanted the eighth to splash me. And just as I'd finally hailed one, a sexy woman from the next building would take three giant leaps and steal it. It would speed off, this time totally drenching my long winter coat and expensive Italian shoes. I would then throw my briefcase down in disgust, yell obscenities and be late for my dinner date. And that was to be my New York moment. I had it all planned.

Oh well.

So I sat in my yellow cab with my Italian driver and tried to speak slowly, clearly and succinctly. Due to my accent this was how I would have to speak for the next month if I was to achieve such luxuries as sandwiches and knowing where toilets were. To another New Zealander I would have sounded like a four-year-old. To this Italian man, I sounded like, well, a four-year-old. But it's really not fair; if Americans or Brits travel to other English-speaking countries they don't have to adjust their speech one bit.

New Zealanders and Australians, on the other hand, have to speak like Forrest Gump.

One thing that never disappoints me about taxi drivers is this: no matter where you are in the world, they seem to think life's main aim is to get into fifth gear as quickly as possible. Even if they're only driving to the end of the block, it's as if they get a pay rise if they hit 'five'. Maybe it's because in a city like New York you can only dream of getting there. It's the Holy Grail of gears, something to celebrate when it happens.

'Hit five today, Barry.'

'Really? That's two days in a row now.'

My Italian driver was no exception; he achieved this feat with alarming regularity. Although I wasn't about to mock him, as he understood my Gumpisms and dropped me off right outside the building where Seinfeld works.

A friend had given me the name of a Lucy in New York who would let me share her floor for the night. Ogilvy's advertising agency is where I would find her and what seemed like the rest of the world's youngest, trendiest, most beautiful people. This seemed like *the* place to work. Living it up in New York with like-minded people from all over the world. Parties every second night, walks to Central Park at lunch time and gigs in Greenwich Village. That they all probably worked till midnight six days a week, paid too much rent and could only afford two-minute noodles for lunch was beside the point.

Golf bag searched on the ground floor, I rode to the 14th and found Lucy by her desk.

'Hi Lucy, I'm Justin.'

'No, I'm Sherene. Lucy's over there.'

'Oh, sorry.'

And there she was, busy typing an email, surrounded by family photos and souvenirs from all over the world. I had heard she was an avid traveller. Other pictures were from parties: friends arm in arm, big smiles. Yep, that's Lucy; I'd been told she also liked a drink.

'Hi Lucy.'

'Lucy? No, I'm Bettina. Lucy's over there,' she said, pointing to nowhere in particular.

Of course it would help if I actually knew what Lucy looked like.

We eventually found each other and headed to the cafeteria where we ate Chinese food. Lucy ate like a bird — I ate like a potbelly pig. She talked, I ate. In between mouthfuls I spared a moment to look out the window and mumble, 'Holy hell, we're in New York.' Lucy waxed lyrical over the essential things to do in New York and just as I was reaching for my credit card I remembered why I was here.

I had to find some newspapers.

'You can leave your golf clubs here if you like,' Lucy offered.

'Great idea. I think I'll just take the seven iron.'

I bought three papers — the *New York Times*, *The Onion* and *Newsday* — and found a seat in an Eighth Avenue café. I was now officially scared. I mean, who *would* be on the front page? What if they were criminals (and there was a very good chance of that)? Would I have to get them a day-pass? More to the point, would they be allowed to carry a five iron around in public? Who would want to play golf with a homeless Kiwi anyway? Would the Americans even like me? What if they didn't even *play* the game? (One thing that'd never even crossed my mind before I left; I just assumed most Americans would have an old set of clubs in the garage.) How was I going to afford green fees? Would I have to pay for them as *well* as me?

I decided to cross those bridges when I came to them.

A stressed-looking woman cleared the table next to me. She was wearing a T-shirt that read, *I've got PMT and a handgun — any questions?* I didn't ask any. Her shirt, though, at least inspired me to bite the bullet and lay the front page out on the table.

This was it. I couldn't stall any longer.

It did feel strange reading the newspaper for an entirely different reason to normal. Others in the café read to check out the weather for Independence Day or to discover that the mayor hadn't escaped scandal. The remaining few just stared at my seven iron. Meantime, I read on and just hoped the mayor (even if he *was* in the middle of a scandal) had a spare four hours tomorrow.

And a country club membership.

Actually it would have been a grand thing if the mayor *had* been on the front page; it may have been a damn sight easier than getting hold of the high-profile husband and wife who were entangled in a bitter divorce. ('Hi, can I speak to your ex please, it's about a game of golf.') Unfortunately, the only other story to make the front page was an extremely brutal murder case involving an 18-year-old victim.

Hmm, yes, suddenly the Ellis Island ferry, Statue of Liberty and New Museum of Contemporary Art were looking very attractive indeed. And that credit card was only inches away. With the diligence of an ox, I resisted. After all, I only had two days in the Big Apple and I was already halfway through the first.

I had to get my skates on.

Luckily, just over from the murder case was a story about a deli owner from Lower Manhattan who, while walking his dog in Queens, had stumbled across a four-foot-long alligator. Now this was more like it! How I was to

This Tale No Croc

Dog-walker helps officials bag gator in Queens park

'It is quite tame, but maybe a little stressed out.'

— *Joe Abene, a wild-animal keeper at the Bronx Zoo*

Newsday, *New York, New York*

get hold of this deli owner I had no idea, but at least I was that bit closer to my first round of golf.

All I had to work with was the name of the owner who had found the 'gator: he was Michael Georgatos and he worked at a Lower Manhattan deli. I found the nearest Internet café and found an article about another Georgatos, Peter (possibly Michael's brother), who featured in a business article just after September 11:

> Business owners and workers who were allowed back into the financial district for the first time this weekend seemed dazed. Back out on the street, there were only a few signs that everything wasn't OK — the smell of something burning, the people wearing masks because of the smell, and the light dust that covered many of the storefront windows. As he and his nephews cleared out the melting frozen food from the Stagedoor Deli at 99 Maiden, Peter Georgatos, 57, talked about the regular customers who came from the twin towers. 'There's a lot of people who never have to say what they want. I just know,' Georgatos said. 'One guy is always corned beef on a bagel every day for five years. Another guy, a lawyer, is juice, a cup of ice and a bagel, three dollars.'

To be honest, I wasn't looking forward to visiting Ground Zero. After all, this was my first time in New York and that's the last memory anyone would want. However, if I was to track down Michael, that's where I'd have to go.

I found the number for the Stagedoor Deli and started dialling. It was 3.30 pm, probably far too late in the day.

'Hello, Stagedoor?'

'Hello, is Michael there please?'

'What?'

Damn accent. Slow down, Forrest.

'Michael, is Michael there please?' I repeated, slowly.

'Mikey?'

'Yes.'

'Mikey?'

'Yes.'

'What about him?'

'Is he there?'

'What?'

'Is he there?'

'He'll be here tomorrow!'

'What time?'

'Early!'

'Don't suppose you happen to know whether he plays g—'

Click.

I was ecstatic having located Michael. Granted, it may not have been the most conversational of calls but just knowing I had the right workplace was very pleasing. A few short hours ago he was just a stranger on the front page of a tabloid; tomorrow I would be playing golf with him. I re-read the business article and wondered whether the nephews that were helping Peter after September 11 were in fact . . . Michael's kids! That would make perfect sense. Hey, we could all go out for a round! Ah, happy families in the Big Apple. Where in New York we'd play I had no idea; we'd cross that bridge when we came to it. Meantime, I could relax for the evening.

Lucy took me to the Cowgirl Hall of Fame for dinner, a Tex Mex-style restaurant which apparently is an institution in New York. All I could think about was Michael. What if he wasn't there tomorrow? What if he was sick? What if that wasn't his workplace at all? Did that guy on the phone *really* understand what I was saying?

Lucy laid the subway map in front of us and told me how I'd get myself to Maiden Lane in the morning. Kinky Friedman played on the stereo while we scoffed margaritas and carne quesadillas, then went for a walk around West Village.

'So, working in a big advertising company, do you ever get famous people coming through the building?' I asked, munching on fat-free ice cream.

'Sometimes, yeah. We had Seinfeld play at our Christmas party a few years back.'

'Seinfeld!'

'Yeah, it was either a choice of him or Sting. He just came on and did a half-hour stand-up routine. He's on our payroll, you see.'

'What for?'

'He does our American Express ads.'

'So he pays tax at *your* company?'

'Yep.'

'Seinfeld pays tax?'

'Sure he does,' she laughed.

'So today, when I walked into reception, I walked where he walked?'

'You walked where he walked.'

'Wow.'

Had they not been my only pair of shoes I would have dropped them off at Lucy's house and never washed them again, but I kind of needed some form of footwear if I was to make my way around America. Plus, getting into nightclubs or fancy restaurants may be a little difficult in bare feet:

'Whoa, whoa, not so fast, mister. Where are your shoes?'

'I'm not wearing them 'cos I'm not washing them 'cos I walked where Seinfeld walked.'

'*Right* — security!'

Like most people I'm a huge fan of Seinfeld, although I was more than a little disappointed to see Jason Alexander (aka George Costanza) parading around as a game show host on a KFC ad. You've got to draw the line somewhere.

Lucy's mini-tour of New York continued; first we went to an open-mike night at a comedy bar and then on to a well-known speakeasy. If you're like me, you'll not know that speakeasies were illegal drinking holes in the 1920s, so called because once you've 'had a few' you speak easy. Makes perfect sense. This particular speakeasy, Chumley's Bar, had no signs on it or anywhere around it. In other words, you had to *know* where it was.

I like that — a bar that makes you work for your first drop.

It also rather sneakily boasted two exits. One was easy to find; it had 'Exit' written above it and a knobby wooden thing that you turned when you wanted to leave. The other was a little more elusive, but one could normally find it (and the middle of the street) by drinking 13 beers and leaning on 'the bookcase in the corner'.

This was indeed a bar with a literary past, a place where original copies of

Sophie's Choice and *Of Mice and Men* adorned the walls. A place where not a lot had changed since Jack Kerouac, William Faulkner and John Steinbeck all shared a drink here. A place where the inspiration for your next work could come just from looking at an Ernest Hemingway or Dylan Thomas book sleeve. And a place where students *still* gathered, philosophised, argued and debated over 'which reality TV shows sucked' and 'whether it's okay to fuck on first dates'.

I tried to keep the soles of my shoes as clean as possible on the way home (still hoping I could get $100 from avid Seinfeld fans), but it was all in vain as Lucy chose a route through a central city park. This is where I discovered surely one of the more individual ways to deal with the lack of space in Manhattan. Imagine a fenced-off piece of dirt the size of a tennis court in the middle of a park. Now imagine people chatting to their dogs, sometimes to other people, but mostly to dogs. This concept (entirely foreign to a New Zealander used to open spaces and ample coastline) is called a dog run. This is where people come to run their dogs. And it's a real club! They have real meetings, and if they're lucky, after a while, they become 'dog-run buddies'. I'm told if you live in Manhattan it's not uncommon to hear conversations like this at work:

'Oh God, I got so drunk last night.'

'Who with?'

'Pam.'

'Pam, how do you know her?'

'Oh, she's my dog-run buddy.'

I'm sure this idea was originally created so your poor little dog could give his poor little legs a little exercise, but from where I was sitting it was hard to get my head around the fact that this so-called dog run had surpassed the supermarket as the ultimate pick-up joint. I met one guy who was walking dogs just for the hell of it; they weren't even *his*. I stood there fascinated, asking questions, obviously cramping his style, when the girl he was chatting to told me:

'You know, a while ago they had to cordon off this dog run.'

'Why's that?' I asked.

''Cos every eight months a big dog would eat a little dog.'

Why this particular incident happened every eight months was anyone's guess. Surely, though, as a responsible dog owner, an irresponsible choice would be to go and see your dog-run buddies after seven months and 28 days.

Unless, of course, you were really desperate for a date.

I WOKE UP in the middle of the night feeling like a train had hit me. To this point I hadn't been introduced to jet lag but for the next couple of days at least the little bugger wouldn't be leaving my side. I was so wide awake the urge to visit Michael at 4 am seemed entirely feasible. Instead, I reached for the papers Lucy and I had found on the way home. The *New York Press* had a photo of Hans Blix, *The Village Voice* an article featuring the entire Supreme Court. It was hardly reassuring knowing that if my plans fell through with Michael, I would have to fork out green fees for 12 wealthy judges.

With a third of the energy I had at 4 am, I rose at eight and sleepwalked to the subway, trying my best to find my way around a new city.

I'm told New York is relatively safe these days; even so, it's still a re-assuring feeling marching down Eighth Avenue with a seven iron under your arm. I recommend it to anyone new to a city.

The rain fell as I searched for Maiden Lane, an area in Battery Park at the bottom of Manhattan. With a bit of luck that's where Michael would be, practising his putting and awaiting my arrival. Before I knew it I was there, standing outside the Stagedoor Deli. This is it, I thought. This is where the real adventure would start. I looked at my hands — they were shaking. What was I going to say? What if I only had 10 seconds to grab his attention (which shouldn't be too much of a problem, given the seven iron)?

Oh my God, what have I done?

Why am I doing this?

I stepped into, unfortunately, one of the busiest delis I'd ever encountered. There were at least 10 men serving a sea of customers. I was not making any friends waving a stray golf club around between an assortment of bagels and mushroom soup. Sadly, there were no pictures of golfers among the posters of Greece on the wall.

I did, however, see the photo of Michael and the alligator — proof that at least I had the right guy. And there he was, in real life! Michael! Hard at work behind the counter, with muscly arms and a sparkly white apron.

But did he look like a *golfer*?

'Fore, playing through,' said a customer behind me, trying to get past.

'I rang yesterday,' I said to the big man who seemed to be running the place, presumably Peter. 'What is the best time to talk to Michael?'

'Come back at 10.30!' he yelled back.

10.30? Sorry, not good enough, I had a lonely seven iron to tend to. I decided to go straight to the source and hit Michael up. The man from the front page seemed very busy indeed, handling hot coffees and giving orders to sweaty couriers. I tried to explain to him what it was I was doing which, given the strange accent and potential weapon over my shoulder, was no mean feat.

'Come back Monday!' he yelled across the counter.

Monday? This was getting worse. It didn't help that Michael clearly thought I was trying to sell him something.

'I just want to talk to you, it won't take a minute,' I smiled.

'Come back Monday,' he yelled again. (I tell you, everyone seemed to be yelling in this place.)

'Monday?' I asked. 'But today's only Thursday.'

Michael was too busy to even hear me. Somewhere in among the 'One coffee to go!', 'Two vegetable soup, one orange!', 'Three dollars fifty, do you have change for a twenty?' was a lone voice: 'Michael, I'm only in town for 23 hours. I'm on annual leave and I need a game of golf.'

I continued to be in everyone's way. I watched Michael and smiled. Didn't he know I had come all the way from New Zealand to meet him? Course not; he was an honest man making an honest living. But didn't he wonder what I was doing here? No, he had invoices to write. If only I could get through to him that all I was after was 18 holes.

He continued to serve hot coffee and bagels; I continued to make a nuisance of myself which, if I was to be completely honest, was getting me absolutely nowhere. After 10 minutes of winking, smiling and practising golf swings I felt the time had come to move on. I had to face facts — if I was to get a game with the alligator hunter I would just have to hope that he would be there later in the morning.

With a bit of luck I hadn't blown it already: 'If that weirdo comes back, tell him I'm not here.'

I felt decidedly miserable walking down Maiden Lane. It had been drizzling all morning and the dark, heavy clouds made it feel like four in the afternoon. Already this whole adventure was starting to look like a glorious failure. After all, my only hope of a game in New York thought I was either an escaped nutter or an encyclopedia salesman.

I found a bakery, ordered some food and while paying heard the song lyrics 'I'm an alien, I'm a legal alien, I'm an Englishman in New York'. Substitute 'New Zealander' for Englishman and Sting knew exactly how I was feeling.

Come on, snap out of it, I told myself. Would Tiger Woods let jet lag get to him? Would Tiger Woods let an opportunity become a problem? Would Tiger Woods give up so soon? More to the point, would Tiger Woods ever walk around Lower Manhattan on a piss of a day and beg Greek alligator hunters to play golf?

I just had to be persistent, that's all. So after persistently scoffing one croissant after another I sauntered across the street to a map shop, hoping that it of all places could at least give me *some* direction.

'Hi, I'm wondering if you could help me please?'

'Not a problem, sir,' said the girl behind the counter. 'But first can I ask you to put the club behind the counter?'

'Pardon me?'

'The golf club.'

'Oh, right, no problem,' I said, forgetting it was even there. She placed the seven iron underneath the cash register as if this were a daily occurrence.

'Do you know the men in the deli?' I asked. 'The Stagedoor, just down the road?'

'Yes, why?'

'Are they good people?'

She looked at me strangely, looking unsure of what to say next.

'It's just that, I mean, all I'm trying to do is go around America, find the local paper in town and play golf with whoever happens to feature on the front page of the newspaper on that particular day.'

'*Right*,' she said, unconvinced.

'Serious,' I said.

'Really?'

'Do you really think I'd carry that thing around town for any other reason?' I asked, pointing to the counter where the club was hiding. 'Don't you think it looks a bit weird walking down Broadway with a golf club?'

'If there's one place you *can* get away with it, it's New York.'

Once she realised I was only going to use the confiscated item for leisure activities, she warmed up a little. She told me she'd known the men in the deli for 10 years.

'Yes, but will they talk to me?' I asked.

'They're nice people, of course they'll talk to you.'

That's if they can understand me. To be honest their English wasn't great; then again my Greek was nonexistent. And our accents caused a major problem. If the deli was as busy as before, I feared I'd once again turn into a bumbling mess. I just needed to explain myself.

It was still hosing down outside and I had an hour to fill if I was to talk to Michael. Seeing as my address book wasn't exactly bustling with friends to see in New York, I reluctantly walked to Ground Zero.

The first thing I noticed was the hole. I had never even seen this part of the world, or the towers, but it was obvious the skyline they once filled was, as Bruce Springsteen sings, now just 'Empty Sky'. It didn't help that it was still drizzling and not a little depressing to see what was only *once* there. New York was still crying. People were taking photos in front of what is a construction site ready to be something. What, people still don't know. Seedy men flogged off September 11 memorabilia, calendars, books and pins laid out on cheap tables. I looked up at Liberty Plaza, which in itself seemed a tall building, but had been just a baby compared to the towers.

Bastards.

I was nervous walking back to the Stagedoor. I felt this could be my last chance with Michael. The encyclopedia salesman/nutcase was walking a fine line between getting what he wanted and getting a bagel around the ear. The last thing I wanted to do was piss him off.

When I arrived I smiled a lot, and waited some more.

'Mikey! Oi, Mikey!' Peter yelled, when he spotted me. Mikey was leaning against the freezer having a cigarette. It's fair to say he didn't seem ecstatic to see me. Luckily I had a new plan in my bag: a copy of my first book, *UK on a G-String*. I figured this would at least break the ice and make him realise I wasn't bound for the nearest straitjacket. Upon looking at the book, his eyes lit up:

A Greek, a New Zealander and a seven iron

'Are you from New Zealand! I visited New Zealand in '64, worked on a cruise ship. Wellington's my favourite city in the world.'

Now we were warming up.

'Come back at midday, then we can talk,' he said, flicking through the book.

Yes! I wanted to jump for joy. The alligator hunter wanted to talk!

As I was leaving, a small boy, Napoleon (most probably one of the nephews), came up to me and asked for an autograph.

'Wow, I've never met anyone famous,' he said.

'You still haven't, buddy,' I replied, 'but I'll sign your napkin.'

THE PEARL DINER offered one-dollar coffees and Seinfeld-like booths to sit in. I was as happy as a pig in shit knowing Michael was going to talk to me. I then had a one-dollar hot dog and a rather nutritious doughnut at the bottom of Wall Street. The ground was slushy and smelt of fish (not a smell I would have instantly thought of when dreaming of New York; then again, it is near the water and fish do seem to like the stuff).

Eventually, after an hour and a half I skipped back to the deli with my seven iron and Michael took me down to the basement. He was on a tea break. We found two old drums and sat down. He checked avocados and smoked while I listened to his life story.

Originally from a small Greek island, he had visited New Zealand in the sixties and moved to New York 32 years ago. He and his brother had owned the deli for the last 15. They were obviously honest, hard workers who had made a great business with happy regulars.

'This deli used to be a great place,' he told me. 'There used to be a lot of big companies here, but ever since September 11th they relocated. It's now a ghost town.'

'Did you know anyone in the towers?' I asked.

'I used to serve a lot of people from the World Trade Center and at the time of the first attack I had my delivery boys in the second tower. Thank God nothing happened to them . . . but I do know a lot of people that got killed.'

'And what about this bloody alligator?' I asked, noting his appreciation that I'd changed the subject.

'Here, have this,' he said, handing me a photo of him and the 'gator. He then started telling the story, which although he'd probably told it a hundred times or more still didn't seem to bore him.

'I got home and took the dog for a walk in a park located in southeast Bayside in Queens County. It was 3.30 in the afternoon. My dog got lost in woods and started barking at a 'gator. I was very surprised to see a 'gator in New York, but there it was. Then the 'gator started attacking the dog, pulling his head and I was afraid for the dog, so I called 911. They didn't believe me — they thought I was joking.'

'So you said something along the lines of, "I'm in a park in New York City and my dog is being attacked by an alligator"?'

'Yes, and they started making fun of me. During this time I had to wrestle the 'gator because it was attacking my dog! So I called 911 again, and they *still* didn't believe me. Twenty minutes passed.'

'Twenty minutes? What was happening with the 'gator all this time?'

'He was still trying to attack my dog, I had to hold him down.'

'You were holding the alligator down! Weren't you scared?'

'No, I grew up in Greece, I was around snakes all the time.'

'*Right*, of course,' I said, unconvinced.

'So I called 911 for the third time. By this stage I was getting tired of holding this thing.'

'I bet.'

'This time they believed me and a special unit turned up and took it to Brooklyn Zoo.' He seemed a little embarrassed to conclude. 'And then . . . the *New York Times* called . . . and then I was on TV.'

'Where do you think the 'gator came from?' I asked.

'I think it was a pet. Some people go to Florida, get a baby 'gator, keep it at home for a couple of years and when it gets to a certain length they let it go. Those 'gators can grow to 30 feet. I wanted the police to come because I didn't want this thing to stay in the park and keep growing. A lot of kids play there.'

Tomorrow would be Independence Day, so I thought it fitting to ask Michael who was his favourite American of all time.

'JFK,' he said without hesitation. 'For his ideas, the way he brought up his country. Later I don't think politics helped this country much. I think everyone hates not necessarily Americans, but American policies.'

'Least favourite?' I asked.

He paused. 'I'd rather not say.'

Enough of the small talk: it was crunch time.

'Michael, I don't suppose you play golf?' I asked.

'Golf? Of course not, I'm Greek, I play soccer.'

'So you wouldn't like to have a game tomorrow?'

'No thanks,' he laughed. He told me to help myself to anything as I left.

New York, New York, where I never rode the Ellis Island ferry or walked through the New Museum of Contemporary Art. Hell, I never even saw the Statue of Liberty.

But I *did* meet a Greek who caught a 'gator.

The next morning, 4 July, I got a cab to Penn Street Station and, again, was comforted to see my driver trying to achieve fifth gear as quickly as possible. My journey would now be taking me to Richmond, where I knew not a soul.

DAY 5: RICHMOND, VIRGINIA

THE WOMAN FROM ISAID SAID: 'I said, it's not the money it's the principle. I said, there are too many people out there with too many needs; I said, now listen; I said, tell me about your family. I said, I said, look, I said, they were left high and dry and you thought you knew everything about me. I said, let me tell you something, you have no idea who I am. I said, I'm not the only one who thinks like that. Now listen, I said . . . are you there? Are you there? Kevin, can you hear me? I'm in a tunnel, Kevin. I said, I'm in a tunnel. I'm gonna have to call you back.'

The next month would be spent on the train: an all-you-can-eat pass, getting on and off wherever I chose. Which, if the woman from Isaid had anything to do with it, would definitely be the latter.

It's funny, your first instinct (well, mine anyway) is not to talk to anyone on the train. Or the bus for that matter. It's far easier to make out you're enjoying reading the safety instructions for the fifth time. But there's only so long you can keep quiet. It's not in our nature.

Meg and I had been sitting next to each other all the way from Philadelphia to Washington DC and the only words we'd muttered were 'Excuse me', 'Whoops, sorry' and 'It should come out with a bit of baking soda.' When we eventually broke the ice she told me she was on her way to a wedding in Richmond and, being on a tight schedule, hoped the journey would be free of delays.

'Excuse me ladies and gentlemen, we have a train broken down on line one. We are going to need every available seat. If you're taking up two seats, you're gonna have to move on over. If you got an ugly grin on your face, you better get rid of it.'

A collective groan sounded and the lady from Isaid called Kevin again.

'Hopefully there are no more of those,' said Meg, when after half an hour the first problem seemed to be resolved. Then a new one arrived:

'Excuse me ladies and gentlemen, can I have your attention?'

'What's the problem?' I asked the conductor who was in between breaths, putting on her best DJ voice for the intercom.

'It's a K276,' she said, playing with what seemed at least a hundred keys on her belt.

'Oh, right,' I said. 'And a K276 is a . . .?'

'Freight train, fulla garbage.'

'Excuse me ladies and gentlemen, we have a freight train in front of us!'

'Not coming towards us, I hope,' Meg mumbled.

'Shouldn't they have given way to us?' I asked. 'After all, they're only a freight train, we have passengers.'

'You'd think so,' she sighed. 'But this train is given no respect.'

Politics, even in the train world.

Although Meg was now officially late ('Sorry all, was held up by the K276'), it wasn't the first thing to go wrong for the wedding party that afternoon. She had learnt on the phone from her friends in Richmond that the bridal party was supposed to go white-water rafting but there had been an accident on the river and they thought someone might have died. Second thoughts, maybe it *was* safer on the train.

'So, you're here to play golf then?' she asked, realising that panicking, huffing, puffing and constantly looking at her watch were getting her no-where.

'Yep,' I replied.

'But you haven't played yet?'

'No.'

'And you only spent two days in New York?'

'Yep.'

'You do realise you've come at the worst possible time of year?'

'So I hear.'

'Regarding the weather I mean.'

'Yep.'

As you can see, I'm not much good at conversation on a train.

Meg and I had covered the basic Where, When, Why and How by the time we reached Richmond (three hours late) so thought it only appropriate we share a cab. She was in a hurry to get a feed with the wedding party; I was in a hurry to get the local paper.

Luckily, there was one lying on the back seat.

'Fred, do you mind if I read this?' I asked our driver, whose name appeared on a photo on the dash, which of course bore no resemblance to the man in the front seat.

It took a few miles before Fred believed my reason for being in America. When I finally convinced him and told him I wanted to keep his paper ('Got 50 cents?' he asked; I gave him a dollar), we decided to try to track down Betty, an 87-year-old who was on the front page. She lived in a local rest home and had made a huge quilt in the colours of the US flag for Independence Day.

'If you're going to play her, you'd better get a cart,' said Fred.

Fortunately, Fred was wrong; it said on the front page that Betty was very 'sprightly' for her age. Yes, but would she play golf? Meanwhile Meg showed me a photo of her baby (this was the first time both she and her husband had been away from her newborn at the same time) and Fred continued to impress with his navigational skills.

Before Meg had the chance to curse 'that damn K276' one last time, she arrived at the restaurant only three and a half hours late. There, she very kindly paid the whole fare and wished me luck.

It was dark when we finally arrived in downtown Richmond. I asked Fred the stock questions about which areas to avoid and found accommodation in an ex-brothel. Correction: *current* brothel. I paid an exorbitant price for a room whose bed had no doubt seen some very lively action over the years. The room was clean enough, just seedy.

As it was only 9 pm and Independence Day was still in full swing, I felt it my duty to at least see how Richmond was celebrating. Besides, it was probably a little late to call Betty at the rest home.

I headed downtown (where most street parties were just finishing) and, rather predictably, ended up in an Irish bar having a Guinness and reading the paper. I figured I should at least find some other front-page stories, keeping my options open for tomorrow should Betty be at football practice or away on a sales conference.

As it happened I needn't have worried: Betty's was the only story on the front page that didn't involve murder, terror or infant death rates.

The saddest story was of a mother who was living the horror of losing both sons to violence. Lenny died in 1990 when someone shot him through the head. He was 19. Lamar, aged 16, was shot and killed five days prior to the article.

The mother now just walks around town in her son's Nikes clutching onto family albums. Unbelievably, the shot that took Lamar's life wasn't the first time he'd been hit. He was almost killed in March just outside their home. He and his mother were on the way to their apartment when he was shot in the left wrist and twice in the stomach. After a week in intensive care he was released.

I finished my Guinness and wondered if I still had Fred the taxi driver's number. After all, who would want to walk back to their brothel after reading that story? I plucked up the courage to leave without a bouncer and soon discovered, after walking for a few minutes without losing my wallet or passport, why it was that people came here.

This was a city with a deep, rich history of civil war. Monuments of revered Southern heroes stood overlooking wide, tree-lined boulevards. Hazy, midsummer air hung low with the smell of Southern cooking. I wandered through the Shockoe Slip, a quaint, unevenly paved street packed with restaurants housed in 19th-century stores and warehouses. I found the larger-than-life aluminium statue dedicated to the late Bill Robinson, otherwise known as Mr Bojangles, who was born in Richmond in 1878. The monument is near the intersection to which he once donated a traffic light so kids from his old neighbourhood could safely cross the street.

Then I took a ride on 'Banjo, Bones and Boatmen!' where we relived the carefree days of canal pack-boat travel on Richmond's historic canal. An old local dude entertained us along the river, playing tunes from the 1840s to the 1860s on his banjo, while an embarrassed bunch of strangers sang along and learnt to play the bones.

IT MAY HAVE BEEN a brothel but I slept like a baby, although not until I had watched all 59 channels. I love American TV — there's nothing on, but who cares? It's therapeutic, it's mindless, it's a sport in itself. Though, it must be said, the downside of such choice is always feeling like you're missing out on something — like someone's having a better party on the other channel. So you flick and flick and flick. You can't relax. What time is it? Isn't there a movie on four? Wonder what's on six? Honestly, these actors have no chance; they can't even finish a sentence before you've gone from the shopping channel to *Friends* to *Star Trek* to the baseball.

So you lie there and say, okay I'll do one more round, I'll go from one to 59 and if there's nothing on I'll turn the light off. So back to one you go. Then you find a rerun of *M.A.S.H.* on five. Hey, I didn't know *M.A.S.H.* was on! You then make an executive decision that stopping at five doesn't count as part of your final flick. You decide to watch *M.A.S.H.* for five minutes, but only if this means you qualify for the bonus round. The bonus round means you can go all the way back up to 59 (which was part of your original plan) but you don't *have* to stop at channel one on the way back because *M.A.S.H.* was on channel five, remember? You're actually allowed to go all the way to 59, back to one and then back to five. And so on. And so on.

Okay, it's not therapeutic at all — it's bloody frustrating.

I HAD THE PHONE NUMBER for the *Richmond Times-Dispatch*, the paper which featured Betty with her quilt on the front page. Andy Taylor was a contact I had seen on the web when I was in Lucy's office in New York so I just prayed that he'd be working on a Saturday. I also hoped his office was close to the brothel; I didn't know how far I could walk in 95-degree heat with a set of golf clubs.

'Our building is just across the street,' were Andy's magic words.

And it was. It was a lovely building, plush, posh and, most importantly, *cool*. Andy offered me a cup of tea and seemed genuinely interested in my adventure. I can't even begin to explain how wonderful it is when someone doesn't just show you the nearest door. This was, after all, a rather bizarre trip and I never took it for granted when people gave me the time of day or helped me get hold of people.

Or showered me in money.

'You can leave your gear here for the day if you like,' Andy offered.

'Thanks. Say, do you know Betty?' I asked, pointing to the front page.

'No, I didn't write that story.'

'Is this rest home far?'

'About 20 bucks in a cab.'

'What are the chances she plays golf?'

Andy laughed.

Betty returned my call half an hour later. She seemed lovely. Very clear, concise instructions followed about where we could meet should I wish to talk to her about her quilt. I hadn't mentioned golf. Baby steps.

'I'll meet you in the care wing at 1.30,' she said.

Yes! Could this be my first game in America? Would Betty be the birdie queen of Richmond?

Just as I was sitting down to enjoy a celebratory drink (a flat Diet Coke courtesy of *Richmond Times-Dispatch* journalists, who no doubt left the bottle lying around after Friday night drinks), Paige, the crime reporter (apt name for a journalist, don't you think?), walked in.

'Paige, hi, what are you doing here?' Andy asked.

'I'm off to a clown wedding.'

'A what?' I scoffed, dribbling warm Coke down my shirt.

'Paige, this is Justin,' Andy said, telling her about my trip. Paige was normally a serious journalist covering serious issues. The previous night, for example, she'd ridden with the police, where after only 10 minutes they had found a black man who'd overdosed. Needless to say, two clowns getting married wasn't a typical story for her but she just couldn't turn it down.

Nor could I.

The only problem now was calling off my meeting with Betty in the care wing. Unfortunately, the clown wedding was booked for the same time. Sadly, I didn't know the clowns well enough to ask them to cancel just so Betty and I could go out for a hit. And there was no way I could get to both places.

I wandered down to change some money and prepare myself for a day I'd never forget. What should I wear? I wondered. Would I need to write a speech? Who was organising the flowers for the reception? Who *were* these people again?

It was 11 in the morning and I hadn't eaten so found the nearest convenience store. While the smooth sounds of Al Green reverberated around the shop, I couldn't help but notice the man behind the counter bore an uncanny resemblance to the Reverend himself.

'Al Green,' I said, pointing to the speakers. 'You look just like him!'

The Al Green lookalike just laughed. 'What can we do for ya, man?'

'I'm starving, Reverend, what can I eat?'

'Well,' he said, plunging his hand into the chest freezer. 'These frozen sandwiches are pretty good.'

'Frozen sandwiches?'

'Yeah, they're good man!'

I ordered two. He popped them in the microwave and told me that he was an ex-Marine from New York, but had deserted the madness of the big smoke for a quieter life in Richmond. I ate the two frozen sandwiches, which were not only worryingly edible, but also somehow fresh. Even scarier, though, was next opting for a frozen cheesy pizza to chase them down. The Reverend spotted that I was either very, very hungry or the heat had been playing tricks on me. He decided to try his luck for one final sale:

'How about a frozen sausage biscuit, they're pretty good too!'

'Okay,' I smiled deliriously.

So with food (?) in my stomach I rather hurriedly sweated my way back to the *Richmond Times-Dispatch*. I was almost running which, given the heat, was not entirely sensible, but it's amazing what the prospect of an air-conditioned building can do. Paige was all ready to go when I returned.

It was official — we were going to a clown wedding!

On the way Paige told me she grew up in Delaware, one of the smallest states and, to be honest, one I'd never heard of.

'My parents are actually down for the weekend — you should join us for a drink tonight.'

This was getting better all the time. Richmond hospitality was indeed exceeding any expectations that may have been dampened from reading yesterday's violent front page.

'I've been there twice in the last two years,' Paige said, pointing to Richmond Hospital. 'It's a bit of a running gag at work. I had my gall bladder removed first, then a year later my appendix. I've had bad luck lately.'

'Well, that luck's all gonna change today, Paige, 'cos we're going to a clown wedding!'

All I can say is I'm glad *we* weren't the ones wearing layer upon layer of make-up today. These clowns had chosen the hottest day of the century to tie the knot. We couldn't even walk from the car park to the Ridge Baptist Church without losing half a gallon of water via our foreheads.

But it was worth it, and nothing could have prepared us for what we were about to see. Bonkers (aka Mike Cox), the groom, was in full costume waiting out the back with the celebrant, who was also dressed as a clown. Paige introduced herself to both and I squeezed past with my golf bag. I tried to explain to Bonkers what it was I was doing in America, but this was a little difficult. I mean, here was a man dressed as a clown; about to get married to another clown; the 70-year-old woman next to him was *dressed* as a clown; and he had a bloody clown from New Zealand asking him for a game of golf! No wonder he looked confused.

As sweat dripped down his face and make-up ran past his ears all he could muster was, 'All the way from New Zealand? Well, thanks for coming to my wedding!'

We'd gotten here just in the nick of time; the ceremony was about to start. Bonkers wiped his brow, Paige grabbed her notebook and I left my clubs by an unlocked door.

'Do you think they'll be okay there?'

'This is a church,' Paige replied.

She had a point.

The celebrant (who had bells on her feet) led us through to the front of the church where I discovered our day was about to get a whole lot stranger. There, peering from the pews, were no less than 70 clowns, in full costume. What was even stranger than seeing so many wigs, red noses and size 16 shoes was the feeling of normality and restraint. Not only were the clowns sitting still, they were incredibly quiet. It was all rather eerie. Surely they were dying to unicycle past the altar or juggle hymn books?

Soon, though, they started to fidget, whisper and, like any wedding, eagerly anticipate the arrival of the bride.

Who just happened to be a clown.

Everyone received red noses on arrival and although I was having trouble

With the newlyweds, Bonkers and Sweet Thang

breathing through mine, I tolerated it for Bonkers' sake. This was his day after all.

He was waiting at the front, smiling while the organist played 'Send in the Clowns'. The other clowns may have been smiling also, but it was very hard to tell with their painted-on, exaggerated expressions. Some looked like they'd just won the lottery, others like they'd just lost their family and entire belongings in a house fire. One clown had to contend with not only two kids but also a bald, rather scruffy-looking cockatoo. Paige and I shook our heads in disbelief — we had arrived on another planet.

The next trick involved Sweet Thang (aka Barbara Ford) walking down the aisle to join Bonkers at the altar. Sporting a red wig and a red heart for a nose, she looked like a . . . clown. The celebrant's shoes rang as she walked over to join them.

'Right,' she said, 'I want you all to know that this is a Christian marriage. That means no horns, blowers or noisemakers.'

That includes that damn bird, she should have added.

For the next hour we witnessed the tying of the knot. Surprisingly, the readings were apt, the hymns were well sung and the bird kept his mouth shut. Bonkers, at 52, was a few years older than his bride. They met as neighbours at a time when Sweet Thang was going through a rough divorce. Bonkers, already into clowning, suggested she give it a try. She hadn't looked back since.

'I found out how wonderful the world of clowning was and we always said if we ever got married, we'd get married in clown outfits,' she told me after the ceremony.

'So, what do you and Bonkers, I mean *Mike*, do for a living?'

'I work at an insurance company and Mike works for the Department of Game and Inland Fisheries.'

This was only small talk on my part; I was stalling. I was too nervous to ask whether her Bonkers played from bunkers. What if, after all this effort, he didn't even play golf? Unfortunately, if I was going to ask it would have to be now.

Because Paige was about to leave.

In her car.

With air conditioning.

'Get out of the way, you stupid clowns,' I mumbled, finally grabbing Mike's attention. He had been swamped by friends and relatives, i.e. people who were *supposed* to be there. He spotted the golf bag on my back and asked, 'Is that your Big Bertha?'

'Not quite, Bonkers, but it does bring me to my point. Do you want to play golf tomorrow?'

'Tomorrow? I'm going on honeymoon with my beautiful wife.'

'Right. Okay, just out of interest, do you play golf?'

'No,' he replied, smiling.

It was a wonderful feeling knowing that whenever I see Richmond on a map I'll think about clowns and cockatoos. It wasn't so wonderful, however, finding two 'Front Pagers' who also happened to be non-golfers. To make

You may now kiss the clown

'Sweet Thang', 'Bonkers' wed in costumes, makeup

BY PAIGE AKIN
Times-Dispatch Staff Writer

JOE MAHONEY/TIMES-DISPATCH

Barbara Ford and Michael Cox exchanged their wedding vows clown-style yesterday.

There was enough foundation and eyeliner on the audience at Ridge Baptist Church yesterday to cover a hundred Anna Nicole Smiths.

But seriously — enough clowning around.

Friends and family gathered for the nuptials of Barbara "Sweet Thang" Ford and Michael "Bonkers" Cox, two stars of the local clown community. Half of the audience, about 50 people, were dressed in full clown regalia and made silly faces at each other across the aisle.

Audience members who came dressed in traditional wedding attire received red clown noses to brighten their outfits.

Just before the ceremony began, the organist played "Send in the Clowns."

It's not all fun and games for Ford and Cox.

She works during the week for a local insurance company, and he's employed by the state Department of Game and Inland Fisheries.

But each weekend, "Sweet Thang" and "Bonkers" shed their stuffy work clothes to paint faces and sculpt balloons at children's birthday parties.

They met more than 10 years ago when they lived around the corner from one another. She was going through a rough divorce when Cox, already into clowning, suggested she give it a whirl.

Since then, she has traded her high heels for clown shoes.

"I found out how wonderful the world of clowning was," Ford said. "And we always said that if we ever got married, we'd get married in clown."

Backstage before the ceremony, the groom swabbed his face, which dripped with sweat. But it wasn't the nerves — it was the 90-degree temperature combined with layer upon layer of clothes and makeup.

He wore rainbow overalls and an oversized bow tie. The bride wore a dress of hearts and lace, with a veil over her trademark red wig.

They were married yesterday at Ridge Baptist by Barbara "Pee-vie" Moss, also a clown.

As she carried the rings to the couple, bells jingled atop her giant, yellow shoes.

"This is a Christian marriage," she warned the audience, "so that means no horns, no noisemakers."

The couple will honeymoon in Nags Head, N.C., this week.

And they're leaving their makeup behind.

matters worse, I had tried to call the rest home to let Betty know I wouldn't be able to make it to the care wing. Repeatedly, I got the answer machine. I tried, Betty.

Sorry, I really am.

'You're not going to stay in that brothel again tonight, are you?' Andy asked when we arrived back at the *Times-Dispatch*. He was a little concerned after having found out what I'd paid the previous night. Actually, 'little concerned' is probably the wrong term; 'nearly lost his lunch' would be more appropriate.

'Eighty-five bucks? It's a brothel! That's outrageous!' he'd barked.

I didn't have the heart to tell him I'd be staying again tonight. I had little choice: either I bunked on the *out*skirts of Richmond or stayed *with* the skirts closer to town.

Plus, I couldn't afford a taxi. I was determined, however, to get a better price than last night.

'No,' said the half-deaf, half-blind man at reception.

'But all I need is a *single* bed,' I pleaded.

'We only have doubles.'

'But I've seen a room with one bed in it, why can't I stay in there?'

'What?'

'I said, I've seen a room with one bed in it.'

'Where are my glasses?'

'On your forehead.'

'I said, where are my glasses?'

'I know what you said. They're *there*,' I said, pointing to his shiny top.

Confident he'd located them, he continued: 'I only work here, I don't set the rates.'

Now, I have no problem with someone being half deaf and half blind, as my friend here so obviously was. I do, however, have to question his survival techniques at four in the morning in one of Virginia's seediest brothels. How would he know it was me, not a burglar, going into my room? Would he give us a call should the fire alarm sound, or would he check the kettle?

'Yes, officer, I would know exactly how much money went missing from the till, if I could only *see* the thing.'

Okay, I was in a bad mood because I couldn't get a cheap room.

48

It had been a big day. I decided to do my washing in the bath; it dried in about an hour. Lack of energy denied me the 59-channel flick. Instead I met Paige and her family for a drink at an Irish bar run by a guy whose claim to fame was that he once served the Beatles. Paige's parents very kindly bought me a few beers, although it was obvious I had some catching up to do — Mrs Paige was already pissed.

She was giggling, cursing her daughter for smoking and telling stories of how she and Mr Paige used to go out till four in the morning — and then have a beer for breakfast.

'So what's New Zealand like?' she asked.

'It's lovely,' I replied, finishing my beer, and at least making some attempt to catch her before her stool fell backwards.

'Are you part of the Euro?' she asked.

'What do you mean?'

'The Euro, are you part of the Euro in New Zealand?'

'No, to be part of the *Euro* you have to live in *Europe*. We live at the other end of the planet.'

She then started telling me about the differences between Paige and her brother.

'My son, he's charming, he's intelligent, his friends love him, the *ladies* love him, and . . .' She paused, trying to find the right word. 'What can I say . . . he's a sex god!'

Paige then intervened, concerned her mother was starting to tell the wrong kind of stories: 'One time Mom knew he had taken a girl upstairs but he didn't know she knew. She sneaked up the stairs and found the dog at the top with a condom hanging out of his mouth.'

'*She*'s sensible,' Mrs Paige said, proudly pointing to her daughter. '*He* on the other hand,' she concluded with a hint of mischief in her eye, 'is a ladies' man.'

What surprised me next was not only seeing Mrs Paige make it to the next bar, but also managing to down a couple of mojitos in the process. They were all fine company and very hospitable, though. It was standing room only in the Havana Bar so we drank more mojitos (rum, sugar, ice, lime juice and sprigs of mojito mint — mmm, one more please), played cards and bet with toothpicks.

I WOKE UP HUNGRY. Even though I *knew* the fridge in my room didn't have food in it (there was none when I arrived and I sure as hell hadn't put any in since), this didn't stop me opening and reopening it every time I walked past. I guess old habits are hard to break; some of us *still* believe if we give the fridge 10 minutes to itself, next time we open the door a KFC feast will be staring us in the face.

The café downstairs had greasy spoon written all over it, but it was close and cheap.

'Do you have Dr Pepper?' I asked, once ensconced in a booth. To me, Dr Pepper is *the* taste of America.

'Pardon?' she smiled, obviously trying to understand my accent.

'Dr Pepper,' I repeated.

'We got Mr Pip. It's close, and if you don't like it we can get you something else.'

How sweet!

What Mr Pip lacked in taste it definitely made up for in size — it arrived in a bucket.

Meanwhile two truly obese people were occupying the booth next to me. One of them ordered beer at 11 in the morning and made the waitress go through the list of specials three times — just because he could. He was rude, obnoxious and I wanted to hit him (but he was real big and I've never been in a fight).

'Fried chicken, with lots of gravy!' he barked. 'And some biscuits!'

When the food arrived, they prayed.

Bags packed and (over-inflated) bill paid, I met a man called Fred in the reception of the brothel. I had seen him the day before. He was a short, stumpy man with a walking stick. He had short little arms and a voice like Mickey Mouse. Bald around the bottom half of his scalp, his hair was dyed black on top.

He shook my hand and said, 'I'm Fred.'

Fred and I chewed the fat for a bit then heard the doorbell ring. Gwen, the lady at reception I'd met earlier that morning, answered it. Fred then told me, 'That lady, she feeds the birds every day, even though she can barely get down the stairs.'

'Gwen?'

'Every day.'

'No, I think her name is *Gwen*.'

'Every day I say!'

'No, her name, it's . . . oh, don't worry.'

After a pause, Fred spotted my passport.

'My grandfather had a clock that was made in New Zealand. He used to collect things, much like me. I collect things, like cars.'

An uncomfortable silence ensued. I had no jokes about clocks.

'I'm on the disability allowance,' Fred continued, clearly not happy with the gap in proceedings. 'I been sick mosta my life. I got cancer ever since my mom died. It's a slow kind of cancer.'

Well, if I thought the *clock* comment had me stuffed, his latest offering had me *speechless*. Thankfully, Fred moved on to a more user-friendly subject.

'There's so much history in Richmond, that's why I love it. I come here for a month four times a year. This hotel is the cheapest in Richmond.'

'I don't think so, Fred — $85 for a double?'

'You should do what I do, just get a single.'

I looked over to reception. Count your lucky stars you're not working today, ol' boy.

Even though there seemed no reduction in the outside temperature, I walked (much to the surprise of locals driving by) to the infamous Hollywood Cemetery. Perched above the James River rapids, this stunning part of Richmond contains the graves of two US presidents, one Confederate president and over 18,000 Confederate soldiers.

Fred was right; there was a lot of history in this place and, rather surprisingly, where you'd normally expect to find a depressing graveyard was an uplifting final resting place. Just a pity I felt so nervous walking there.

A big old red, white and blue gas-guzzler was waiting for me on my return.

'Yeah, well, make the most of it 'cos it'll have to be off the road come January,' the taxi driver said of his pride and joy.

'You're joking, why?'

'It'll be 12 years old.'

'You've got to take cars off the road when they're 12 years old?'

'Them's the rules in Richmond.'

'Just Richmond or all of Virginia?'

'Just Richmond.'

'So, who's your favourite American?' I asked, aware that I'd exhausted my knowledge of cars. Maybe we should talk clocks?

'Martin Luther King,' he said, without a pause. 'Now that may sound strange for a white man to say, but the older I get the more I respect that man. I believe he was a *good* man. He was everything to everyone. He would have made it to president; I truly believe that, him and John Kennedy were awful close.'

'What about least favourite?'

'Hmm, I'd have to say Jesse James. I didn't care for Bill Clinton much neither. Anyone who has never served in the army does not get my vote. He ran away to Canada when he should have gone to war. Anyone who's too chicken doesn't get my vote. He was a sleazeball. Did a good job, though. He surprised me. I'll give credit where credit's due. He's still a sleazeball, though.

'In terms of favourites, John Glenn would be up there as well, first man on the moon.'

'I thought that was Neil Armstrong?'

'Don't ever let anyone tell you that; it was John Glenn. You take a look at the history books real careful and you'll see it was John Glenn.'

I was confused. I felt cheated. What about what my teachers had told me?

'But that's the beautiful thing about America,' he continued. 'That's why I love it so much, we could agree to disagree and still respect each other. I mean, you might love Bill Clinton.'

I thought it was Neil Armstrong.

'Ever been out of America?' I asked.

'I been to Vegas.'

I waited and waited and waited at Richmond railway station. I wondered how Meg had got on at her wedding. I thought about Betty and her quilt and Bonkers and his honeymoon. A garbage truck driver from New York was telling me how he couldn't wait to get back to Brooklyn to see his son.

Little did I know, in the next few days I *too* would become a father.

DAY 7: CHARLESTON, SOUTH CAROLINA

MESSAGE OVER INTERCOM: 'Okay, listen up everybody, the wash-rooms at the back of the carriage are now closed because people keep using them!'

Well. *sorry.*

I was back on the train, my second home. It's always a great feeling knowing you haven't missed your connection and have found your seat safely.

Well, what I could see of it anyway.

You see, the first problem I had encountered this morning was the lady sitting next me. It would be fair to say most women on this train had one arse — the lady in seat 18H, however, had three. Sadly, 18G (me) would spend eight hours wedged in a small space by the aisle armrest. 18H would sleep most of the way, sometimes lean on 18G and, if he was really lucky, dribble on him. 18G decided pretty early on this was going to be the longest trip of his life.

Luckily, the carriage had entertainment in the form of a 10-year-old boy who was a cross between Gary Coleman from *Diff'rent Strokes* and a pre-teen Michael Jackson. Having spent the first two hours saying nothing, he certainly made up for it in the next six when he sang, mimicked Austin Powers and threw baseballs from one end of the carriage to the other. We were best friends by the time we reached Charleston, which is where I'd hoped he would then say, 'Justin, meet my Aunty May. Hey, we could give you a ride to your hotel if you like!'

Travel, though, as we know, is not plain sailing.

And I was about to spend the next hour overboard.

The problem started with only having $10 in my wallet. I realise I should have cashed another hundred back in Richmond but I was trying to avoid the inevitable: spending more money. So while most people on the train drifted into a light slumber and watched North Carolina gently roll by, I jealously watched them eat, drink and congratulate each other for having cashed a hundred before they left.

Meanwhile, 18H had not only woken up, she'd also managed to eat the café carriage out of house and home. As I looked through my wallet for spare change she proceeded to polish off burgers, hot dogs and a large plate of fries.

I wasn't too concerned about my cash-flow crisis as I assumed Charleston train station would be open 24 hours, with all the amenities. Assumption, however, is not the smartest of travelling companions. Having spent only three dollars in eight hours, I departed a proud man. Unfortunately, 30 others departed at the same time to find only two taxi-vans waiting. I jumped in one with three other people, once again *assuming* that seven dollars would cover the trip. One thing I *had* done was book accommodation, which was just as well really as Charleston station had no staff, no money machines and no food. I'm surprised they even left the lights on for us. Not that it mattered — I was just glad to be in a cab bound for bed.

'How much is it to La Quinta?' I asked, once we'd already left.

'Twelve dollars,' the driver replied.

'Shit, I've only got seven,' I mumbled.

'What's that?' the driver asked.

I said nothing, embarrassed. I wanted my bed. This situation felt bad.

And was about to get a whole lot worse.

'I think he said he's only got seven dollars,' a man from Boston said in a loud clear voice. *Too* loud and clear a voice if you ask me.

'Seven dollars?' the driver demanded.

'I could always walk,' I muttered, still embarrassed.

'Ha! Walk? Around here? It's too dangerous to walk. In the day, no problem — not at night.'

I had become a charity case. Ladies fished around in their handbags and passed money back. 'I hope they're only ones,' they said, passing notes in the dark that could easily have been fives or twenties. This was too embarrassing; I knew I'd never see these people again, but even so. I thanked them and skulked back into my seat.

'I sure hope you plan the rest of your trip better than this,' the taxi driver said. The rest laughed. Don't tell me about planning trips, buddy! You have no idea the hell I've put myself through in the last week. I have only 28 days to get across your whole country. I'm *planning* to go to places you've never even heard of. I've spent three dollars in eight hours. I've had no sleep because the woman next to me had an arse the size of a bus. I stayed in a brothel. For two nights. I've had to book more hotels, flights and train trips than you've had hot dinners. And yes, all I want is a game of golf. So don't sit there all smug in your comfy front seat and tell *me* about planning. You should have planned your career better, then we wouldn't even be having this imaginary argument in my head!

I think someone needed a sleep.

I clutched those dollar notes like my life depended on it. The last thing I needed now was to lose them on the taxi floor or out an open window.

'Don't worry about it,' said the woman in front of me, after I'd apologised for the second time. 'We've all been in that situation, I've been stuck many times when I'm travelling.'

'Well, I'm sorry, I just feel bad.'

'Don't worry about it,' she repeated.

The first stop we came to was my guardian angel's hotel. I thanked her again and she wished me well for the remainder of my trip. The driver seemed to take some time unloading her bags. Meanwhile, an uncomfortable silence ensued between the couple from Boston and the penniless New Zealander. I still felt bad for having taken their money.

Things took another turn when the driver rejoined us.

I couldn't be entirely sure (as I was sitting down the back), but I *think* the driver said to the Boston couple that she had ended up paying my full fare. The man from Boston confirmed this by saying, 'Oh really? That was nice of her.'

This was proving to be one bizarre ride. First, no money; now I was loaded. From rags to riches in less than 10 minutes. And my fare had been paid! Was I now *up* out of all this? I daren't turn the lights on to count my earnings. You gotta know when to hold 'em . . .

There was still one thing bothering me: if my guardian angel really had paid my bill, as the driver had suggested, wouldn't that mean the woman from Boston would now expect her money back? And why did he tell them and not me? I would now have to assume that she *hadn't* paid and hope the driver informed me otherwise.

This was getting confusing.

I decided, as a gesture, to offer the driver the full fare of $12 once we got to the hotel, assuming he would then say, 'Oh no, don't worry, your lady back there paid for you', and I would say, 'Really? How lovely', and because he was honest, give him a tip.

Or maybe I had gotten the whole thing wrong? Maybe she hadn't paid my fare at all. Maybe all the driver had said to the Boston couple was that his wife had made him chicken gumbo for lunch three days in a row.

'Oh really? That was nice of her.'

I know this may sound like a pathetic little 10 minutes but you've got to remember I was delirious, starving and still traumatised by my time with 18H. So upon arrival at my accommodation I reached into my pocket and hesitantly handed the $12 to the driver. He looked surprised, then elated. In fact, he looked like a man who'd just been told he would never have to work again.

'Well, God bless you son!' he said. 'Thank you *so* much.'

Damn, she did pay. And he didn't tell me.

'Do you have funds for the rest of the trip?' he asked, quickly putting the cash in his pocket. 'I mean, how are you going to get around now?'

'I'll manage,' I grumbled.

Back to rags.

I often wonder where travel stories end up. Everyone on that harmless little taxi ride saw the same thing but would tell it a different way. Somewhere in California right now the guardian angel would be telling her travelling buddies about a young New Zealander who didn't have enough money for his ride. Her friends would all agree that she had 'done the right thing' and 'what goes around comes around; someone will help you next time you're at Nairobi airport'.

Alternatively, somewhere in Boston right now an argument would be erupting about how many times people get ripped off while travelling.

'Not necessarily mugged, as some might imagine,' the husband would say. 'It's the little things; remember that New Zealander we had on that taxi ride in Charleston, honey? *Supposedly* he had no money. I mean, who gets into a cab at midnight with no money? He probably did the same thing in every town. Hell, he's probably in Vegas right now spending our money!'

And somewhere in Charleston a 60-year-old taxi driver is telling his wife the reason she's drinking French champagne tonight is because 'I helped out this young lad by telling him if he was going to have a successful trip he would just have to plan things a little better.'

Unfortunately, I was on the outskirts again. Beautiful, historic Charleston lay just miles away but for all I knew I could have been on any American highway, anywhere in the States. All I could see from my room were a Motel 6, a Mr Waffle, a Super 8, an Arby's and smoke-bellowing 18-wheelers roaring past every 30 seconds. This is a view I would have to get used to if I wanted a bed across America. These charmless, identical hotel chains were everywhere, all sitting on cheap land, miles out of town.

I surveyed my new room. There were two king-size beds (one I'd never use), a 28-inch TV I'd barely watch and a table and chairs I wished I could fill. Why couldn't they just give me a room with a single bed and air conditioning? That's all I needed. Maybe only *couples* came to America? Maybe I should have brought a golfing *foursome*, then we could have filled both beds and shared the costs? That would also have solved the problem of finding potential partners. But it wouldn't be nearly as much fun.

AFTER SCOFFING my free breakfast in the hotel lobby the next morning (why do you eat so fast when you're by yourself?), I asked how long it might take to catch a bus to the historic area. 'A bus — *is* there one?' one clerk said to the other.

Not a good start. Eventually a woman who, given her knowledge of public transport in the area obviously rode it every day, told me a bus to town would take 20 minutes. She was very helpful. But so, so wrong.

Two hours and 10 minutes later I disembarked from a vehicle that was dragging its feet in the heat as much as the rest of us. This tired old piece of metal chugged, spluttered and stalled the entire journey. In fact, to call it a bus would be a lie. This thing was obviously beaten up at school and still bore the scars. To make it worse, the guy driving seemed to have no concept of time. He stopped at every bus stop, even if no one rang the bell!

As a result, for the second time in 24 hours, I had an imaginary argument with my friend behind the wheel. This time, however, I didn't tip him.

For all its beauty (and I have rarely seen a more historic or stunning town) Charleston sure did have its problems. The headlines from the front page of the local paper, *The Post and Courier*.

Police Officer Kills Man During Stop

Woman Gives Birth and Leaves Baby in Restaurant Toilet

18-year-old Girl Runs Over Two Teenagers, Killing One of Them

Needless to say, unless I wanted to visit the local prison, police station or cemetery (Buddy Ebsen, the old guy from *The Beverly Hillbillies*, had just died as well), a game of golf definitely wasn't on the cards. Not for the first time I began to wonder whether this whole venture was a waste of time. The States is a big place and I felt lost. I craved familiarity, a beer with my mates; hell, I just craved a newspaper with some good news. While holidaymakers waited in line for free maps at the Charleston information centre, I went to the community newspaper stand and found a copy of *Island Life*. This is where my day, and indeed my life, was about to change.

I was about to become a parent.

The Carolina Youth Development Center was holding its annual Million Dollar Duck Race, which raises money for kids' shelters. 'Help a Child . . . Adopt a Duck' was the headline in the paper. What happens is you adopt a duck, put him in the water on race day with all the other rubber ducks, and one lucky person wins a million bucks. Unfortunately, the day of the race had already been and gone. I still wanted one of these ducks, dammit, so I adopted one. It cost me $17.95 and I named him Charleston.

When the lady from the Youth Development Center handed me my receipt I wondered what I had done. Had I even *thought* about this? After all, adoption is not a spur-of-the-moment kind of thing. It was a big decision and this was not a small duck. But let me tell you — I never thought I'd say this because it sounds so clichéd — but once I actually held Charleston in my arms and looked into his beautiful blue eyes (then at the receipt), I decided the little bastard cost too much to abandon.

The only problem now was taking him everywhere I went. I hadn't exactly been winning friends and influencing people carrying a seven iron around town; God knows what they'd think when I coupled that with a duck the size of a soccer ball.

The midday heat was relentless but walking around historic Charleston

Carolina Youth Development Center

Help A Child...Adopt a Duck

By Victoria Marshall
Special Events Manager

Thousands of yellow rubber ducks have been spotted flocking towards Berkeley County. On July 5, 2003, the Home Telephone-Santee Cooper Million Dollar Duck Race to benefit the Callen-Lacey Center for Children will take place in Old Santee Canal Park, Moncks Corner, at 4:00 p.m.

One lucky duck may have the opportunity to win a $1 million dollars, along with many other prizes that include a Disney World vacation package, Mystery Get-A-Way for two, Health & Beauty Package, rocker/recliner, Jim Booth print and many, many more prizes.

This will be the fourth year the ducks have raced to benefit the local shelter for abused and neglected children, which has served more than 400 children, aging from newborn to 17, since the doors opened in 1998.

"This is the only major fundraising event for Callen-Lacey Center, and this year's goal is to raise $40,000. The proceeds of the event will help keep the

emergency shelter open for the children who have no other place to go until a suitable home is found," said McBee Zimmerman, Director of Shelter Services for Carolina Youth Development Center.

"We are very grateful to Home Telephone and Santee Cooper Power for sponsoring this family event and helping us create awareness that there is a need in our community for the service we provide at Callen-Lacey. We are one of two emergency shelters that service the tri-county area and the only shelter for children in Berkeley County," said Zimmerman.

Callen-Lacey volunteers have duck adoption papers available for $5.00 (1) each; a six-quack (6) for $25.00; Very Important Duck (30) for $100.00, and the Big Duck on the Pond (130) for $500.00.

There will be a corresponding numbered duck for each adoption form. On race day, thousands of ducks will swim down the waterway towards the finish line to win their adoptive parents great prizes, hoping for their chance at a million dollars. The adoptive parents

Island Life, *Charleston, South Carolina*

Charleston, the media megastar

(the city, not the duck — this is going to be confusing till we get to the next chapter) was worth it. Ladies wove sweetgrass baskets in the market while housekeepers swept the verandas of elegant three-storey homesteads. I felt like I was in *Gone with the Wind*. It's the sort of place where instead of just concentrating on the 'now' and taking photos with your mind, you find yourself repeating, 'This is too beautiful, I have to come back some day.'

At Jestine's restaurant I had to choose between deep-fried pork, beef stew, pecan-fried catfish or a BBQ pork sandwich. To make life even tougher, I had to somehow find room for either coconut cream pie or a generous serving of banana pecan pie. You would be right in suggesting that not a lot of golf had taken place in my day so far, but I knew I would be playing a Front Pager by nightfall.

In the meantime I felt it only appropriate to join the glamorous housewives who were doing their part to help the country's economy. King Street was obviously *the* place to shop and they were doing their darndest to keep it that way. It's also probably the only street in the world where you don't see one ugly person. It felt unreal, like a film set. You almost expected to see producers jump from the bushes, rugby tackle, gag and evacuate the first pimply-faced, fat woman they saw. Lucky those same producers never caught sight of the golf club-wielding Duck Dad; all hell could have broken loose.

It was during my tour of the old city that I discovered a new phenomenon: Jimmy Buffett's store, Margaritaville. I tell you, this guy has got it made. He wrote a few top 10 hits in the seventies, drank a bit of tequila, convinced middle-aged men and women to turn up to his concerts in shirts they wouldn't normally be seen dead in, and now, some 30 years later, invites those very same punters to buy Margaritaville beach towels, rubber parrots, T-shirts and guitar picks. Apparently he's making more money now than he ever has, and all because he's living and *has* lived the life we all crave. He's still basking in the Florida Keys, still writing songs and still not taking life seriously.

These shops are popping up everywhere. It seems people can't get enough. Many faithfuls even go one step further, leaving behind the snow of Chicago, heading to Florida and becoming officially Buffettised.

Funnily enough, when I walked into the store, a Jimmy Buffett record was playing.

'How sick of the music are you?' I asked the teenager behind the counter.

'Pretty sick of it,' he said.

'How long did it take before that happened?'

'We work in seven-hour shifts and hear the same thing all day — it doesn't take long.'

Just as I was about to jump in a cab (I wasn't about to get on that bus again), I noticed a rather peculiar sign outside a boutique. I couldn't work out whether it was a brilliant marketing ploy or just a mistake: *Hundreds of prices inside*. I didn't have time to find out.

The cab driver, in his forties, had been born in Britain but spent two-thirds of his life in the States. And he had bad teeth.

'So you haven't played any golf yet?' he asked, when I told him why I was in Charleston.

'No,' I replied.

'Not surprising really, you do know you've come —'

'— at the wrong time of year, I know. Can you please take me to this address?' I asked, handing him a brochure.

'You come to Charleston and you want to go *there*?' he said, pointing at the desired address. 'What do you wanna go there for?'

'It's a long story,' I said, lounging back in the big old leather seat, just happy not to be on that bus. 'Ever been to New Zealand?'

'I'll go when I'm retired. I hate planes. I tell ya, something that big should not be able to sit up there in the sky. I'd freak that something would happen.'

'Who's your favourite American of all time?' I asked.

'Well, at the moment it would have to be the Dixie Chicks. Supposedly, this is a free society; yet they speak their mind and get censored. Hell, their careers were even on the line for a while there. That's bullshit.'

'What about least favourite?'

'Hmm, least favourite, that's a tough one. Ah, I know . . . Snoop Doggy Dogg. That man thinks he's all that, but he's gotta be the most butt-ugly man I've ever seen!'

Twenty minutes later, Charleston and I teed off at Frankie's Fun Park mini-golf course while our driver watched — a little puzzled I might add — from the car park. Sure, part of me bought the rubber duck for the cause (who wouldn't want to support homeless kids?), but it didn't do any harm that Charleston happened to be on the front page.

Okay, so I was stretching the rules a little, and indeed, some may look upon playing golf with a toy as a little desperate, but I needed a game. Plus, from a competitive viewpoint there was no chance of losing.

Back at the hotel I had a message from Harriet, a reporter from *The Post and Courier*. She had been in touch with Andy from the *Richmond Times-Dispatch*, who had told her there was a mad New Zealander in town. I returned her call and asked whether she could shed some light on a person I might play golf with. Unfortunately, she just repeated the morbid front-page stories I'd already read that morning. She also told me of a story about how a number of dogs in the area were dying after having been left in hot cars. Honestly, dead dogs and plastic ducks; this trip was getting more bizarre by the second.

'Does Charleston normally have this much crime?' I asked.

'We don't normally get a lot, but if it happens it tends to happen all at the same time. You're in for a treat, though — South Carolina has some of the best golf courses in the world.'

'I'm only here for two days,' I said. 'And so far I haven't found anyone to play with.'

'You're joking, you haven't played golf yet? You've been in the country a week!'

'Okay, I lie. I did actually have a game today.'

'Really, who with?'

'Oh, just a friend of mine.'

THE NEXT MORNING I rose early, drank bad coffee and was delighted to find a lovely story on the front page:

Blind commentator leaving baseball

By Gene Sapakoff

River Dogs' Don Wardlow retires, saying 'Family has to be No. 1'

It isn't that it just wasn't fun anymore. Don Wardlow enjoyed broadcasting Charleston River Dogs' games as one of the sport's most respected radio analysts. He also appreciated the opportunity to inspire other blind people with his unusual, high-profile place in minor league baseball history.

But because he loves his wife even more, Wardlow on Friday officially announced his retirement from broadcasting. His Braille typewriter has made its last appearance in a press box. His tape recorder will be used for music, not interviews.

Wardlow, 39, and partner Jim Lucas, 40, began broadcasting baseball games as students at New Jersey's Glassboro State College in 1983 and have worked together as a minor league duo full time since the 1991 season, including the last three seasons with the River Dogs.

'I'm just somebody who after 12 years and almost 1500 ball games and a lot of bus rides realises that was a lot of nights away from Melanie,' Wardlow said after breaking the news to the River Dogs staff. 'The longer I did it the more I didn't get used to it. Family has to be No. 1.'

Melanie Wardlow has been Don's biggest fan. She attended as many River Dogs home games as possible, though had to miss a few due to complications from hydrocephalus — the excessive fluid in the skull she was born with.

Typically, Melanie Wardlow handed out line-up cards just inside the front gate at Riley Park.

'At some point,' Don Wardlow said, 'I had to see she'd done enough for me. I need to be there to say "Baby, you're wonderful" more often.'

I spent the morning trying to track down this amazing man, which was easier said than done given the rather confusing dialling codes in the local phone directory:

Before you dial a local number use one of the following codes for Charleston and North Charleston:

200, 202, 207, 209, 214, 218, 219, 220, 223, 224, 225, 243, 255, 259, 261, 266, 270, 276, 277, 278, 289, 296, 297, 302, 308, 323, 324, 327, 329, 343, 345, 359, 364, 367, 371, 377, 402, 404, 406, 408, 412, 414, 425, 434, 442, 452, 460, 469, 475, 478, 509, 512, 514, 518, 529, 532, 534, 552, 553, 554, 556, 557, 559, 566, 569, 570, 571, 572, 573, 574, 575, 576, 577, 579, 607, 637, 670, 693, 696, 697, 708, 709, 720, 721, 722, 723, 724, 725, 727, 728, 729, 740, 743, 744, 745, 746, 747, 760, 762, 763, 764, 766, 767, 768, 769, 789, 792, 795, 797, 805, 807, 809, 810, 813, 814, 817, 818, 819, 820, 822, 824, 830, 834, 852, 853, 860, 863, 864, 870, 876, 901, 906, 937, 953, 958, 961, 963, 964, 965, 967, 973, 974, 991

I mean, really!

Try as I might I just couldn't find a Wardlow anywhere in the book so I headed to reception and asked whether they'd heard of the local legend.

'Don Wardlow? Sorry, the name doesn't ring a bell,' said Angie, wearing an envelope-sized name-tag. 'But I have just found out there *is* a bus that goes into Charleston. It leaves from right outside the door and only takes 20 —'

'Minutes. Yes I know, and I challenge you to ride it.'

Eventually I got through to River Dogs management, who informed me that although Don had never said no to an interview, he really didn't enjoy the limelight. Even so, they very kindly provided me with his cellphone number, which I rang about 30 times. Typically, the more it went straight to answer machine the more determined I became to get through. Much like the coin in the slot machine, it's always the *next* one you think will be the winner — but never is. Likewise with Don's phone. That thing was off and staying off. So I called again. And again.

I do realise that in my quest for 18 holes with a complete stranger I was becoming a stalker of sorts. Walking around one's hotel room in nothing but a towel, barking, 'Come on, Don, pick it up, we gotta play golf, show me what you're made of' to a blind man who just wanted to quietly retire is not exactly normal behaviour. I had to be content leaving messages; probably too many. Chances are he didn't understand a word anyway. I probably resembled a nervous teenager asking someone out on a first date, but I didn't want to leave Charleston without meeting this inspirational man from Goose Creek, South Carolina.

So I rang one more time for luck.

I had been so hell-bent on finding Don that I'd failed to keep track of time. I now had less than 24 hours left in a town where my only game had been with something made in China and destined for the nearest bath.

At the bottom of *The Post and Courier* front page was a story about Paul Conway, a professional soccer player for the Charleston Battery, who had recently been injured:

> The latest blow came last Wednesday, when all-time leading scorer Paul Conway left the second half of a game at Pittsburgh with ligament damage in his left ankle that could sideline him until next month. Conway injured the ankle while attempting a header. He said he landed in a small hole in the field, and his foot turned over.
>
> 'It turned straight over, and I heard pop-pop-pop,' Conway said. 'I've done it before, about five years ago, so I knew exactly what I'd done. I came off and it blew up like a balloon, even though I had it in a bucket of ice.'

'Where's Blackbaud Stadium?' I asked Angie at reception, after finding where the Charleston Battery played their home games.

'Long way,' she replied.

I then asked something I thought I'd never repeat in South Carolina.

'Do buses go there?'

Angie laughed, hysterically — not at my joke, but quite the opposite. 'No, but you could get a bus into town, that would only take 20 minutes,

BATTERY GETS KICKERS

The Charleston Battery's Ryan Trout dives over Richmond's Peter Luzak during first-half action at Blackbaud Stadium.

Henderson, Conway score against rival Richmond

**BATTERY 2,
KICKERS 1**

BY DAVID CARAVIELLO
Of The Post and Courier Staff

Richmond forward Kevin Jeffrey found Josh Henderson at midfield after the game ended, and the two shared a friendly embrace. Kickers goalkeeper Ronnie Pascale offered his former teammate a warm handshake. Henderson may play for the Charleston Battery, but Tuesday night he had plenty of friends on both sides.

"They're some of my best friends in the world. It's always fun to play against your best friends," said Henderson, who joined Charleston during the offseason after two years in Richmond. "It's a little more competitive. It's not like playing your brothers, but it's damn near close. You just feel that spark."

Henderson scored what proved to be the game-winner, and Paul Conway scored his first goal since returning from an ankle injury as the Battery defeated Richmond 2-1 in a matchup of A-League divisional rivals played before a crowd of 1,513 at Blackbaud Stadium.

With the victory, Charleston (11-3-2, 36 points) became the first A-League team to reach 11 wins, and built a nine-point advantage over second-place

Richmond (8-8-3, 27 points) in the Southeast Division. The win also snapped a two-game winless streak for the Battery, which continues its three-game homestand against Toronto on Saturday at 7:30 p.m.

"Soccer-wise, we played very, very well," said Battery coach Chris Ramsey, whose team was coming off a scoreless draw against Pittsburgh and a 2-0 loss

See BATTERY, Page 6C

The Post and Courier, *Charleston, South Carolina*

then you could get a —'

'How much would a cab cost from here?'

'That'll be expensive, about 40 dollars.'

I had to do it.

IT HAD TAKEN a good hour to get hold of Paul Conway but compared to Don it had been a walk in the park. It was 3.40 pm. Paul had told me to meet him at the stadium before 4 pm, which is when he would have to be at training, even if he did have an injury.

My driver, a recovering New York cabbie, seemed to delight in the fact that we had to get there in record time. He lit a cigarette, rolled up his sleeves and told me to hang on. He sped, swerved and abused his way to Daniel Island. He even had time to take the odd call: 'Hello? No, Kerry. I said no, Kerry! No, the answer's still no!'

He then hung up. 'Wives and cellphones, huh?' he said, looking at me in the rear-vision mirror. 'This is fun,' he added, lighting another cigarette, accelerating even more and passing on a blind corner. 'I used to drive limos in New York but ever since the towers came down, so did the limo business. Cut it by about 70 percent. Driving down here is more fun. You smoke?'

I covered my eyes.

Daniel Island, a purpose-built settlement only six years old, surrounded by three slave cemeteries, is where I waited for Paul. Five minutes later a black pick-up arrived and he drove me to his brand-new house, which lay just minutes from the stadium.

Paul was in his sixth season for the Battery (so called because of the battery downtown, used during the Civil War) and had played for the US under-23s as well as the United States B side. At the ripe old age of 33 he was no longer the new kid on the block. Others at the club called him Veteran, Elder Statesman or, some, Old Man.

When we arrived at his house I met his wife and two young kids, Gwen and Maddie. We sat on the couch sipping lemonade and talking sport. Paul's father is the legendary Jimmy Conway who played for Ireland (30 caps), Manchester City and Fulham. Paul himself was born in London.

'Long way from London to Daniel Island,' I said.

'I'm actually from Portland, Oregon but let me tell you, this island is great. No one has bad memories; we're the first here. No one has any baggage. Life is good, I can train down the road, plus it's a great place to bring up the kids.'

I didn't mention yesterday's front page.

'Do you play golf?' I asked.

With Paul Conway, Blackbaud Stadium, Daniel Island

'Uh-huh, I'm on a one or two.'

'Really?'

'Yeah, I like my golf.'

'Do you think we could get a round in?'

He grimaced a little and alluded to his leg: 'I gotta train for tomorrow night, but we could bash some balls in the stadium.'

So we did. Finally my seven iron was being used for something other than a walking stick or backscratcher. And before you call me a neglectful father, I should point out that Charleston also joined us for the ride.

Paul indicated the course he normally played at on our drive to the stadium. It was difficult knowing that just inside those gates lay the real thing, a real course with real people, putting on real greens and wearing real collared shirts. I was so close, yet so far. I had done all the hard work. After two days of searching and calling and risking my life with retired New York cabbies, I now sat in the front seat with a Front Pager.

Who just happened to be injured.

Kate, the secretary for the club (that's unkind; she probably calls herself

First Impressions Manager or Club Coordinating Account Managing Executive Director, but to me she answered phones and passed yellow Post-it Notes to passers-by), very kindly offered me a ride home after my photo session with Paul.

'How come we never see any alligators around here?' I asked, once in her black four-wheel-drive monster. 'I was led to believe they were everywhere in the South.'

'Didn't Paul show you? We've got two at the ground.'

'At the ground!'

'Uh-huh, they live in the marsh behind the scoreboard.'

What Paul did tell me, however, were his favourite and least favourite Americans: George Bush and Bill Clinton respectively.

Having saved me 30 bucks and rear-ending a trailer at the traffic lights, Kate wished me luck back at La Quinta. The little red light flashing on the phone next to my bed meant I was about to receive my best news of the day: Don had called back!

He was on his dinner break at Alamo Car Rental when I caught up with him. Little did I know that being interviewed was nothing new for Don; along with Jim Lucas (his calling partner) he'd featured on CNN, ESPN and *The Today Show*. It hadn't been easy in the beginning though, his job-application pitch being rejected by 176 minor league teams before Mike Veeck (the owner of the River Dogs) admired his gumption and awarded him and Jim a full-time gig.

Now, if you're anything like me, you'll no doubt be wondering how on God's earth anyone could commentate on a game of baseball when they can't even see the bloody thing! This is how it worked: Jim Lucas would describe every last detail, down to the number of tugs on a batter's glove, in order to edify his audience and his partner. Don, on the other hand, offered statistics and titbits, all of which he gleaned either through chats or over his audio-enhanced Internet, from which he transcribed notes in Braille on his bulky typewriter.

Together, they made a great team. I'm sorry I never heard them.

'Who would be your favourite American of all time, Don?'

'I'd have to say my favourite, if he's still around, would be Bob Murphy, the broadcaster for the New York Mets. He'd be 84 now.'

'Anyone you don't feel so positive about?'

'Anyone who is against our war efforts, anyone who gets in the way of what our troops are trying to do over there, like the Dixie Chicks.'

Glad you weren't in the cab today, mate.

'Do you miss commentary?'

'Don't miss working 16- or 17-hour days, and the travel is hard with baseball. I do miss being at the microphone, yes, but I'm glad I can now be at home for my wife. The commentary was a great deal of extra work because of the blindness. I was too long away. I wanted to be a better husband.

'I now work for Alamo Car Rental. South Carolina is a very big employer of blind people because the amount of unemployed people is shocking.'

'This may be a stupid question, Don, but do you play golf?'

'My wife taught me mini-golf about a year ago but, like a lot of things, it can be difficult for blind people.'

'Do you think we could play tomorrow? There's a mini-golf course down the road.'

'I can't see how. I have to work.'

'You're an inspiration, Don.'

'Well, I appreciate that very much.'

Speaking to Don made me think of the time my first book, *UK on a G-String*, was accepted by the New Zealand Foundation for the Blind to be recorded as a talking book.

At the time I thought, great, I could voice it myself, as it is *my* story involving a bizarre trip around England. Course, you don't get paid for this sort of thing, but it truly is a privilege. The only problem was I failed the audition. I failed to be myself!

'Sorry, not enough in character. Next.'

DAY 9: TYBEE BEACH, GEORGIA

THE THING I LOVE about America is that it features in countless songs. Subconsciously you find yourself humming 'Philadelphia Freedom' or 'The Only Living Boy in New York'. I couldn't even tell you where Massachusetts is but I sing along with the Bee Gees as if it were my home town. Ironically, often these towns or cities are nothing to write home about:

'Well I'm standing on a corner in Winslow, Arizona,

And such a fine sight to see . . .'

You know the song: 'Take it Easy' by the Eagles. My friend *went* to Winslow, Arizona, stood on a corner and thought 'what a shithole'. I've been to Penny Lane in England — it's a dog of a street. Though when you think about it, it's all free advertising and can do wonders for a town people had never even considered. Imagine the tourism boom for Eastern Europe if it had've been 'Sweet Home Albania', or 'Welcome to the Hotel Chernobyl'. You can't *buy* that sort of publicity.

The journey from Charleston to Savannah took just three hours, in which time I ate, drank and watched other people fret for not having cashed money before they left. This would be my third train trip in America and also the third time the conductor would tell us today's movie would be *Chicago*. It's a movie I must have caught a glimpse of at least 40 times while on the way to better things, such as food, beer or relief.

Not seeing the movie in its entirety didn't faze me as the 'moving movie theatre' wasn't exactly built with comfort in mind. Imagine, if you will, a carriage with plastic seats facing the window to enhance scenic viewing.

Now imagine 50 irritable people squashed in those seats, bending their backs, craning their necks, cursing, leaning backwards and forwards as people walk by, all in an effort to catch a glimpse of a 14-inch screen some 30 metres away.

Enjoy the movie!

I found refuge in the cafeteria, where two granddads were playing cards with their loved ones, at the same time quizzing them about the Civil War. These kids knew their history; I was impressed. Not so impressive were the conductors who, while only doing their job, weren't making any friends by asking the old guys to take their money off the table.

comments were very rude and we won't repeat them.

Radio has become the homeplace for political incorrectness. We don't think it should rent out space for political opinion at all. Radio wasn't always sarcastic, cynical, didactic, strident, ill-informed and offensive. Radio was a place you called to ask the deejay to play something by Pearl Jam, not to be *assaulted* by the deejay. Radio used to be *fun*.

RADIO LAND: Maybe in New Zealand it still is.

A radio guy from Auckland called GMLc to ask who might be on today's Page 1.

He has a book contract (from Random House) to travel the states in 28 days and play golf in each city he visits with whatever local is pictured on the front page of that city's newspaper. His book will be called "USA On A Golf Swing" (his last book was "UK On A G String" — don't ask).

Justin Brown... that's his name... started his project in June in New York "and I haven't had a round of golf yet," he said. "I've got to

get my skates on if I'm going to have any golf... But I did go to a clown wedding in Richmond! Seriously. It was two clowns who were getting married and they were in clown outfits. And everybody there was in clown outfits as well. It was *fantastic.*"

If Brown can't find a human to tee off with, he has adopted a rubber duck from last Saturday's Biggin Creek charity duck race. He's named it Charleston, and he'll play putt-putt with his little buddy today.

If you want to play golf with him, he's staying at the La Quinta.

RADIO CONTACT: Crumpet Too and what's left of her tea are expected to make landfall today in Horta, Azores ending a nearly month-long odyssey from Stono Marina for Sailor Boy GMLc, who accompanied — via amateur radio — James Island's Huntley Brownell. Brownell was crew on the 42-foot sailboat for captain Graham Axford of Southampton, England.

So it's time to tell the story of how Axford, the longtime, self-de-

The Post and Courier, *Charleston, South Carolina*

'Do pennies *count* as money?' one asked.

The guard said nothing, rattling his keys as a sign of authority and motioning for him to get rid of the coins. This didn't seem to deter the game or the mood one bit. After all, you don't live for 80 years without harbouring *some* ingenuity. Within minutes, the old boys had substituted pennies with peanuts. The youngest boy started munching on his.

'Don't eat all the profits now, son!'

Calls of 'Great day, you gotta full house!' echoed around the carriage while I ate junk food and got out my copy of today's *Post and Courier.* I was shocked and stunned to find that Charleston, my little bastard child of a duck, had made it into print. And I thought this trip was all about me!

Harriet had written a piece about my failures so far. Subsequently, I wouldn't be surprised if the phone in Room 218 was ringing as we speak:

> A radio guy from Auckland called us to ask who might be on today's page one. He is travelling around the states in 28 days and playing golf in each city he visits with whatever local is pictured on the front page of that city's newspaper. If Brown can't find a human to tee off with, he has adopted a rubber duck from last Saturday's Biggin Creek charity duck race. He's named it Charleston and he'll play putt-putt with his little buddy today. If you want to play golf with him, he's staying at the La Quinta.

(No he's not, he's on a train to Savannah, try his cellphone.)

As I never got to meet the 'gators behind the scoreboard at Blackbaud Stadium I was thrilled to see a story on the front page of *Business Savannah,* which happened to be sitting on a table in the café carriage:

Crab Shack Sees Reptiles as Bottom Line Boost

> It's known as a place where the elite eat in their bare feet, but now patrons might want to put on some shoes, or at least watch where they dangle their toes. The Crab Shack on Tybee Island, an area seafood restaurant favorite, has

been renovated to include a Gator Deck and Lagoon. What used to be the restaurant's front parking lot next to its 'party shack' now has twin cascading waterfalls and houses 78 American alligators. 'This is one of the biggest tourist efforts by a small business in the area for a long time,' said Jack Flanigan, owner of The Crab Shack. 'It's a great attraction for Tybee Island and Savannah.'

Flanigan buys his baby alligators from a 'gator farm, and he considers the exhibit a lifesaver. 'Put it this way, they are out of the food and pocketbook chain now that I have them,' he said. 'They are the original Georgians, here over 150 million years ago.' Flanigan said the only drawback is that customers now have to watch where they dangle their feet.

I had no idea where Tybee Island was but as long as it had hotels, washing machines and a golf course I would be happy. Oh, and it would kind of help if Jack and his 'gators were home, too.

I stepped off the train into the sweltering Savannah heat where Bill, the taxi driver, drove me through the city he loved, then (due to my need to get to the island) straight out again. We negotiated a fare to Tybee (can't be much of an island if we can get there by car!) and I wondered how I would get back in a few days' time. If the public transport was to match Charleston's, I might have to apply for a green card.

Bill told me he used to be a tennis pro but lost all his trophies (as well as half a house) when fire ripped through his New Jersey apartment. He also trained in opera and was in the middle of rattling off an impressive list of sopranos when we nearly took the shell off a turtle, who for some reason thought it a sound idea to walk across a busy four-lane freeway rather than go cross-country.

'Stupid idiot,' I said, looking through the gaps in my fingers. 'He'll never make it!'

'The Almighty will look after him,' Bill screamed with delight. 'The Almighty will look after him! You do believe in God, don't you?'

'Um, yes, I think,' I said, feeling this was the right thing to say. If believing in the man upstairs meant we got to Jack's in one piece and Jack played golf and Jack shouted me dinner and a bed; if saying my Hail Marys before bed tonight meant that turtle back there saw another sunrise then sure, I believed in God.

'Thought so,' he said, grabbing his ringing cellphone from his pocket. 'You look like the sort of person who believes in God.'

I looked back. The turtle was safe.

For now.

'What?' Bill barked down the phone. 'I ain't wit' your wife! Whatya talking about, I'm wit' your wife? Look, I gave you my social security number already. Now go, you're wasting my minutes.'

He turned it off and threw it in the glove box.

'Wives and cellphones, huh?' he cussed.

'Apparently so. Bill, I wonder if you could tell me if there's a golf course on Tybee Island?'

'No.'

Course not, why would there be?

There was a lot of renovating going on at The Crab Shack; obviously business had been good since the newspaper article. Meanwhile Bill, looking a little hot and flustered, took my money and gave me a business card. It had not been an easy journey for him. He'd gotten lost three times. I was proud of him when he finally relented, mentally chopped off his penis and asked for directions.

Jack Flanigan was to be found shirtless, walking around with his Labrador in tow. He was as brown as a berry (Jack, that is) and it was obvious judging by his swelling, healthy belly that there definitely wasn't a shortage of good food around these parts. He appeared to revel in the fact he could walk around his workplace in nothing but shorts with his best friend by his side. 'Course I'll talk to you,' was his response when I told him I was all the way from Down Under. He sat down (probably for the first time that day), ordered a sweet tea and told me to make myself at home.

Seventy-eight alligators lay in the pond next to us. A ''Gator Girl' was showing kids around, putting some sort of chicken product on the end of bamboo poles from which, if the 'gator could be bothered moving in the midday heat, it would snatch it and run.

Jack was born in Arizona but moved to Savannah with the air force

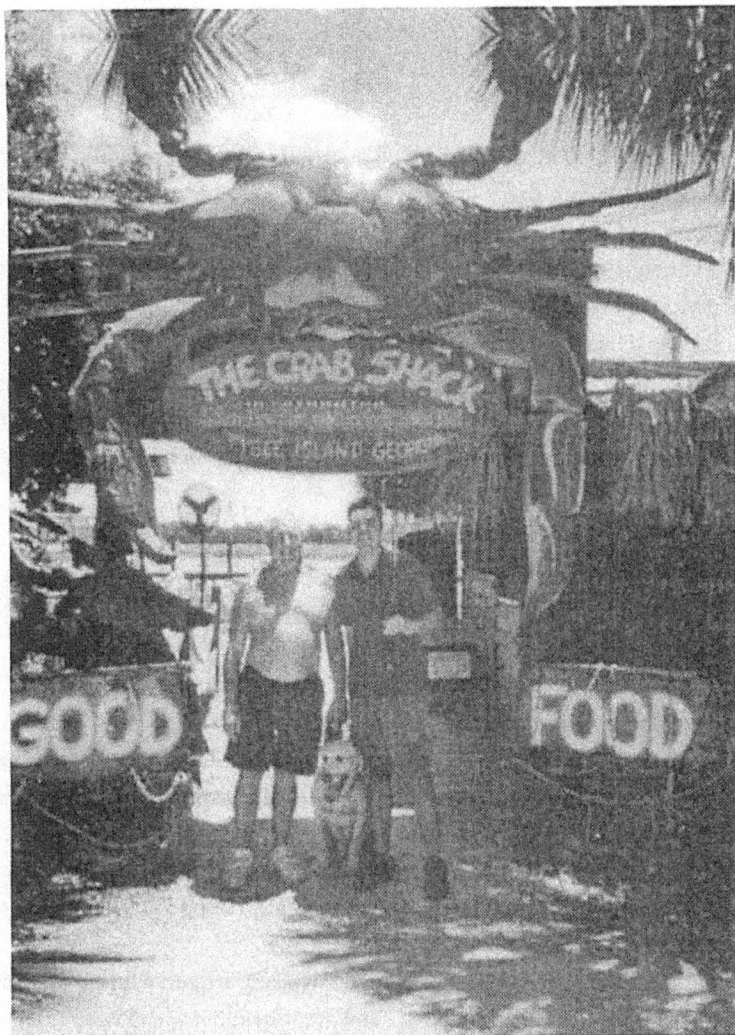

Jack Flanigan at the Crab Shack, Tybee Island, Georgia

during the Korean War. Having served his time as a Master Captain in the food and beverage industry, he bought the land the restaurant now sits on 21 years earlier when it was a fishing camp.

'I used to be barman, dishwasher and server. Then we started serving food on Fridays and Saturdays. Soon we needed to be open seven days a week. Now we're open 363 days a year.'

'So why alligators?' I asked.

'I like all kinds of wildlife. I even used to own an otter, but 'gators are synonymous with the area. These are only babies,' he said pointing to a group that hadn't moved since I'd been there. 'We get them at a year old. They grow about a foot a year. At four feet they start to breed. These ones will never be released back into the wild.'

'So where do they go when they're four years old?'

'We trade them in for younger ones.'

'Trade a 'gator — what an interesting idea.'

'Georgia 'gators used to be endangered, then they started alligator farms, now it's so successful they're raising them for meat and skin. This is the first year when they'll actually open the alligator season. In the wild they live to about 50 years, in captivity to about 80.'

'Do they ever escape?' I asked, hoping for stories about dishwashers and bartenders losing limbs in the dead of night.

'Well, I'm never gonna say never . . . but it's very secure in there.'

'Out of the 78, how many boys, how many girls?'

'There's no way to tell, you'd have to surgically find out.'

'Think we'll leave that one, Jack.'

'I tell ya one thing, though, the female's pretty onto it. She can determine the sex of the eggs from where she lays them. If the eggs are where the temp is 90 degrees or over that means they'll be male. If the temp is say 86, 83 or less, all the babies will be female.'

'Do you *serve* alligator?'

'No.'

Like his cooking counterpart in Lower Manhattan, Jack's favourite American was JFK.

'Now there's a man with all the money in the world and he still had time to think about the little fella,' he said, pulling on his Lab's ear. 'As for least favourite — I don't dislike too many people. I don't deal with people I don't like.'

'Do you play golf?'

'Golf? No, that game takes too much time for a working man. It's a game for a man who doesn't have to work eight- or 12-hour days.'

I felt guilty for having ever touched a club.

Jack was a busy man and busy men don't play golf. Meantime, I had no home, it was over 100 degrees and I was starving. Jack saw me sweltering under the shade of a tree, wiping sweat from my brow and unsuccessfully searching for a dry piece of clothing on which to dispense it. How his dog could stand the heat I'll never know. Even the 'gators were suffering — they hadn't seen weather like this in 150 million years.

Jack quickly directed me to the restaurant where fans expelled a cold, watery spray and diners ate overlooking a piece of water where no doubt half their plate once lived. Before I knew it a Dr Pepper and the biggest plate of seafood you've ever seen (all boiled, not fried) was placed in front of me. No knives or forks either. A portion of the table top was cut out to accommodate a large bin underneath into which you threw unwanted crabs' legs, prawn heads or veggies you didn't want Mum to see.

'This is on Jack,' the waitress said when I reached for my wallet.

Sitting next to the fans was very pleasant indeed. I wasn't in a hurry to move, not before the sun buggered off anyway. I got chatting to one of the builders who was working on the renovations.

'You want me to catch one of the 'gators for ya?' he asked.

'Catch one? Are you allowed?'

'No, but I can catch one for you, when Jack's not looking. You can hold one if you like. Don't tell Jack, though.'

I looked over at the big man himself. He was patting his dog and telling off builders.

'No, don't worry, maybe another time.'

Barry, a guy who seemed to be doing the crappiest jobs while the rest of us ate, offered to take me into the main part of Tybee. Actually, he didn't offer at all; Jack did the rounds and asked who was going into town. Barry drew the short straw, but not before he shifted a few more kegs, loaded and unloaded food off trucks and shed half a kilo in half an hour.

He dropped me off at the Royal Palm Motel, which boasted colour TV, cable, a pool and air conditioning. The last two amenities were all I desired. Actually that's not true; my main desire was to feel human again. To do so, I would have to shower and shave — maybe even wash my clothes in the shower at the same time.

Unfortunately, I was subjected to one of those showers where the water hits everything but *you*. You dance around in the cubicle entertaining the thought that one of the droplets must have your name on it, but no, the prehistoric nozzle seems to think it a far better idea to soak the floor and anything that's not waterproof. Before you know it your bum is glued to the shower curtain (one thing that *doesn't* seem to have a problem following you) and you're somehow drier than when you first stepped in.

I was no closer to a game of golf but upon ordering a beer at a beachside bar I was filled with tremendous confidence. I picked up a copy of *Connect Savannah* and saw that a Korean War vet from Savannah had written a book about his experiences.

Now there was a man who would play golf!

It was happy hour at the next bar whereby I got three beers and a generous serving of jalapeño nachos for 10 bucks. It was here that I met Jim, a man who'd left the cold of Cleveland for the laid-back life of Tybee. He would have been 50, wore a tank top and shorts and had what looked like a year-round tan. He confirmed my thoughts when he told me, 'I been Buffettised, man. Came down here from Ohio and never went back. Half my gear's still up there. I'm living the life Jimmy sings about. It's escapism.'

This bar was obviously his *Cheers* so the question had to be asked: living in essentially a holiday town with a good bar and a good beach with good weather, how does one avoid drinking and partying every night?

'I come to the bar most nights but only drink on Tuesdays, Thursdays and Saturdays.'

'What day is today?' I asked, quite genuinely. It could have been December for all I knew. I hadn't had a good sleep in days. I was running on pure adrenalin and the odd happy hour.

'Tuesday,' he said, raising his glass.

'You'll be happy about that then.'

'You've got to have some sort of system,' he said, ordering another.

I was impressed — restraint and Bohemia living side by side.

Jim introduced me to Bill and Rose, two more regulars. When I told them what I was doing in Tybee, Rose swiftly produced a copy of the *Tybee News* from her handbag.

'You can't leave the island without meeting Miss Iva, can he Bill?'

'No, she's a doll,' Bill replied.

The front-page headline read: *Miss Iva, 91, crowned Tybee Island's Beach Queen*. In the last few days the Mayor of Tybee Island had proclaimed 26 March Lady Iva Day.

'So she's fit and active?' I asked.

'She's probably fitter than you or I. She's the most incredible woman, a real party animal. She's got grey hair in that picture,' she said, pointing to the article. 'She dyed it blonde for years, but finally did the grey thing on her 90th birthday.'

We had a great old time in that bar overlooking the ocean. Jim relished being able to drink, Rose told me stories about Iva, and Bill (having lived on Tybee for a while and no longer sporting rose-tinted glasses) told me one of the problems of the area: 'Around here, people arrive on vacation and leave on probation.'

'Come back tomorrow,' Rose said, getting into the lift at the end of the night, handing me a business card. 'We'll see if we can bring Lady Iva.'

Rose was one of those people who, when telling you they would give you a call, felt the need to put her hand to her ear to indicate an imaginary phone. Similarly, if she were going to email you, she would type on an imaginary keyboard. Given our closest friends (presumably) all speak the same language, I find these hand signals completely superfluous, necessary only in rowdy nightclubs.

'Thanks Rose, I will. Hey, I forgot to ask, does Iva play golf?' I asked, falling into the same trap, swinging an imaginary club.

'Don't know. I know she plays pool!' Rose yelled, chalking up an imaginary cue, just before the doors met.

'What a friendly bunch,' I said to Chris the barman. 'I really like it here.'

'It's a good place,' he said, giving me the thumbs up.

With a full stomach and a smile on my face I walked back to my hotel in the cool(er) evening air. My night was about to take a bizarre turn; I was about to have a beer with Billie Holiday.

It all started when I saw a teenager attempting to hit golf balls around a park. From where I was standing, though, all he seemed to be doing was digging up scotch fillet-sized divots and distributing them to another part of the ground courtesy of a five iron. His diligent father (who looked just like the dad from *Family Guy*) stood by his son and confirmed that he was indeed playing like crap. It reminded me of my Dad taking me to the park and doing the same.

Having one more person join the gallery didn't seem to help the teenager, who sprayed his next ball onto the road. We exchanged niceties, talked golf and that seemed to be that, until I started heading back to my hotel for a much-needed lie-down.

'Oi!' *Family Guy* yelled. 'What are you doing?'

'Going back to my hotel,' I replied.

'Why don't you come home and have some lasagne with us? Or a beer?'

'I've just eaten . . . but I'll join you for a drink.'

Bill and his son William showed me the way to their home where we sat outside by the cooler and drank beer. Upstairs, we joined the rest of the family who were making lasagna and mojitos. (What is it with Americans and these awfully strong, awfully good drinks?)

'You could have a game of golf with me, I'm famous,' said Bill, offering lasagne for the third time even though the nachos sat in my stomach like a dead weight.

'What for?' I asked.

'Last name's Holiday.'

'Bill . . . Holiday,' I mused. 'Billy Holiday! Hey, we should play. How 'bout tomorrow?'

'Gotta work tomorrow. Anyway, don't I have to be on the front page?'

William, already onto his second mojito, then asked, 'How do *I* get to play golf with you?'

'Like your father says, you've got to be on the front page.'

'What about if I rob a bank later on tonight?'

'Yeah, that should do the trick. You rob a bank, I'll take the photo just as the police arrive, then we'll hit the course.'

'I would be most happy if my 18-year-old played golf with you,' said his mother, 'but I don't know about him robbing a bank.'

'William!' his father barked as he caught his son bringing a fresh (in)edible concoction to the table. 'It makes me wanna throw up seeing what you've eaten in the last hour: beer, mojito, shrimps, lasagne, cranberry and vodka and now chocolate milk and vodka! It's disgusting!'

'Mmm,' William slurped.

William's family reminded me of my own. Friends of his seemed to drop in constantly, clear the fridge and crack jokes. One such friend was Chris, who caused quite a stir when I asked who his least favourite American was: 'Lennox Lewis,' he told the room.

'Lennox Lewis? He's not American!' William spat.

'Isn't he?'

'No, he's British!'

I may not be one of the smartest men in the world but knowing what country the heavyweight champion of the world hails from sure could save you some embarrassment in a bar brawl. William agreed to forgive his ignorant mate if he told the New Zealander about the unique present his parents gave to him and his sister.

'Mum and Dad didn't want to give us middle names at birth, so as a present they let us choose one on our 18th birthday.'

'What did you choose?' I asked, jealous of such a good idea.

'Danger,' he smiled.

'Why Danger?'

''Cos then I can say to the birds, "Danger's my middle name".'

IT WASN'T UNTIL I set out into the searing heat the next day that I realised I might have been a little overzealous with my consumption of jalapeños the previous night. Consequently, I couldn't walk more than 10 metres without taking a pit stop. Those damn things really can interrupt an otherwise free-flowing day. At least alcohol only makes your head hurt; any vegetable that causes you to require medical attention after consumption should be illegal.

It was while hobbling to the next lamppost that I spotted William on his bike, heading towards the beach.

'Why ya walking funny?' he asked.

'What do you mean?' I said, disappointed it was that obvious.

'Looks like you've got a carrot up your ass.'

'Long story.'

'I was going to call you,' he said, handing me a drink from his bike carrier. 'We're all going down to the beach — you should come.'

He then took great delight in relaying the contents of his oversized plastic margarita glass: 'Vodka, juice, ice, chocolate milk and Sprite,' he smiled.

'Your father would be proud.'

After a game of pétanque with William and his friends on the beach, I battled the heat and walked towards my favourite bar. After all, I had a date with a 91-year-old.

When I arrived, Chris the barman was welcoming customers and mopping floors. It was Wednesday and Jim, true to his word, was drinking soda water.

I can't begin to explain how nice it is to run into familiar faces after nearly two weeks of meeting strangers. Obviously I'd never see Jim or Chris again (they were 'two-day' friends, but a 'two-day' friend is better than none at all) but at least I didn't have to explain myself every five minutes. It felt comfy, like old slippers.

'The usual, thanks Chris,' I said smugly, grabbing a bar stool with my name on it.

He handed me a drinks menu.

Just as I was explaining to Chris where he'd seen me before ('No it wasn't university, I was here last night, remember?') in walked Bill and Rose with Lady Iva. She smiled when she saw Jim and me at the bar. I couldn't believe she was 91.

'Justin, let me introduce you to the one and only Lady Iva,' Rose said, organising some chairs. Lady Iva took my hand and smiled. She was a charmer. Better still, she drank whisky. She had a sense of humour, too. Upon spying Jim nursing a glass of soda water she remarked, 'Come on, it's not every day we have a New Zealander in town.'

'No.' Jim remained stoical, folding his arms in defiance. 'If I have one I'll have another, and then I can't have a big Saturday.'

Lady Iva and I found a quiet corner where for the next hour she would show me pictures and tell stories. And there was no shortage of those. She was just three weeks old when the *Titanic* sank. Her twin sister died at birth, strangled by the umbilical cord. When she was two and her mother 26, her father died of consumption. He was 28.

'What would be your earliest memory?' I asked.

'In 1918, when the war was just over, the navy boys came home to Pittsburgh, Pennsylvania and marched down the main street. I still remember it like it was yesterday.'

Iva's eyes lit up when she told me about her soulmate, Roy, to whom she

Teeing off with Lady Iva, Tybee Island, Georgia

was married for 49 years. The two of them ran a grocery store in Pittsburgh during the Depression. He passed away in 1985.

'Do you have any children?' I asked as she sipped her whisky.

'My son died when he was only five days old — phlegm got caught in his throat. They couldn't get it out. He was the only child I ever had — I wasn't allowed to have any more. I shouldn't have had a natural birth, I should have had a Caesarean. But it was 1942 and a lot of nurses were doing war work. They didn't notice my baby was in trouble and there wasn't enough help. By the time they got to him it was too late.'

I didn't know what to say. Iva filled the gap.

'I nearly died when I had my son, so my husband and I had to choose. He used to say to me, "*You're* more important than anything in the world".'

After a few seconds she added, 'He was a very careful lover.'

'How do you get through that sort of thing?'

'We're sturdy folk, we lived through the Depression. You get your hard knocks and you live with them. You don't dwell on the past; the past is gone. You remember it and you look ahead one day at a time. I take good care of myself.'

I hated history at college. It's an obvious thing to say but what the subject needed was life, people, something you could touch. It would have been a different story had the teacher brought in a 91-year-old from Georgia who drank whisky, chewed the fat and handed out advice to upstart, spoilt teenagers who thought the world would end if they didn't have the latest MP3 player. Iva would sort them out.

'So what's your secret to longevity? You must have a comfy bed.'

'No, I sleep on the couch,' she smiled.

'You sleep on the couch! Are you serious?'

'My apartment's not big enough to have a double bed so when I go to bed I just grab some blankets and a pillow and lie down on the couch.'

'So do you still feel like you can do anything?'

'I do. I was line dancing up until three months ago. The only problem I've ever had is carpal tunnel syndrome, after knitting too much. I knitted nine afghans in one summer!'

'Did you ever think you'd live this long?'

'No, and I have no idea why I have. I smoked for 25 years. I enjoy my beer, but I never overdo it. I'm a very small eater; I can never eat all they put on my plate. I don't take any medication. I do love younger people; I would go out every night if I could. You gotta mingle with energetic people. I'm also part of YEEPIE, which stands for Youthful Energetic Enthusiastic People Interested in Everything. Tomorrow night I'm serving food at the bingo group.'

Iva was an angel; I felt lucky to have met her. I'll be honest, I had a tear in my eye when she was telling me about her family but felt just as affected when she told me how she managed to get through the tough times.

'So what's your advice for a good life?' I asked, swallowing a mouthful of beer that my date not only endorsed, but encouraged, for longevity.

'Be interesting, *give* a little bit of something.' Her eyes smiled. 'And don't burn the candle at both ends for too long. Don't overdo it.'

It seemed superfluous, even somewhat superficial given the heartfelt stories Iva had told in the last hour but I had to ask anyway:

'I don't suppose you play golf as well as line dance?'

'No, but I really wish I had time to learn when I was young; the grocery store was just too busy. I play pool. But not golf.'

Once happy hour was over, Bill and Rose asked if I'd accompany them and Lady Iva to the American Legion. This is something that literally blew me away as a New Zealander in America. In the States, not a day passed when I didn't meet someone who served in the Second World War, Korea or Vietnam (particularly the last). At home you'd be hard pressed to find anyone who fought that recently.

Bill, who served in Korea, showed me around his second home where his war buddies lined the bar and told jokes. He introduced me to a soldier my age who happened to be parading around with some sort of rifle. Having not spent much time around guns, I peppered him with questions. And before any mothers in near proximity had the chance to yell, 'If you boys are going to play with those guns, go outside!' my armed friend informed me that, although this one *looked* real, it was just for practice.

(Note — don't make the mistake I did: 'So that's just a toy one then?')

Outside, having watched him perform all sorts of tricks and spins — behind the back, over the shoulder, load it up, shoot your mate, march over there, dive in there, pretend he's the enemy, shoot that, hide under there — I asked him what attracted him to the army.

'It's obvious,' he said in a deep voice, gun resting on his shoulder. 'I'm committed to my country, committed to my president and committed to the cause. I would go anywhere, do anything and save anyone if it means I can serve my country and fly the American flag. What about you?'

'I just want a game of golf, mate.'

'I think Rose has had too much too drink,' Iva said, handing me my bag while George Bush's mate continued to swing his weapon about the place. 'I think you're leaving.'

Bill offered to drive me home so I said my goodbyes to my new friends who promised they would visit me in New Zealand. We even foolishly exchanged addresses. Like most travellers in this situation, I wish I had the balls to say, 'Nice to meet you Bill, or Bob, or whatever your name is. Hey, thanks for the beers. Sorry about the wine stain, should come out with a bit of baking soda. Hey, since we have more chance of being eaten by a great white shark than ever seeing each other again, let's just leave it at that, okay? Bye.'

However, one person I did want to exchange addresses with was Lady Iva. I had a lump in my throat saying goodbye. It was hard to believe this divine woman was no one's grandma.

Be interesting, give a little bit of something.

She waved from the bar. I waved back and thought to myself, I'll never see her again.

'You wanna play golf with Sandra Bullock?' Bill asked as we were leaving.

'What do you mean?'

'She lives on Tybee.'

'Get outta town! Does she really?'

'Sure, but I doubt she'd be home. We can always check.'

We pulled up outside a house with a large fence and intercom.

'We'll get in trouble, Bill, we should leave,' said Rose. 'Bill, the police will —'

Before she had the chance to finish I leapt out of the car and rang the intercom buzzer. There was no answer. So I swung a club, posed for a picture and thought to myself what might have been: golf on Tybee Island with Billie Holiday, Sandra Bullock and 78 alligators. Now *that* would have been an interesting round.

DAY 11: SAVANNAH, GEORGIA

WILLIAM SAVED ME 30 bucks by driving me back to Savannah. He was impressed that my date had gone so well, not so impressed that once again I had found a Front Pager who didn't play golf. It was hard to believe it was just over a week since I was with Lucy in New York. In that time I had covered a fair chunk of the States and met six news-makers. Unfortunately, the only one who played the game couldn't get off the couch.

'So you're not really doing that well, are you?' William asked.

'Well, that's all a matter of perspective, William. I mean I . . . no, not really.'

'What's your plan for Savannah?' he asked, turning up the Grateful Dead.

'There's a Korean War veteran on the front page of the local paper who's just written a book about the war. I'm pretty confident that if he served in Korea he'd be in his sixties or seventies by now. And as we all know, William, men of that age do what?'

'Wear leisure suits and eat baby food?'

'No, William, they play golf.'

William dropped me off outside the youth hostel (a rarity in the States) where I was informed they didn't open till 5 pm, so I would have to carry my bags around until day's end. However, once the guy at reception realised my bag contained 14 clubs and a duck, he made an exception — out of fear, I hasten to add.

He showed me the way to the sauna, I mean my *room*, which was housed on the fourth floor in an attic. This room was either an afterthought or the forgotten child. It was so far away from anything that even resembled civilisation that should anyone have felt the need to visit, they would have had to hire extras from *Jack and the Beanstalk*. After an exhausting climb we found a room where sweat dripped off the walls and the smell of wet towels and previous guests filled the air. I dumped my golf clubs in the corner and wiped my brow.

'If you really need it,' my new friend offered, 'there's an air-conditioning unit by the bathroom. But only use it if you have to.'

'Oh, don't worry mate, I probably won't need it,' I said, cranking it up to full as soon as he left. 'Give us a call when you reach base camp,' I mumbled.

World-record hikes aside, Savannah was indeed something special. Having once again found where *not* to go I headed toward the historic district, River Street in particular, where I walked along the brick and cobblestone waterside promenade. Once a wealthy shipping centre (Savannah was a main hub for the exporting of cotton and the importing of slaves), the city was hit hard by the collapse of cotton prices in the late 1800s. Although this meant a serious economic decline, it may have also been a blessing in disguise; a lot of locals believe that if the city had prospered during that period, the timeless streets which still stand may well have been bulldozed in the name of development.

Live music bellowed out from the main square where I scoffed pizza and watched passers-by. I couldn't have been happier, watching a city overflowing with artists who strummed, picked and sang for a living. Everywhere I looked, blackboards outside bars boasted free jazz, rock or bluegrass. Had I not been on a mission, staying here would have been a very attractive option (for several weeks even).

Meantime, I had a Korean War vet to find.

James McAleer initially told me he'd be happy to meet in the central city. This was top news and meant I could save on a taxi fare and have another slice of pizza. However, no sooner had I done this than he called back to tell me to meet at his law firm.

Which just happened to be on the other side of town.

Leighton, a 23-year-old and new to the job, picked me up in his big old

Connect Savannah, *Savannah, Georgia*

family station wagon (which doubled as a taxi) and took me to Commercial Drive. Even though my golf bag was back in the four-storey sauna, I had my trusty, under-used putter and seven iron in the back seat, just in case. It was still hard to take the staring — a guy wielding two clubs does look mighty suspicious — but the last thing I needed was to find a Front Pager who was keen, only to be marooned on the other side of town with no clubs.

Of course, a *logical* person would just ask the person in question whether they played the game before they set off. However, I figured just *meeting* them was often a bizarre enough request; if I asked from the outset if they'd care to embarrass themselves on the nearest fairway, my phone calls may have been a lot shorter. Baby steps.

90

Leighton's favourite American was actor Will Smith.

'Why's that?' I asked, glaring at my watch, praying we weren't about to hit rush hour.

'He's straight man, he raps but he doesn't curse. He's a good actor and he's got a *beautiful* wife. Man, he's cool.'

Unfortunately, for all of Leighton's laid-back charm and youthful exuberance, his driving bore an uncanny resemblance to what I experienced with Bill back on Tybee. It made me wonder whether Bill himself had penned an international bestseller, *How to Scare the Shit out of Your Client and Still Get Them There on Time*, closely followed by the ever-popular *Asking for Directions is Not a Crime*. Leighton had obviously devoured both books and sadly (judging by his response of rubbing his hands together when I said I was new in town) appeared to be contributing to the last book in the trilogy, *Haven't We Passed that Church Already?*

James had been expecting me and led me down the hallway to his air-conditioned office. He was indeed in his sixties or seventies and although there didn't appear to be any golf trophies among the various framed certificates, I still had a very good feeling about how he spent his Sunday mornings.

James was 17 when he joined the Marine Corps and 22 when he went to Korea. He studied law in between, which he had practised for the last 50 years. He spent nine months in Korea. I started to read aloud an excerpt from the article on the front page of *Connect Savannah:*

'In 1940, 182 Savannahians left to serve their country as Marines during the Korean conflict. This book is about what they did and experienced. Over 100 of them went to Korea. Five died, one was blinded and one was emasculated.'

'That's right,' he said.

'What's emasculated, if you'll excuse my ignorance?'

'Had his balls blown off.'

Silence from both parties. James took the reins while I crossed my legs.

'You *can* live after it, but I don't know how much living you could actually do. At my age it would be okay, but at 22 it would be pretty bad.'

'Did war change you?' I asked, feeling a change of topic was critical to the way I sat.

'War doesn't change you, just reinforces who you are. Course, if you fought for six years it would be different. Six years would change what you did with your life. But it's not actually the combat itself, it's the time. The guys who moan about war would never have become anything anyway. A lot of them just use the war as an excuse: it's sad to say, some actually love the sympathy that comes with it.'

I thought back to the soldier on Tybee and wondered how I would react in such a situation. James continued: 'The greatest fear isn't "How well will I react?" In my experience I found most people worried more about not *performing* than they worried about dying. You had to brace yourself for the next day and the next day and the next. Eventually this will get most men. The English have a name for it — old sergeants' disease — where a man can be very brave for years and then one day he just can't get up. It could happen to any of us.'

Do you play golf?

Not yet, ease into it. Ask more questions. Don't scare the poor man.

'So what is it you're doing exactly?' he asked. 'I didn't quite catch it all on the phone.'

This was a typical response from a Front Pager. Often my phone conversations were so hurried and the person on the other end so confused, it wasn't surprising they remembered only a few words. Of course, having an accent didn't help.

'I'm basically going around America trying to meet up with people who feature on the front page of the newspaper.'

'Oh, that sounds interesting.'

And play them at golf. Not yet.

'Who is your favourite American of all time?'

'That would have to be Thomas Jefferson. He contributed more to the foundation of this country than any other. He put some balance in the constitution that was very favourable and he had a great mind. It was a unique time in American history with great men like Washington, Adams and Franklin.'

'What about least?'

Without hesitation he said, 'Jane Fonda.'

'Why's that?' I asked, not wanting to ask another stupid question. (Wasn't she in *Speed*?)

'She was a traitor and not treated as one.'

Or was that Sandra Bullock?

'Whether you believe in war or not —'

No, it wasn't her. It was the other Fonda, the daughter, what was her name? *Bridget*, that's the one. What was that movie she was in, the one where her roommate starting dressing like her and tried to kill her in that apartment?

'— you don't go to the country and comfort the enemy.'

Single White Female, that's it.

'Such as was the case in Vietnam.'

Crap movie, but we all liked it for some reason — kind of embarrassing to admit now.

James was a very engaging and intelligent man who had obviously led an interesting life in which history was a big part. 'While we're on the subject,' he said, 'I'd say my other least favourite American would have to be Benedict Arnold.'

Oh no, not again. Surely I wasn't expected to know about Mr Arnold's adventures as well. One thing was for sure, he wasn't in *Speed*, but that's about all I knew. And James could tell.

'He was a traitor in the Revolutionary war in the 1700s. He sold out to the British. He was a general in the American army and switched sides to the British.'

'I can see why you don't think too highly of him. And do you have any children?'

'We . . . we had four children, lost the eldest in February.'

James continued to tell me about himself while I proceeded to accidentally bang my teeth on my teacup and carry on as if nothing had happened. Thankfully James didn't notice.

'Do you play golf?' I finally asked.

'Golf? I'm only 75; I'm too young to play golf.'

'You're kidding me!'

'How many games have you played so far?' he asked, obviously noting my disappointment.

'With people from the front page you mean?'

'Yeah.'

'Counting you?'

'Yeah.'

'None.'

James laughed. I was too embarrassed to tell him about the duck I had beaten back at Frankie's Fun Park. Being a lawyer, surely he had sued people for less.

'So you really don't play?' I asked a final time, figuring maybe he'd been fibbing all along; hoping he was really a life member at Augusta National.

'No,' he smiled.

'Don't even have any clubs in the garage?'

'Nope.' Dammit. 'I'm surprised you haven't found more golfers,' he offered. 'They're everywhere in this country.'

'Not where I'm looking, James! What do you do for kicks then, in the weekends?'

'I like to fish for salt-water trout and bass. When I'm not doing that I'm normally hunting bird and game with my brother, normally deer. Georgia is overrun with deer.'

Deer hunting around America — always an option.

James and I went outside and took a photo with Charleston. His wife came out asking what I was doing in America with a seven iron and a rubber duck. James did his best to explain. Unfortunately, instead of offering names of friends or relatives I could have taken out for a round, all she could offer was a bemused smile.

'How lovely — we've got friends in New Zealand.'

Meanwhile I had to get back to town before nightfall. When he'd dropped me off, Leighton had given me his business card and a verbal guarantee of a seven percent discount (strange number, I know) but I decided to wave down a cab that happened to be outside James' office.

My driver took me on what appeared to be a direct route, which I appreciated very much. Along the way he told me his president was 'a good man doing good things' and that he had 'absolutely no time for that idiot Jesse Jackson'. Still on the topic of politics, we drove past a sign advertising the local elections. One candidate's name seemed less appropriate for a civil servant than for the latest cleaning product: *Dicky Mopper for Mayor.*

James McAleer putts — Charleston looks on

'You look pretty good for 74,' I told the driver, after I caught him boasting about his age.

'Eat a lot of seafood,' he said bluntly. 'Been playing golf, have ya?' he asked, spying my golf club.

'Hardly.'

'My son plays a lot — every day in fact. Rain or shine. He retired from the army and became semipro. After his wife died he got right into it.'

'I should give him a game,' I said, perking up.

'Sure, I'll give you his address. He lives in Richmond.'

EVEN THOUGH the sun had done its dash for the day the heat still hadn't faded and finding a spot on your shirt where you hadn't already wiped sweat appeared to have become a national pastime. That and avoiding fumes from cars, fumes that seemed only to intensify in the gluggy, mid-evening air. They say Savannah is a great walking city and I sure did my share. The result was dehydration. All I wanted was a bottle of water, but in a truly surreal moment (and one which will add weight to my next CV, I'm sure), I found myself getting kicked out of a supermarket for having bare feet.

Rock'n'roll.

The next shop wasn't so discriminatory so I purchased some sunscreen for an already reddened nose, and a copy of *USA Today*. The front-page headline read *Sausages are People, Too* and showed a picture of an Italian sausage mascot being hit by an obviously upset Pittsburgh Pirates baseball player, Randall Simon. Not only had this story dominated the papers but I found it had also been replayed on TV all day — purely, one suspects, for the sheer comedic value of seeing a player so frustrated with his own form that he takes it out (slapstick-style) on some poorly paid university student dressed as a hot dog.

Having decided not to get in touch with Mr Simon for a game (it would appear he had some anger management issues to deal with) I decided instead to mull around Franklin Square and the Old City market.

I couldn't keep away from the live music; guys with plug-in acoustics sang American classics in the main street and refused to leave until punters filled their buckets with change. Couples sat around drinking in the balmy weather, cruising Georgian style. Art galleries (no doubt popular because of their latest work: air conditioning) were to be found all around the main square along with what seemed to be thousands of copies of the book written in, and about, Savannah: *Midnight in the Garden of Good and Evil*. (A book I really must read some time, but know I won't.) Irish bars down by the river belted out live music while tourists bought Georgia Bulldogs hats, scarves and ashtrays.

What a great feel this city had. From the footpaths of Martin Luther King Boulevard to the history-soaked Forsythe Park, this was the Deep South I had hoped for.

If only one could get served in bare feet, then it would be perfect.

Feeling a tad guilty having to leave such a memorable city so soon, I found myself in yet another cab the following morning, this time bound for the train station and, ultimately, Florida. The newspaper lying in the back seat confirmed something I really didn't need to know: Las Vegas (which was where my trip would end), was currently basking in 112 degrees.

Mel, a lovely old black man with bad speech and arthritic hands, made sure I arrived in one piece. We weren't going to break any speed records getting there but this made for a pleasant change. Mel reminded me of Morgan Freeman in *Driving Miss Daisy*, although that's where comparisons with the movie and its famous car would start and finish. Besides, who needs a 1950 Hudson Pacemaker when you've got a beat-up Dodge with no air-con and a noisy fan belt?

After he got out of the army, Mel decided he'd like to drive cabs for a living and had been doing so for 32 years. And as it seemed to be taking us that long to get to the station, what better opportunity to chew the fat about past and current-day favourite Americans?

'Well, that's a hard one,' he said in a slow drawl, lightly gripping the wheel, one arm hanging out the window. 'I suppose most people have been saying presidents, have they?'

'Some, yeah.'

'Well my favourite American would have to be my mother. I would have said some president but I can't, because they come and go. But my mother was always there.'

I DID HAVE a contact in Jacksonville, Florida, although to be honest I was a little wary of calling a friend-of-a-friend and asking for a bed and a meal. Not that it's ever stopped me before, but I just had the feeling this contact wasn't happy that the friend-of-the-friend had given out his number in the first place. Sometimes, though, in travel and in life, you've just got to bite the bullet. And not biting this one would have been a huge mistake.

Because if I hadn't, I wouldn't have met an ex-CIA agent who lived a crazy James Bond-style existence and once played with golfing greats Chi Chi Rodriguez and Lee Trevino.

DAY 12: JACKSONVILLE, FLORIDA

'GOOD AFTERNOON LADIES and gentlemen. We apologise for the delay, we had line problems leaving New York. We trust you will enjoy your journey with us. You'll be pleased to know that today's movie, showing now in the dining car, is . . . *Chicago.*'

Translation: *Not you again! Yeah, yeah, we're three hours late, so what? You need to know why? Why do you need to know why? We're just late, okay? Got held up. Want to complain? Too bad. Crap movie in dining car if you can be bothered.*

I sat next to a middle-aged couple from Albany, Alabama, who were on their way to Miami to meet their three-week-old grandson for the first time. They showed me photos of the latest addition, fed me chocolate and told me to visit them some day.

'I know *three* New Zealanders,' the husband said proudly, when he discovered where I was from. 'Bob Charles, Steve Williams and you!'

'You're dead right, and they're all golfers,' I replied. 'Do you play a bit?'

'Every day.'

'Maybe we should have a game. Have you ever been in the newspaper?'

'Last time I was in the paper was when I was in the military in 'Nam.'

The trip to Jacksonville was a short one, just three hours. In that time I watched the world go by, caught the credits of *Chicago* and devoured more chocolate from my companions who, as it turned out, actually *owned* a chocolate shop back in Alabama.

This was one fine choice of seat.

Forty minutes into the trip the husband/golf nut opposite (who had seemed completely preoccupied with other thoughts) broke into a gleeful fit:

'And Michael Campbell — that's four New Zealanders I know!'

As I disembarked we said our goodbyes and I promised not to write. Pockets filled with chocolate, a nose still like Rudolph's (damn sunburn) and blisters on my feet, I stepped onto Florida soil — but not before I slipped on my golf bag, causing my sandal to fall under the train.

'Cinderella, eh?' I said to the conductor.

She laughed. 'Don't you mean Cinda*fella*?'

Thunder was imminent and for the first time on this trip I had to put on a sweatshirt. Having booked a hotel in advance (not a good idea — a room that cost me a non-refundable $70 on line was only $50 when I got there), my only challenge was finding a cab at the busy Jacksonville station. Eventually a Steve Martin lookalike with no teeth and a scruffy beard agreed to take me. This man (along with his redneck girlfriend from Jersey) spent the next 30 minutes smoking, coughing and filling me with utter dread about my impending time in Florida.

'Oh man, this is bad,' he said, trying to find his way around various back streets.

'Oh, no. Oh no, no, no,' the redneck mumbled, taking another drag, covering her face as she eyed a bunch of youths sitting on a car.

'What?' I enquired rather innocently, thinking perhaps they were joking.

'We shouldn't be driving down here, this is not good.'

'Why?'

'Cab drivers don't normally come to this area,' he told me. (Another good reason not to book on line; what seems a good deal in the comfort of your bedroom can actually be, as was clear in this case, some kind of drug-dealing ghetto.)

Rain continued to fall and my depressants in the front seat continued to smoke. The cab now resembled a bushfire. I was becoming more and more convinced the lady from Jersey was an extra from *Deliverance*. Steve Martin, lighting up his third fag in 15 minutes, told me he used to earn $6000 a week, but now earned less than $300.

'Six thousand, really?' This figure was obviously as inflated as his lungs but I wasn't about to give any cheek — not here, not in this area. 'Why the drop in salary?'

'All the Marines have gone to war,' he said. 'That's my *business*.'

'So I guess Bush isn't one of your favourite people at the moment?'

'That man is sticking his nose where it don't belong, and it's costing me.'

Steve Martin's favourite American was Babe Ruth. I didn't ask the redneck; she scared me. In saying that, the whole area scared me. People we drove past looked bored. Cars were abandoned. No one seemed to be walking along the streets. This was the kind of place you saw on the news, that you thought was a million miles away.

'We've had two cabbies shot in the last week,' Steve Martin said, just as I was trying to think about sun, sand and Jimmy Buffett songs. 'One guy, eight times at point-blank range. He walked out of hospital the next day.'

'Yeah,' the redneck sniggered.

'The other guy was stupid — he took a customer to a drug neighbourhood and the deal went bad. He was shot three times.'

'Do you carry a gun?' I asked.

He reached in his back pocket and showed me one: 'Hell, yes.'

'Aren't you afraid it'll go off?'

'No, I'm a good shot — plus, it's got a safety lock.'

Welcome to Florida.

Things were not going well. I was tired, depressed and soaked; not a good time to argue with hotel staff about dubious room rates. Coupled with that, I felt it necessary to do some homework if I wanted to stay alive walking to a restaurant later that night.

'Is there anywhere I *shouldn't* go?' I asked Carl at reception.

'Yep, over there by the new housing — that's some bad shit goin' down over there. Directly across the road, that bunch of apartments, stay away from there. Oh, and it's probably best to stay away from that road straight across from us. Other than that, you should be fine. If there's anything else you need, just let us know.'

'A bodyguard would be nice.'

Once inside my room I bolted the door and found the phone number for my one and only contact in Florida. Funny how a solitary phone number scribbled on the back of a card can mean so much! Contrary to how I felt yesterday, this was not a time for shyness or feeling as if I didn't know people well enough to ask for a favour. After all, I was alone, stuck in the middle of nowhere and not entirely convinced there were enough locks on that door.

Thankfully, Jesse Vaughn was home and promised to pick me up the next morning, adding it would be his family's pleasure to have me for Sunday lunch.

'Lunch, only lunch? Please, you've got to get me out of here!' I wanted to say but didn't, realising just in time what an ungrateful little bugger I was turning out to be.

A good old Southern thunderstorm had accompanied the rain, convincing most of Jacksonville's power to switch off at the same time. The fast-food restaurant (20 metres from the hotel and the only place I was guaranteed not to receive a bullet) had suffered as well; its staff, congregating by the front door, gloated to punters that they were getting paid for doing nothing. A collective groan sounded when the traffic and street lights came back on.

A fat truck driver jumped out of his cab and headed straight for the buffet. It occurred to me when he squeezed past, plate piled high with deep-fried shrimps, cheeseburgers and fries, that there was one thing I hadn't actually seen on this trip: an American eating fruit.

I, on the other hand, was determined to eat well tonight. True, it hadn't been a great day but tomorrow was a new one. Against all odds, I was going to find something healthy on that slippery, fat-ridden menu. I needed sustenance, dammit. I needed vegetables or salad and I wouldn't be leaving until I had them.

Having read the menu three times, I looked out the window and weighed up my options should I wish to try another restaurant.

Don't go near the apartments.

Stay away from the new housing area.

There's some bad shit goin' down over there.

'Deep-fried shrimps, cheeseburgers and fries coming right up.'

I'm sure Jacksonville was actually the entrance to something beautiful, i.e. Palm Beach, Daytona and the Florida Keys, but from where I was sitting it was a hole.

But travel's like that. It all depends on one's experiences. Had I been picked up at the train station in an air-conditioned Humvee, ushered to one of Jacksonville's many PGA-rated golf courses and had fish of the day with a bottle of sauvignon blanc for dinner, I would have raved about the place. As it was, I ate badly, inhaled more smoke than a volunteer fireman and didn't want to leave my room.

Ever.

To make matters worse, if I was going to get to the other side of the States on time (i.e. before my plane left) I would have to do some major reshuffling and planning. Hence I spent the evening having a brain-melt working through train timetables and calling 1800 numbers. On the odd occasion I actually spoke to a real person:

'Sorry sir, but you can't book tickets over the phone if you have a New Zealand address.'

'But I don't *live* in America. I'm travelling.'

'I'm sorry, then we can't book tickets.'

'So unless I have an American billing address I can't buy anything on credit card?'

'That's correct, sir.'

Short of purchasing a property in Nashville (why didn't I think of that before I left?) there seemed to be no solution. I looked outside. The hotel pool was inhabited by ill-behaved rug rats. The only thing between it and America's noisiest freeway was a flimsy plastic fence. It was far from what you would call a stress-free environment. Even so, it seemed far more inviting than negotiating with the real person I now wished *was* a computer:

'What is your zip code?' she barked.

'I don't have one.'

'You must have.'

'I don't, I live in New Zealand. We don't have zip codes.'

'You must have.'

'We don't.'

'But you *must* have.'

'We don't.'

And so on.

NEXT MORNING I jumped out of bed like a kid on his birthday. The sheer excitement of not having to take another cab in Jacksonville nearly reduced me to tears (happy ones). Families who had donned their Sunday best and were bound for church slurped coffee at reception. Little kids, much to the dismay of their well-meaning mothers, untucked pristinely ironed shirts. I grabbed a cuppa Joe myself, settled down with the morning paper and waited, hoping my conversation with Jesse wasn't all a dream.

Front page of the *Florida Times-Union*:

Woman Accused of Trying to Fake her own Death in a Fire

CIA takes Blame on Uranium Dams

Is There Anyone who can Carry on Lynard Skynard's Rock Tradition?

Jesse arrived in a pick-up truck and was surprised to see I was travelling so light. He may have also wondered why I was bringing *all* my bags just for Sunday lunch. Little did he know I had other plans, i.e. never setting foot in that drug-dealing neighbourhood ever again.

We hit the road, and Jesse pumped up the country tunes. For a man who at first seemed quiet and reserved, he sure dispelled any notions that my next few days were going to be boring. It's the quiet ones you gotta look out for; Jesse Vaughn of Jacksonville, Florida, would turn out to be one of the most interesting people I've ever met.

Upon arriving at his home Jesse introduced me to his lovely wife, Angie, and their son, Dominic, who greeted me wearing swimming medals he'd won in 1988. Apparently it was his custom to show them off to every new person he met. Within minutes I was in his bedroom, where George Strait and Bee Gees posters covered the walls, country music tapes were scattered across the floor and the TV showed a video of him swimming, winning those medals. Dominic was born with Down's Syndrome and obviously a love of music.

I looked back to find Jesse standing at the door:

'Come on, Dominic, leave him alone, he's only just arrived.'

Jesse and Angie were impressed I'd managed to dine without a gun the night previous. I told them I was just happy to be out of the area.

'Lot of drug murders around there,' Jesse said.

Needless to say, I felt happy and safe in their home. They told me Sunday was the one day in the week where they all got to put their feet up, have a beer and watch the baseball. This was sounding better by the minute. Having discovered some pretty interesting photos in the lounge while Jesse fetched

The name's Vaughn . . . Jesse Vaughn

some cold ones, it wasn't long before the stories came out. Jesse described his career as 'golf at the beginning, golf at the end and smoke and mirrors in between'. He told me all this while he was *supposed* to be watching the chicken on the barbecue. Angie, obviously noting her husband was going to be a while (and had more than his fair share of stories to get through), took the tongs and did it herself. 'She's 100 percent Italian,' he boasted, gladly surrendering the kitchenware.

Photo number one — Alice Cooper and Jesse playing golf.

'Believe it or not, he is the nicest guy in the world. He's good, too — plays off about a five. That day I was playing him at a celebrity tournament. He said to me, "Jesse, I wish we could play again tomorrow but my wife says I gotta go to church." Church, can you believe it? Alice Cooper!'

Photo number two — Jesse playing cricket in Milan.

'When we lived in London I played for the MCC, Milan Cricket Club.'

'Get outta town, you actually played cricket?' I said.

'Sure I did.'

'You are the first American I have ever met who played cricket.'

Nostalgia does funny things to a man and I got the feeling Jesse was enjoying this trip down memory lane as much as I was. Consequently, while Angie prepared a beautiful meal, Jesse was to be found rummaging through the garage looking for old cricket scorecards. He came back triumphant.

'My best was 50 not out, look,' he said, pointing at the official MCC booklet. 'And that's us playing against the Munich Spies. I was bowled by Onion for 18.'

'Didn't you find it difficult playing a game you'd never played before?'

'If you've got a good eye you can play anything. I even learnt to bowl with a straight arm.'

I was floored: an American who played cricket. I wanted to hug him. (If you haven't noticed already, I love the game.) Even stranger than finding an American who played the game was discovering where they actually played: namely Germany, France, Switzerland, Monte Carlo and Italy. This is akin to playing baseball in Egypt, the Ukraine or Australia.

'I remember once I was having a particularly bad season so headed to the indoor nets at Lord's. A middle-aged black man came up to me and shook my hand. When he found out I was American, his reaction was much like yours; "Wow," he said, "this is the first time we've had an American in the indoor centre at Lord's." He then said, "My name's Gary." I said, "Hi, the name's Jesse." Anyway, after I'd finished batting practice, a teammate came up to me and said, "Do you know who that was?" I said, "Yeah, said his name was Gary."

'Turns out it was Sir Garfield Sobers — the Babe Ruth of cricket!'

Photo number three — Jesse on the same scoreboard as Chi Chi Rodriguez and Lee Trevino.

'When I left the CIA in '92 [told you this bloke was interesting] I decided to take up golf again. Luckily my game started coming back, so when I turned 50 I tried to qualify for the seniors tour. I qualified for a dozen or so tours, including the Nike tour and the buy.com tour. But it's a hard slog. There are only 16 spots on the senior tour. Even if you play well all year but finish 17th you're still out for the next year. It's tough.'

'What sort of guys did you play with?'

'Arnold Palmer, Chi Chi Rodriguez, Bob Charles but never, regrettably, Jack Nicklaus.'

'What was your best-ever finish?'

'Fifth at Pittsburgh and sixth at Grand Rapids, Michigan,' he said proudly. He could tell I was dumbfounded. 'Every day I used to tell myself, try to be the best you can be — *today*. Nobody can ask you to do more than that.'

As luck would have it, underneath the cricket scorecards in the garage were newspaper articles Angie had kept from his golfing days:

> Jesse Vaughn won $4180 with rounds of 78, 74, and 71 — a total of 223.

> Monday, 6 June 1994: Jim Dent $150,000, Bob Charles $73,333, Jesse Vaughn $4100.

> In the same field as Bob Charles, Chi Chi Rodriguez, Lee Trevino, Jim Dent, Kermit Zarley, Larry Gilbert and Tommy Aaron (who later won the Masters) was Jesse Vaughn, a somewhat mysterious man. The self-described Monday-morning scrubber, originally from San Diego, went to San José State on a golf scholarship and missed qualifying for the tour by one shot in 1970. He played in Europe and Asia in 1970 and 1971, enjoyed a third-place finish in the French Open and then disappeared.

'Journalists used to get frustrated,' Jesse smiled. 'I was the Man of Mystery, they knew nothing about me. They tried to find my records but I didn't exist!'

This was too much to take in: senior tour pro, CIA agent and cricketer. I needed a lie-down, or at least a good Sunday lunch. Angie didn't let us down. As the rain continued to fall, we dined on chicken, roast veggies, salad, bread and red wine. Not only was I having my first decent meal in weeks but my dirty washing was getting done, I was sitting with a man who was guaranteed to give me my first round of golf in America, and my gracious hosts kept insisting I use their phone to call home.

I felt I'd found it already.

Dominic, clad in a signed Hooters T-shirt, had joined us for lunch. He asked me to sign his visitor's book while I asked about his girlfriends.

'He thinks he runs the place,' Jesse said, speaking of Hooters. 'He gets all the girls to sign his shirt — he's got five of them.'

Dominic fanned his face with his hand: 'Hubba, hubba,' he said loudly.

'We'll take you there tomorrow,' Jesse said, much to Dominic's pleasure.

'Hubba, hubba!' Dominic repeated.

A scar on Dominic's head revealed that I'd be rooming next to someone that, according to his father, 'had an angel sitting on his shoulder'. Once, when Jesse was on the senior tour, he received a phone call to say that his son had been involved in a car accident on the way back from St Augustine. Dominic was in a coma for three weeks.

'He had a pretty bad brain injury,' Angie said. 'His walking is still a little unstable, but he's doing well.'

We stuffed our faces and laughed for the rest of the afternoon. Jacksonville was a good place after all — I just had to find the Vaughns. Jesse couldn't resist showing me his AK-47 under his bed and I couldn't resist asking about his 'smoke and mirrors' period.

'I'm a Marine from a family of Marines,' he said, filling my glass. 'Then I got the opportunity to join the CIA. We lived in Sydney, Hong Kong, Tehran, Athens, London, Milan, then back to DC. In London I was attached to the Soviet bloc division which wasn't much fun. I was away from the family for six to eight weeks at a time.'

'Basically I've spent my whole life worrying,' Angie added.

Jesse looked at his wife. 'I've put her through a lot.'

'You must have been in some hairy situations,' I said.

'Oh, yeah.' Jesse's eyes lit up. 'Like '78 in Iran. It got really wild there for a while. Looking back I really shouldn't have taken my family there. It was the worst place in the world to live: guns, bombs, the lot. I had to carry two .45s everywhere I went. I didn't mind the work, just didn't like exposing my family. Once in Tehran . . .'

'Oh no, not this story,' Angie said, head in hands.

'Once in Tehran,' Jesse continued, smiling, 'this crazy revolution was going on — it really wasn't a safe place to be at all. We were on the ground and could hear gunfire. Bombs were going off in the distance. It really was scary.'

Jesse reminded me of James Bond: softly spoken, assured and confident. I couldn't imagine him getting too flustered in any situation. Iran had obviously tested his nerve.

'We were trying to get the hell out of there. We could still hear gunfire in the distance and sprinted to a waiting helicopter — only just got there in time. We slammed the doors and the chopper took off just before all hell broke loose. I then turned to check on my wife, who was yelling at me, above the noise of the engine: "Got any other fucking places you'd like to take me to?"

'I said, "Come on, honey, where's your sense of humour!"'

The Vaughn household had another Sunday tradition I could easily get used to: Irish coffees down at the local sports bar. Although this wasn't your run-of-the-mill bar. Six TV screens, each surely the size of a football field, covered the bar's factory-sized walls. Jesse promised every sport, 'maybe even cricket'.

Watching golf balls the size of car tyres on the screens made me realise I still hadn't popped the question. I decided to wait until after an Irish coffee. Or two.

'So, you're travelling around the States for four weeks?' Jesse asked, perched at the bar.

'That's right, from one side to the other.'

'How do you get that amount of time off work?'

'By pleading,' I conceded.

'I only ask because in America everyone gets two weeks' holiday, unless they work for the company for ten thousand years, then they get another week.'

'So, are you working tomorrow?'

'Sure am.'

'You don't . . . want to . . . you know, play golf?'

'Justin, I haven't picked up a club for five years and I don't want to go out and shoot 80. So no, I can't play.'

Wrong answer, Jesse. I'm gonna get you out there.

On the way home I remarked that, as a couple, as a *family*, they had lived a really interesting life. A life Lady Iva would definitely approve of.

'I've been lucky,' Jesse said. '*We've* been lucky, I should say. We've always had good health and in my career in particular, I always seem to have been in the right place at the right time. That's led us to having some wonderful experiences, meeting great people who became our good friends, and seeing places that a lot of Americans would never get to see. Honestly, Americans don't know how easy they've got it. They need to visit some of these other parts of the world.'

'What do you say to all the bad press the CIA seems to get?' I asked.

'The CIA is not popular with Hollywood, that's for sure, but then they don't see all the good work we do.'

'And what do you think of James Bond?' It had to be asked.

'I had friends who worked for MI5 and MI6 and I used to say to them, "How come you guys have got women coming out of the woodwork and you're getting laid every night? Meantime, I got a guy chasing me down the back streets of Cairo with a machete!"'

As the garage door rolled up, Jesse patted me on the knee and told me what I wanted to hear. 'You know what, I'm going to call the office and see if I can't get tomorrow off.'

'That's great, Jesse!'

'I can't believe I'm doing this,' he said.

'*I* can't believe you're doing this,' Angie said from the back seat.

'Don't worry, Angie,' I said, 'I won't get him back on that tour.'

'I hope not, Justin. It's either feast or famine. Most of the time, famine.'

The load was a lot easier that night. I slept like a baby with the reassuring sounds of the Bee Gees and George Strait at full volume in the next room.

And, finally, I had a game of golf lined up.

SECOND DAY IN JACKSONVILLE. Bad news. Jesse called from work to say he couldn't get time off after all. Angie was more concerned, however, that her son had kept me awake all night.

'He stays up all night and then wonders why he's tired all day,' she said. 'Coffee?'

'Yes please, that would be great.'

Bugger — I was really looking forward to that game. A quick look outside confirmed that the rain had eased, but the 53-inch, larger-than-life TV in the lounge informed all that more thunderstorms were due. Too bad. I had come too far not to play this bloody round of golf. Luckily, Angie's offer of taking me to the course still stood; $25 later, I had a game on my hands. Two locals, Bud and Jerry, would be joining me on the first tee at Jacksonville Beach Golf Course. Neither was wearing a collar.

'Be careful out there,' the club pro warned us. 'Severe thunderstorms predicted.'

'Whatever,' I grumbled. It was going to take more than a lightning bolt up the backside to stop me today. I had waited two weeks to spoil my walk with a small white ball.

My over-eagerness hardly paid off. My first shot dribbled 10 yards from the tee, barely creeping past the ladies' tee.

'After that shot, maybe we should be calling you Justine!' Bud said.

Obviously Bud wasn't short of a word or two, which didn't bother me. I like cheeky golfers. 'You'll keep, Bud,' I said. 'You'll keep.'

For someone who was basing his whole trip around golf, I was hardly the game's best advertisement. The first five holes I was in the bushes, in the lake and over the green. I could hardly be blamed, though; I was distracted by a piece of technology I'd never seen before on a fairway, a GPS system in a golf cart.

'You are 125 metres from the green!' the screen flashed.

'You are 50 metres from the green!'

'Are you hungry? Would you like to order a hot dog?'

'How about pizza? Press here!'

Unfortunately, I spent most of the front nine trying to work out whether it was a 'cheeseburger and fries' or a 'hot dog and Coke' kinda day. Hence, my golf suffered.

You might think that through all this I was neglecting my fatherly duties, but Charleston, the attention-grabbing media megastar, was riding shotgun the whole time. He really was a pain in the arse, that duck. Sure, he looked stupid sitting in the front seat and I definitely received more than my fair share of strange looks but hey, that's what being a parent is all about. When meeting people, such as Bud and Jerry, it was easier just to say he was a mascot rather than admit he was the guy who nearly beat me in South Carolina.

Bad golf aside, it was a relief to use my clubs on an actual course rather than on Eighth Avenue or at a clown wedding. (Speaking of which, I had heard from Bonkers. He thanked me for attending his wedding and said he hoped we might keep in touch. Wouldn't that make for a strange moment in New Zealand five years from now: 'So, how did you guys meet?')

Golf being a sociable game, I didn't have to wait long before Bud and Jerry told me how they'd spent their 60-odd years. Unfortunately, most of this information was relayed just as I attempted to play another shot across the water, which never made it. As I dug around in my bag for new balls, Bud smoked and Jerry laughed. Both retired, Jerry (who'd been to New Zealand) used to work for Delta Airlines in Atlanta, while Bud had worked in insurance his whole life.

He told me, 'I was often asked when I was going to get a real job, but the work was so easy and the money was so good, why would I bother?'

Splash. Another ball in the lake. Bud smoked and Jerry laughed, a big Southern, hearty laugh.

I had now given up on my game and decided to enjoy my walk instead. It wasn't a great course — at least six temporary greens proved we weren't on one of Jacksonville's PGA-rated courses — but it was pleasant enough with well-cut fairways and big old oak trees, 'witch's hair' hanging from their branches. Jerry informed the group that his bladder needed a work-out at hole number nine. A quick trip to the urinal brought a new joke:

'Reminds me of a sign I saw in a bathroom once; it was placed three feet from the basin. It said, if you can hit the urinal from here, join the fire department!'

And there were more:

'Justin, over in New Zealand what do you call a nurse with dirty knees?'

'I dunno.'

'Well, over here we call them the *head* nurse.'

Bud smoked, Jerry laughed.

'You can use that one when you get back to New Zealand if you like.'

'Thanks, Bud, but I don't think I will.'

And one more for good measure (hell, he was on a roll now):

'Three nuns go to heaven,' he continued, rolling a cigarette between his fingers. 'Saint Peter says, "You're all allowed one thing you didn't have on earth." "Well, that *sex* looks pretty good," says the first nun. "Okay, no problem," says Saint Peter, "you can have sex. Who would you like to have sex with?" "Clark Gable," she says — he's a movie actor,' Bud added, lighting his new creation.

'I know that, Bud.'

'So they had sex. Next nun says, "I kind of like the sound of that sex, too. Saint Peter says, "Okay, who would *you* like?" "I'd like that Brad Pitt," she says. He's a movie actor here as well,' Bud said, nudging me in the ribs.

'I know that, Bud, we do have TVs in New Zealand.'

'So they have sex. Then the third nun says, "I kind of like the sound of that sex as well, and I tell you who *I'd* like. I'd like Justin Brown." "*Justin Brown*, why on earth would you want Justin Brown?" "'Cos every time I go to New Zealand, everyone walks around saying, 'Fuck that Justin Brown!'"'

Jerry laughed, Bud smoked.

'I been thinking about that one all round,' Bud said, showing his pearly white false teeth. 'You can use that when you get back to New Zealand if you like.'

'Thanks, Bud, but I don't think I will.'

The sky was black and rumblings drew close. Unfortunately, my GPS was no longer concerned about how best to serve my stomach, and instead flashed regular warnings: 'Lightning storm approaching, head back to clubhouse.'

Bud looked up at the clouds. 'Looks like the good times are over.' And he should know — his father-in-law was struck by lightning on this very course, on the 13th hole. The bolt went right through the metal grommet in his hat and came out his belt.

'He didn't die,' Bud told me, 'but it knocked him unconscious, and he couldn't quite hear the same. Funny thing was, up until then he smoked a pack a day. After he was struck he couldn't stand the smell of tobacco.'

'One way to give up, I suppose,' remarked Jerry. 'Maybe I should try that.'

Big fat raindrops drenched us on the last couple of holes and deep, growling thunderclaps warned us what lay ahead. Even my hardy local partners weren't going to risk the last hole, instead opting for the 19th and a cold ale. The severity and suddenness of the storm intrigued me, but not nearly as much as how, and why, they were named.

'How come this new hurricane's called Claudette?' I asked. 'The one in the news that's supposed to be coming any day now. I mean, why not Gavin or Barry?'

'Are you serious?' Jerry asked.

'Sure, I'm serious. Is there actually a reason?'

Jerry took a deep breath:

'In 1953, the United States Weather Service first started naming hurricanes after women. Wives, girlfriends, even Bess Truman, the former first lady, were all honoured with namesake storms. By 1979, men's names were added in response to protests from women's groups. [You'd think it would have been the other way around, wouldn't you?] Anyway, each year's storms start out at the A name of a new list. After six years the lists are used over again. For example, the names for 1999's storms were last used in 1993.'

It appears I'd underestimated Jerry. I thought he just laughed. Of course, what he said made complete sense. If you live in America you probably know all this, but to me it was a revelation, like the day I discovered the only animal with four knees is the elephant, and that most advertisements for watches show the time as 10.08. (Have a look next time.)

All I knew about Claudette was that she was on her way and seemed to be taking up her fair share of primetime TV. Of course, if I'd actually paid attention to the news in the first place, I would have seen that Ana and Bill had already paid a visit to the South before I started my trip. Fingers crossed, the country wouldn't be seeing Danny, Erika, Fabian, Grace, Henri, Isabel, Juan, Kate, Larry, Mindy, Nicholas, Odette, Peter, Rose, Sam, Teresa, Victor or Wanda in the near future.

Jesse picked me up and took me home where we watched the *Home Run Derby*. I couldn't have been happier: feet up, glued to a 53-inch screen where

10 blokes lined up to bash baseballs around a stadium. Simple concept: get the best hitters from the competition, put them in front of 50,000 expectant fans, person with the most home runs wins. One guy hit 14 in a row. Entertaining stuff!

'The Tornado should be home soon,' said Jesse, speaking of Dominic.

Sure enough, we soon heard a whirling noise approach the front door. He would be extra-hyper tonight knowing that 'we'll go to Hooters tomorrow' was no passing comment.

'Hi, everyone!'

Slam. Crash. Bang.

The Tornado had arrived.

Dominic had received a five-dollar pay cheque from work. He hung it on the fridge, convinced he would never have to work again. Jesse would have to break the news later.

While Dominic decided which Hooters shirt to wear (they were all the same, covered with various signatures from scantily clad waitresses) Jesse invited me to his boss's house for a drink, which happened to be just down the road. Wally, an ex-navy officer, was a solidly built man with a pregnant-like belly. He offered us a drink and poured one for himself. At first I thought he was going to have a gin and tonic as a hefty bottle of Bombay Sapphire had found its way onto the breakfast bar.

I was half right: it was gin, just no tonic. A whole tumbler of the stuff.

'I saw him drink *six* of those in one night once,' Jesse told me when Wally was getting some snacks. 'Honestly, he *spills* more than I drink.'

Surely gin brings out the best in people, or the worst. Either way I figured this would be as good a time as any to talk American history.

'My least favourite American,' Wally mused, 'would have to be Clinton. Can't believe he ever got in. He's an idiot, a womaniser and a moron.'

'Don't hold back, Wally,' I said. 'Say what you really feel.'

'Don't you worry about that, I will. Damn Southerners, I tell ya, every time we elect a damn Southerner they screw things up. We should never let them in. Carter was the same. Too nice.'

Wally didn't let me leave the house without two biographies of General George Patton. 'Send them back to me, but you've got to read them. That man is America's greatest hero. Ever.'

The Tornado got away with murder at Hooters. He hugged the girls, kissed the girls and had pictures taken with them. He said things other men only dreamed of. He fanned his face, stared at cleavage and screamed 'Hubba, hubba!' at the top of his voice.

Angie ordered. Jesse and I tried not to look.

THIRD DAY IN JACKSONVILLE. It would be difficult to leave behind my comfy double bed, en suite and free Bee Gees concert, but tonight I would again be watching *Chicago*, this time on a train bound for New Orleans. As it was an overnight trip, and I'd managed to save some coin by staying with James Bond and family, I decided to splurge, leave cattle class behind and get some rest in my own room. This wasn't a cheap option but who wants to arrive in New Orleans tired?

Angie, the ever-amiable host, had promised to drive me to America's oldest city in the morning, so we grabbed a paper, brewed a coffee and hit the road. I took great delight in the fact that today was, after all, a rest day. Granted, I only played 17 holes yesterday, and yes, I accept I played like a nun against two men who didn't even feature in the paper, but at least I could now say I'd played a round of golf in Florida.

Plus, I had a few new jokes up my sleeve (ones I'd never use).

Even so, I still had to check on a few papers in the car. Front page of *Florida Times-Union*:

County Debates Same Sex Marriage

Gambling Problems on Rise Among Teens

Why Children Shouldn't Sleep in Their Own Beds

Front page of the *St Augustine Record:*

City Opposes Idea of Water Trolleys

Leaders Discuss Housing Programs

Manfred Schroeder, Leader in Economic Development of County, Dies at 73

Honestly, how was I ever supposed to play golf if potential partners kept dying on me?

I don't know about you but I had no idea America's oldest city lay in Florida. St Augustine was settled in 1565 by Spanish explorer Don Pedro Menendez de Aviles. Having been attacked twice by the British, the residents of St Augustine built the Castillo de San Marcos (a massive fort which still attracts visitors) and for the next century and a half the city changed hands three times: the Spanish, British and eventually, the USA.

Keeping up with tradition, I ordered Russian-style fish in a Spanish restaurant. Afterwards Angie and I wandered St Augustine's narrow cobblestone streets, bought tacky postcards and had a coffee in the historic Casa Monica Hotel.

Jesse dropped me off at the train, waiting with me (like your parents would) until it had actually arrived. I kept telling him to go but he refused. He gave me a hug and I boarded the train. It was hard to believe I was already halfway through my trip and, thanks mainly to Angie, still had clean washing.

DAY 15: NEW ORLEANS, LOUISIANA

WITH A BAG FULL of clean washing and golf clubs that had finally seen some action, I walked to the far end of the track, past cattle class ('Hi all, enjoy *Chicago* and no sleep!'), and boarded a train bound for New Orleans. At the end of the platform Cynthia greeted me:

'Hello sir, I'll be your hostess for the trip. Please go upstairs, turn right and make yourself comfortable. If there's anything you need just let me know. Help yourself to soda, coffee or tea and I'll wake you when we get to New Orleans.'

Holy hell, was this ever worth the money! A clean toilet, a shower and as much Pepsi as I could drink. Sometimes you've just got to splurge.

'Are you hungry, Mr Brown?' Cynthia asked as I downed my second bottle. I was lying on my bed reading *Patton: The Man behind the Legend*, wondering whether I'd actually taken down Wally's address.

'Come to think of it, I am feeling rather peckish,' I said.

'Well, if you'd like to adjourn to the dining car, dinner is being served.'

'Lovely, I may just do that.'

I put the dog out and locked my room. The alarm wasn't necessary; I was only going down the road. Having made the obligatory comparisons with other rooms, I made it safely to the dining car but was disappointed to be joined by three complete strangers.

Surely part of the package could have included dinner with friends or was I expecting too much bang for my buck? Or had I just had too much sugar?

My steak was cooked medium-rare; the roast potatoes were just crispy

117

enough and for dessert I opted for the chocolate mousse pyramid (purely for the name). This was all washed down with a glass of Perrier sparkling mineral water. I did toy with the idea of getting the waitress to put my peas in a doggy bag for the paupers downstairs, but decided instead to use them as cannonballs.

Make them suffer!

The elderly gentleman opposite kept stroking his neck which, judging by the scarring and rawness, had obviously seen some major surgery in the last month. He confirmed this by telling anyone who would listen that the reason he was eating so slowly was that he'd had a couple of bouts of cancer. The woman next to him, in her late thirties, was helping with his dinner and stroking his back. This is where I started playing the rather dangerous sport of assumption, a game we've all played and a game where we're nearly *always* wrong.

Assumption: sitting opposite were father and daughter. He was obviously very sick. Daughter has decided that as a last hoorah she'll take her loving father on a month-long trip around the States; something she's always wanted to do. Her father's illness had kicked her into action.

Reality: 'We're married, we met at church group.'

Assumption: the woman to my right, in her late seventies, is fit and well. Her husband was not so lucky. He died recently. After a lot of soul-searching she finally made the decision to tour the country in style.

Reality: 'I've just been to see my daughter in Florida. She broke up with her husband and doesn't have enough time to look after her boy. I've been his mother for the last six weeks. I kind of miss him now. Miss the chaos.'

Dangerous game, assumption.

This was indeed a fine way to travel. I can see why people, given the option, choose rail over air or road. No maps, no gas or concentration required. And so sociable, too. Take our table — at first shy and reserved, we soon turned into one of the noisiest in the carriage, reciting jokes, throwing food and swapping stories. With nothing to do and nowhere to be, the only thing left to do was to watch the sun go down over the swamps of the South.

UPON RETURNING HOME, I let the dog back in and made my bed. I was knackered; unfortunately my neighbour wasn't. Short of coming over and welcoming me to the area, she told me she'd been visiting her sister in Miami. Had her story not been about alligators, I may not have been so accommodating.

'My sister, she lives right by the water,' she said excitedly. 'They've only just bought the house. Anyway, her husband often goes out with the weed whacker and does the lawn. But lately, big, four- to six-feet-long alligators have been wandering up while he's right by the water's edge. So he said to my sister, "Look, if you see one of those 'gators, grab the gun, walk up to one of them and just shoot the water." Well, she did just that, but at a time when he didn't even know she was home. She spotted a 'gator, fired the gun, and he nearly died of shock and fell in the water!'

THEY MAY BE RIGHT in saying you're no *safer* in first class, but for some reason you do seem to get there quicker. I awoke to find Cynthia at the door fulfilling her promise: 'We've arrived in New Orleans, Mr Brown.'

It was 7 am. There was no question I had slept better than in cattle class, but I hadn't found the 'clackety, clackety, clack' all that soothing, unlike my neighbour, who said it reminded her of 'being in the womb' (good memory).

I said goodbye to the dog, locked up and stepped into the balmy, midsummer vibe of New Orleans. If the rumour was true that food and music were all people talked about in this part of the world, I might never leave. I wanted jazz, Cajun cooking, crazy people and golf courses. It didn't upset me one bit that I hadn't timed my visit to coincide with the infamous Mardi Gras, either. There's no doubt this festival is one hell of a party, though having heard recently there's not one part of Bourbon Street that hasn't been pissed, puked, spat or shat on, it didn't exactly make me want to take the first bus there.

Little did I know I'd actually *be* there at 3 am, adding to its demise.

Confirming my belief that every cab in America smelt like an urn, I then rode in a moving ashtray with my new driver, Will (is *everyone* called Will or Bill in this country?), and was taken to my hotel.

At first I thought he was ripping me off; 10 bucks to travel what appeared to be a few blocks seemed a little excessive, but he informed me that a standard fare had been introduced so taxi drivers wouldn't rip off tourists. How sweet!

'So where you from?' he asked, extinguishing his cigarette on something that didn't appear flammable.

'New Zealand,' I replied.

'New Zealand? That's w'sup man.'

'Yeah, it's pretty good.'

'Kiwis, right?'

'Yeah, Kiwis — how did you know that?'

'I used to live in LA, man. One night I drove your New Zealand rugby team all over town. I drove them to every fucking strip club there was. They couldn't get enough.'

'Rugby team? You mean the All Blacks?'

'Yeah, man, the All Blacks, that's the one. They're w'sup, man. We went to this one club where the shortest rugby player in the team had the hots for this stripper. She was all right, had a few too many tattoos, but a hot body. Anyway, I was fooling around with this other chick at the time and found out the chick with the tattoos wanted to bag this short guy. He wanted the same but the biggest guy in the team said, "You bed one, you bed 'em all." The short guy said "What?" He said, "You heard me, you bed one, you bed 'em *all.*" And with that the littlest one smacked the big guy clean in the face!'

At first I thought Will had the wrong address. The hotel was exquisite: marble floors, staff dressed in black and a concierge called Brian were awaiting my arrival. He asked if there was anything I needed. A shower, I felt, may have been stretching his job description. Instead, I told him what I was doing in America. He made me promise to consult him should I wish to get hold of any icons from the South. This was sounding better all the time — could it be true that concierges were now helping in my quest for a game of golf?

Maybe they knew I needed all the help I could get.

And before you think I had splurged twice in 24 hours (first the room on the train, now this), let me just say the reason I was able to afford this hotel was because Tim, a friend-of-a-friend (who I'd never met), was staying in New Orleans on business. Having kept in touch over the past two weeks, he had left a message overnight to say I was most welcome to stay with him on the 15th floor, in a posh hotel, in the middle of the French Quarter.

It doesn't get much more felicitous than that.

Fluffy towels, mint shampoo and a view of the Mississippi River were to be found in a two-bedroom suite high above the old city. Tim had done well; this was mind-blowing. I set up camp and showered till I ran out of songs to sing. I jumped around the room in my underpants, unable to believe my luck. I wanted to call all my mates and brag, 'I'm in New Orleans, in my underpants, staying with some bloke I've . . . never met!'

It appeared that most people staying at The W were on some sort of Microsoft conference. Riding the lift to the pool, I couldn't get a word in for the TCP/IPs, protocols, BACPs and RAACMs.

Still, if it hadn't been for these guys, this marvellous hotel wouldn't have been built and I wouldn't be swimming for free.

Tacky as it seemed, I had to visit Bourbon Street. I grabbed a copy of the New Orleans *Times-Picayune* and, against my better judgement, ordered a Hurricane instead of a coffee or lemonade. (William from Tybee had ordered me to try one: 1 oz light rum, 1 oz dark rum, $\frac{1}{2}$ oz passionfruit juice, $\frac{1}{2}$ oz fresh lime juice, in case you're wondering; bloody awful, especially at 11 in the morning.)

It was a seedy bar with no character. Pictures of drunken people, arm in arm, hung on the walls, cowboy hats hung from the ceiling and a barmaid with no teeth hung around like a bad smell. She seemed to think my life wouldn't be complete without the help of another of those god-awful drinks. I paid her and found a corner, where I flicked through the newspaper and found these front-page stories:

Woman Arrested on 25-year Charge

A New York woman wanted on a homicide charge over the death of her infant son 25 years ago was arrested Monday in a New Orleans supermarket parking lot.

Two Men Slain in N.O. on Violent Sunday

A 42-year-old New Orleans man died from a stabbing in his lower Gentilly Terrace home early Sunday and a 27-year-old New Orleans man was killed in Mid-City when someone wielding an AK-47 assault rifle chased him down and shot him.

Brian, my concierge, would have to work overtime if he believed I could get a game with any of these guys. Luckily, a light-hearted story at the bottom of the page grabbed my attention. The Annual New Orleans Waiter Race had taken place at the weekend, which also happened to be Bastille Day. This event, obviously a tradition in the city, involved waiters from various restaurants carrying (and running with) food and wine around a U-shaped obstacle course, in front of nervous bystanders.

Two waiters featured in the article. I called the first at his place of work, only to find he wouldn't be there till the next day. The difficulty came when asked if they could leave a message for their semi-famous co-worker: 'Yes, can you tell him that a New Zealander he's never met is in town. He's easy to spot. He'll be the one carrying around a set of golf clubs and a plastic duck. Please call — he's sick of being rejected.'

Instead of calling the next restaurant, I decided to hike there in the heat. After all, I seem to have a lot more success face to face. There I found that Donald Brebner from the Rene Bistro (the other waiter from the article) *would* be working today but not until later that afternoon. Rebecca, the very friendly maître d' told me to come back at four o'clock, adding, 'Donald is a most likeable man and would no doubt love to talk.'

GETTING A LITTLE TIPSY

Palace Cafe waiter Aaron Young, right, watches water start to spill from his tray of cups as he falls behind in a race against Rene Bistro rival Donald Brebner, left, in the semifinals of the annual Waiters Race during the Bastille Day Celebration in the Central Business District on Sunday.

STAFF PHOTO JENNIFER ZDON

The Times-Picayune, *New Orleans, Louisiana*

'Does he play golf?' I asked.

'Not sure,' she smiled. 'I know he spends a lot of time on line.'

To be honest, I found this a nervous time. I mean, what if after a day of waiting, the one person you've wanted to talk to all day takes one look at you and tells you to bugger off? Or worse still, doesn't play golf (which seems to be the trend)?

SO WHAT DOES one do in New Orleans when one is waiting on a waiter to confirm whether or not he can play 18 holes tomorrow? Well, aside from riding a streetcar through the historic district and gawking, open-mouthed, at beautifully restored mansions, I rather predictably ended up in a second-hand toy shop.

I know, I know, I should have been taking a paddle-wheel riverboat cruise or soaking up culture in the New Orleans Museum of Art, but among the comics and figurines in this dingy, hole-in-the-wall store were two middle-aged guys whose main aim in life was selling a model of Mo's Bar, a Buddy Holly figurine (whose guitar and hand fell off later that day) and Max from *Where the Wild Things Are* to an unsuspecting Kiwi. I *was* going to buy Beaker from *The Muppets* as well but, typically, if you wanted this pleasure you also had to purchase Dr Bunsen Honeydew and the whole lab.

And I had enough to carry.

Tim called to ask if I'd care to meet him and a few of his work buddies for a drink.

In New Orleans.

I liked the sound of that. I agreed this was a fine idea, adding that I would also bring a driver's licence to prove I was the guy he'd be sharing a room with. Meantime, I had a waiter to meet.

Having successfully navigated my way around the city (I count getting on and off a tram as a major achievement), I returned to Rene Bistro where Rebecca welcomed me with a warm smile. Great, I thought, she hasn't forgotten me.

'Donald should be here any minute,' she said. 'Take a seat at the bar.'

Before I saw him, I could hear him, and others congratulating him:

'Don, saw you in the paper.'

'Hey, Donald, great picture!'

'So you've had your 15 minutes of fame, huh Don?'

Thankfully, Rebecca had briefed him about the New Zealander waiting at the bar, though I don't think she'd mentioned anything about golf. He came over, shook my hand and invited me to join him in the restaurant.

Don was an amiable sort of guy who didn't look his 47 years. He also appeared to relish working alongside young people, hence he appeared very young at heart himself.

'It's a problem I run into often,' he told me. 'People often ask me, why are you *still* waiting on tables? The truth is, I love it. I started 25 years ago while at college and never stopped. I couldn't imagine doing anything else. I did study for a while, art and graphic design, but I just loved waiting too much. It's a performance, every day is different.'

Donald was that enthusiastic about his bloody job, he almost made me want to throw on an apron and set the table. His take on life was similar: *Life is mysterious, don't take it serious*, and *Never regret growing older, it's a privilege denied to many.*

'So, what do you do in your spare time?' I asked, jokingly. 'Cook?'

'I do cook, yes.'

'Really?

'Well, sort of. I own over a thousand cookbooks. I don't use any of them, just read them. It's my therapy. What else do I do? I travel.'

'Been to New Zealand?'

'No, I've been to Michigan, Florida, Europe and Hawaii.'

'Got any kids?'

'No, but I do have a dog. I *love* my dog, my best friend has dedicated a website to her, ladythedog.com. She's a mutt; I got her from the SPCA. What else do I do? If I've had a really bad day, I'll go home and paint. I love Jackson Pollock; my paintings are very childlike. We've got a big house so I like to throw paints around. I believe there's no such thing as a bad painting.'

Could be a good thing by the sounds of it.

'Salvador Dali would have to be my favourite American. Even though he was Spanish-born, he lived here a long time. He was fascinating, a really freaky person.'

124

Now, about that meal . . . ? Don Brebner, New Orleans

'And least favourite?'

'Anyone who's not open-minded, anyone who is right wing or close-minded. Anyone who is racist or discriminates. It shocks me living in New Orleans; even though it's a melting pot and a very integrated society, some people still make comments like they're living in the '50s.'

Donald lived with his partner of 26 years on the West Bank of New Orleans.

'We moved to New Orleans 15 years ago,' he said. 'They appreciate older waiters down here — up north they make you feel like a loser.'

'Speaking of losers,' I remarked, 'I tried to call your competitor from the waiter's race today. Did you actually win? I couldn't tell from the article.'

'No, I came second — to someone half my age, I might add. You've got to be quick in that race, and balanced. It's all over in 20 seconds. They judge you by spillage.'

'Any accidents?'

'None, it was an injury-free day.'

I hadn't meant to offend anyone today but did so when declining a meal offered by Rebecca. The truth was, I just couldn't afford it. Normally I would have just opted for street food or a dodgy burger — something cheap, not necessarily nutritious, but enough to keep me going. Rebecca was twice as angry upon realising my failure to understand what she *really* meant: 'Please, you must stay. Have what you like, compliments of us.'

'Done.'

I felt like a food critic, sitting there quaffing white wine and ordering copious amounts of fine French food. I smiled and looked out the window. How had I stumbled across this? What a damn fine piece of luck, and what a wonderful introduction to New Orleans.

'Frogs' legs?' Donald asked, looking up from the menu.

'Not enough left in the world,' I said, quite seriously. 'I feel sorry for the frogs.'

It was great watching Don in his work. He loved serving people, though he felt he was but one of the cogs in the wheel: 'It's the cooks I admire,' he said. 'There's a lot to be said for someone who cooks or serves well — it's an ancient art. No one tips them and no one commends them when, really, they're the heroes.'

Donald continued to talk while I continued to gorge. 'My favourite customer is just the average person who really, really likes food,' he said, while I ate chicken with lemon soup. 'People in New Orleans love to eat, it's a pastime here,' he remarked as I polished off the Tuna Rossini. 'Here, we call them "foodies". They live to eat as opposed to eat to live,' he declared as I scoffed peaches, raspberries and home-made ice cream (against my own wishes, I might add; I was adamant there was no room left after those delightful entrées and mains; Donald proved otherwise).

Suddenly, 18 holes was the last thing on my mind. I had forgotten why it was I had even come here. I was officially becoming a 'foodie' myself. Eventually I got around to popping the question, not minding in the least what the answer might be.

'I don't suppose you play golf, then?' I asked absent-mindedly, eyeing him opening another bottle of French red.

'No.'

'Oh well, no problem, how 'bout a little cheese with this wine?'

Unbelievably, more food arrived. I had to stop. I couldn't move.

'Donald, please, no more,' I muttered.

'How about some dessert wine?'

'I don't understand how you can work here and not be the size of a whale. I mean, you obviously love food, but you're not fat.'

'That's surprising, the chef lets me try everything and I seem to eat twice as much as everyone else.'

I met Tim back at The W and informed him that, thanks to this local eating establishment, I wouldn't be leaving New Orleans hungry. I also remarked, when he insisted on buying the first drink, how funny it was that you never seem to get hangovers on holiday.

Unfortunately, I spoke too soon — tomorrow would be one of the worst of all time.

I blame Donald. He was the one who poured fine wine down my throat. Then I blame Tim's friends, Chuck and Amy, who took it upon themselves to lead a defenseless Kiwi astray in New Orleans. Bar hopping till four in the morning wasn't what I had in mind when I left the Rene Bistro. Still, when in Rome . . .

And at least I didn't have work tomorrow.

Unlike Chuck and Amy.

Contrary to popular belief, *music* (along with golf) was the reason I came to the South, not French food or three vodka shooters for the price of one (though it would be rude to look a gift horse in the mouth), so I was happy as Larry knowing we were going to walk the streets till we found some live stuff that tickled our fancy.

And it didn't take long. In a dimmed, otherwise lifeless bar with sticky floors and cheap jugs of beer, we sat down to watch a blues guitarist who, if he were playing in New Zealand, would probably attract thousands of punters.

I looked behind us; there were six people, including our party.

This didn't seem to deter our entertainer one bit, who took it as his cue to play louder, longer and harder. I sat there in awe. Watching live music in the city where Louis Armstrong, Fats Domino and Huddie 'Leadbelly' Ledbetter were born made me wish I myself had kicked around as a kid in the birthplace of jazz.

Meanwhile, my roommate and next of kin in New Orleans was feeling a little fluey so decided to head back to our room (had I done the dishes?), leaving me in the capable hands of Chuck and Amy. Knowing they both had work the next day made me think: one more bar, one more band and one more for the road.

I couldn't have been more wrong.

First to El Matador (a bar part-owned by Vince Vaughn from the brilliant movie *Swingers*) where a band called the Soul Rebels played Marvin Gaye and Jackson Five songs. This band, consisting of nine black guys the size of professional footballers, played trumpets, trombones and marching drums. These guys didn't just play rhythm — they *were* rhythm. Having grown up listening to predictable four-piece bands, witnessing an ensemble that had recently been described as 'the missing link between Public Enemy and Louis Armstrong' was something special.

The night was capped off by visiting a creepy gothic-themed bar (Ye Olde Original Dungeon), finding happy hour at a student hovel, and lastly (and most unfortunately), running into a middle-aged, severely overweight Latino woman who, no doubt in search of Mardi Gras beads, got her tits out on Bourbon Street. Speaking of which, some say the rumour that New Orleans is sinking is due not to it being wedged precariously between the mighty Mississippi and Lake Pontchartrain, but because of the weight of these beads stored in bathroom cupboards throughout the city!

EVEN WHEN ONE has a clean, clear head, there is too much to see and do in New Orleans. When one wakes up with a thousand voices hissing, 'Never again, you idiot, you hear me, never again!' you know it's going to be a long day.

I woke at 11 am, knowing Chuck and Amy would have been at work for three hours.

A knock at the door was not what I needed. I fell out of bed, rolled to where I thought the noise was coming from and opened the door while on my knees. I hate to think what I must have looked like. I glanced up, squinted through the only eye that seemed to be in working order and focused on a well-dressed, sweet-smelling chambermaid. I was jealous. Wow, you look so *un*hungover. And smell so good!

She turned out to be another guardian angel.

'Here's a bottle of water for you, sir.'

I never wanted to leave. A hotel that read minds!

Of course, I *would* have to leave, sooner rather than later. My easy ride in the Big Easy would be coming to an end tomorrow. My next train ride (in cattle class) would take me to Houston, although a quick look at the timetable told me I'd be arriving at two in the morning. Figuring this was far from an attractive option, another was to stop in a place called Beaumont, which didn't even feature in the guidebook.

'Ever been to Beaumont, Texas?' I asked at numerous bars.

'No, driven through it.'

If I was to be completely honest, it was the trip *after* this one I was dreading most: Houston to El Paso — 24 hours, 800 miles.

I must have exhausted New Orleans' entire water supply while showering, but it seemed to be the only remedy for curing such a self-inflicted injury. Besides, I took comfort in the fact that, since the city sat eight feet below sea level, it needed all the help it could get to prevent serious flooding in future. As was pointed out to me the previous night, this is also the reason some of New Orleans' dead are buried *above* ground. Due to the shallow water table, bodies are placed in raised tombs or long rows of vaults. This, of course, makes complete sense, and I say full credit to whoever thought of such a procedure. After all, a loved one's death is painful enough; no one needs the added stress of knowing if they want to visit Granddad's grave, they'll have to take their scuba gear.

I stumbled down to reception, where Brian met me with a bright, cheery smile. I attempted one in return, though it probably just looked as though I was going to vomit. It was just as well I didn't know how big a day this was going to be either; I wouldn't have been able to handle such a thought. By nightfall I would have visited another drug-dealing neighbourhood and waited till after midnight to meet a jazz singer who cooked turkey necks in between songs. This wasn't what I had in mind to soothe a sore head.

But I was in New Orleans, after all.

Aware that I had to find a potential golfing partner, Brian had scoured the *Louisiana Weekly* and found two Southern icons on the front page. The first, a man called Kermit Ruffins, was going to be playing at Vaughan's bar later that night.

'How late?' I whispered, aware that normal volume might blow an eardrum.

'He'll probably be on about nine.'

'Nine?' I put my head in my hands, adding the hours between now and then.

'Honestly, you've got to see this guy! He's like Louis Armstrong reincarnated. If there's one thing you've got to do in New Orleans, it's see Kermit.'

'Very good, thank you, Brian,' I said, putting the article in my pocket and looking around for a jug of water. None was to be seen.

'I also have another number for you, Mr Brown.'

Wasn't this great — my very own concierge!

'Also on the front page is a woman called Antoinette from the Mother-in-Law Lounge.'

Brian was on the money with this one. The Mother-in-Law Lounge was on my list anyway, having been highly recommended by friends who had visited New Orleans. With a bit of luck, I would find both Antoinette and Kermit keen for a quick round of golf.

But first, I needed a glass of water.

I had agreed to meet Antoinette later that afternoon. As for Kermit, a quick call to Vaughan's had confirmed he was playing later that night. Hopefully I wouldn't get to the gig only to find Kermit, this huge, untouchable megastar, would jump on stage, strut his stuff and then go straight home and I may not even get the chance to talk to him.

This was always a risk, but one I would have to take for the sake of golf.

Not that it seemed to make any difference anyway; I was beginning to wonder whether anyone in America even *played* the game. Donald had been my eighth Front Pager and the closest he had come to a golf course was probably stopping by the trees on the seventh hole so his dog could take a piss. Not counting Charleston, or hitting a few balls around a stadium with Paul, this trip was beginning to look like one big failure.

Maybe it was worth *me* trying to get on the front page; though that would mean I would have to play with myself, and if you're playing with yourself in America, it's probably time to go home.

With four hours to fill before I was due at the Mother-in-Law Lounge I found the various (air-conditioned) art galleries along Royal Street just the tonic I needed. There were some fantastic works in there, as well as free cold water. Other than that, most shops around the French Quarter boasted tacky gifts destined for the garage. Unless you felt the need to purchase voodoo dolls, plastic beads, masks or dildos, New Orleans appeared a very easy place to save money. Until night-time, that is.

In serious need of a lie-down, I headed to my room and thanked my lucky stars I had done my big tour of the city the day before. I witnessed a storm like I'd never seen before. Within minutes roads had turned to lakes, dirt to mud, shop stalls to boats. Thunder, resembling bombs exploding, clapped over deserted streets while car alarms bleated in unison.

More importantly, I lost the reception on the ball game I was watching.

ONCE THE DUST had cleared, I ordered a taxi bound for Antoinette's place. Brian had given me some info for the journey regarding the icon I was about to meet.

> In 1994, Ernie K-Doe opened the world-famous Ernie K-Doe Mother-in-Law Lounge at 1500 N. Claiborne Avenue in New Orleans, Louisiana. One of K-Doe's main reasons for opening the Lounge was to provide a place for New Orleans' living legends to come and perform. The Lounge is a shrine to the immortal legend of K-Doe. The walls are adorned with photographs and artwork of K-Doe throughout his life. Many pictures of K-Doe's family and friends can be seen as well.
>
> When K-Doe was still with us, it wasn't uncommon to have the Emperor himself greet you at the door. Today, Antoinette continues to keep alive the warm, friendly,

hospitable environment that K-Doe's fans have come to expect. You are nothing if not well taken care of at the Mother-in-Law Lounge. Have a drink and play the jukebox, which has one of the best selections you can find of classic New Orleans R&B artists.

My Bosnian-born taxi driver dodged more vigorous rain on the way to the historic Treme neighbourhood, whereby he magnified an already pounding headache.

'I don't normally come to this area,' he said.

Oh no, not again.

He continued. 'Even in the day I stay away. I used to have no problem coming here. No problem at all, but I knew I was getting tangled up in drug deals.'

'How would you know when you were in the middle of one?' I asked.

'Someone will ask you to pick them up, they say "I'm just going to run in to the house and drop something off", and before you know it there's guns and dead people.'

'Can't you just refuse to pick them up?'

'You can lose your permit if you refuse to take someone somewhere, whether they're black or white, yellow, whatever. I just avoid this area now.' He looked weary. 'Bush has made this country so unsafe, no one feels safe any more.'

Considering my driver was my closest thing to a friend right now, I asked if he wouldn't mind waiting while I ran inside to speak with Antoinette. Strange how you can be so far from home and put your life in the hands of a stranger, all for 10 bucks . . .

I *can* see how things can turn bad in New Orleans, and why people tell you to watch your back, however. If you don't know where you're going or what you're doing, you could run into some very dodgy situations. The problem is, many of the best places actually lie on the cusp of bad neighbourhoods. On the one hand, I kind of like that. It means everything's not laid out on a silver platter; you've got to go out and find it. Then again, if you're not in a sound state of mind (and let's be honest, I *wasn't*) and take a wrong turn, your day may end a little differently than you'd initially planned.

I looked behind me. My Bosnian friend had the motor running and was looking nervously across the road at a bunch of bored-looking youths. He leaned over, locked the door on the passenger side and buried his head in a novel.

The distance between the taxi and the Mother-in-Law Lounge was only a matter of metres. Even so, I walked briskly, knocked loudly, and hoped like hell I wouldn't get shot in the interim. A short black woman with long plaited hair, wearing a purple and pink polka-dot dress, answered.

'Hello, is Antoinette here please?' I asked.

'I am Antoinette.'

'Great.'

She held the door open for a bit, staring at me.

'I'm Justin. I called earlier.'

'Right,' she said, still staring.

Well, how 'bout letting me in before I get shot?

Unfortunately, my first mistake was telling Antoinette I might be recording details of my golf (or lack of) for a book later down the track. I figured an honest approach was best around these parts. Putting someone's picture in a book without his or her prior approval could mean the difference between cattle class and free Pepsi (or worse). I just wouldn't risk it (unless that someone was Charleston; I'd exploit that little bastard till the cows came home).

Antoinette told me to take a seat at a small table by the front door. I peered out the window. Wispy smoke trickled from the taxi's exhaust. My Bosnian friend was still there, at the ready but not leaving. A good sign. She sat on the couch opposite and switched on the 33-inch TV. A trashy daytime soap had her glued. I needed water.

'So, can you tell me a little bit about Ernie K-Doe?' I asked.

'Uh-uh, no way,' she said, waving her hand, holding a cigarette.' I noticed one of her fingers was missing. 'You talk to my lawyers first.'

An awkward silence followed. She started doing the 59-channel flick. Lawyers? All I wanted was a game of golf.

Countless pictures of Ernie K-Doe covered the walls. Posters, candles and signed pictures adorned every available space. A slightly stale smell wafted through the lounge. It was so damn hot. Antoinette continued to watch TV. She put her slippers on. Against my better judgement, I asked more questions.

'So, is this shrine all for Ernie?'

'You talk to my lawyer, no way,' she said, waving her finger. 'No questions.'

I was confused; did I have the right woman? Was this 'The Icon of the South?' Okay, so I wasn't expecting to be pampered, fed or even watered, but a sentence with more than five words wouldn't go amiss.

'How long have you been here?' I persisted.

'I can't answer any questions, you better talk to my lawyer.'

My hangover was now so bad that opening and closing my eyes took effort. Why do 'hangover days' seem to last twice as long as regular ones? I wiped my brow and shifted positions on surely one of the South's most rickety chairs, trying to find a comfortable position in which to continue *the* most unsuccessful, unrevealing interview of all time. 'Okay, so if I talk to your lawyer, then we can talk, right?' I asked.

'If you talk to my lawyer, I'll call you in the morning and answer anything.'

I was to find out later that the legendary Ernie K-Doe started his singing in his church choir. Early in his career, he'd practised with Joe Tex at the Dew Drop Inn, this being one of the reasons they both had similar styles of dancing with the microphone, falling down and apparently rolling off stage. Ernie considered the stage to be a ring and once remarked, 'If you don't get out there and move they will kill you.'

His biggest recording was 'Mother-in-Law', which became number one in 1961, sold millions and made him a star. When 'Mother-in-Law' was in the charts, K-Doe was considered one of the Big Five, along with the likes of James Brown, Little Willie John, Joe Tex and Jackie Wilson. All have now passed on, apart from Mr Brown.

Mr K-Doe started the Mother-in-Law Lounge in a bid to restore New Orleans to the glory of its heyday. For his last few years, he had been on a path to sobriety after living in a haze for years. Ernie married the woman now opposite me in January 1996.

'You like watching TV?' Antoinette asked, after five minutes of watching *The Young and the Restless*. The taxi was still outside. I was starting to lose my patience.

'TV? Um, yeah, sure.'

'Watched any TV in New Orleans?'

'Little bit.'

'Hmm,' she said, picking up the remote and switching channels, leaving drama for infomercials.

What the hell, I had nothing to lose. 'Do you play golf, Antoinette?'

'Golf?'

'Yeah, golf.'

'Do I *look* like the sort of person that plays golf?'

'Um, no.'

She put her cigarette out and folded her arms. Her eyes still hadn't left the screen. I had to go; this meeting was going nowhere fast. My driver would be getting impatient and I needed the safety of the 15th floor at The W.

Aside from that, I had a sausage and alligator cheesecake with my name on it waiting at one of New Orleans' finest, but most reasonably priced, restaurants. Plus, I still had to figure out how to find Kermit Ruffins and the Barbecue Swingers. With a bit of luck, a meeting with him would be a little more successful than my time spent in Ernie's shrine.

I held no animosity towards Antoinette — by the sounds of it, the reason she'd been so defensive was because in the past TV crews had bowled into Ernie's shrine, taken pictures, plastered them over the TV, made a profit, and given her nothing. Had I myself been in a healthier state of mind, I may well have been able to get across that I wasn't a TV crew, a journalist, or anyone trying to rip her off — just a hungover Kiwi on a harmless adventure wanting a round of golf.

'Here, call my lawyer,' she said, handing me a business card. 'This is his home number and this is his cellphone. I'll call you in the morning.'

I never called her lawyer and she never called me — not what you'd call a successful first date by any means.

BY DINNER TIME I was still struggling. This had been the longest day ever. The heat hadn't helped. Tim, still suffering with the flu, was embarrassed he wouldn't be joining me for a bite. He did tell me, however, that he'd seen Chuck and Amy at work and they were definitely looking a little worse for wear.

'Worse than me?' I asked, encouragingly.

He looked at me, grimaced and coughed. 'No.'

Like most good things in New Orleans, Jacque Imo's restaurant was not easy to find, though I really shouldn't have had any trouble: it was right next to where I had found Beaker and Mo's Bar yesterday. A table for one, a few lemonades and more confirmation I wouldn't be leaving New Orleans hungry:

> *Fried rabbit tenderloin*
>
> *Soft shell crab almondine*
>
> *Panned rabbit with oyster tasso sauce*
>
> *Grilled mahi*
>
> *New Orleans BBQ shrimp*
>
> *Shrimp and alligator sausage cheesecake*
>
> *Blackened tuna with oyster champagne brie sauce*
>
> *Smothered chicken with biscuits*

At 8.30 I had to leave to find Kermit, who just happened to be performing on the other side of town. Due to overindulgence of jalapeños the day before, the same problems endured in Tybee came back to haunt me. Luckily, a taxi drove past in the nick of time, saving me from a potentially embarrassing gastro experience. Once inside the cab, I was fine. I just needed this day to be over. The sooner I saw Kermit, the sooner I could hit the sack.

The sign on the door read *Vaughan's Bar since 1959*. Judging by the security buzzer and the woman behind the bar not letting me in until she'd taken a good look, this part of town wasn't exactly prime real estate. I set up camp at the bar, wondering why it was so quiet. Two drunken old men hugged the end of the pier, smoking and laughing, while a hooded, depressed-looking woman mulled over a red wine. All I could stomach was a Coke. It would be the first of many.

'What time is Kermit Ruffins on, please?' I asked the jovial-looking bar lady.

A cockroach ran across the bar. She slapped it with the nearest available tea towel. The old blokes laughed harder.

'Eleven, maybe eleven-thirty,' she smiled.

Oh God, stop the madness. Why did I have to have such a good night

Kermit Ruffins outside Vaughan's Bar, New Orleans

last night? It was the first real bender I'd had on this trip and I was being made to pay.

Vaughan's was a cute place. Old posters and photos hung on the walls, along with Christmas decorations. A jukebox pumped out classic Ray Charles, and a table-tennis table in the middle of the dance floor would later be taken down to accommodate Kermit and his band. Eleven-thirty was over two hours away; that's a lot of Coke in anyone's language. And it's not as if I could just cruise the neighbourhood to fill in time — that security buzzer was there for a reason. I was staying put.

Ever so slowly the bar began filling up, first a bunch of guys ready for a big night, then a few couples, then a hens' night, and finally a Swedish couple, who maybe wished they'd never arrived. The reason being, when the atmosphere became a little livelier, the music got turned up and the table-tennis table moved, this Nordic beauty decided to go to the wash–room. Only problem was, when she returned, she did so with a rather large piece of toilet paper hanging out the back of her jeans. Worse still, her embarrassed boyfriend, who'd spotted the offending loo paper, didn't have the guts to say anything in front of all these people. Maybe he was hoping no one had seen it.

Trust me, everyone had seen it — including a regular, who'd been chatting to me. Realising all the other blokes had chickened out, he himself sauntered over to our free entertainment and whispered in her ear. A fair complexion quickly turned beetroot and her boy-friend received a slap for his troubles. 'Why didn't you tell me!' she scowled.

At 11.30, the bar lady handed me my fourth Coke and said, 'There he is.'

Kermit Ruffins was eating crisps and drinking a Bud Lite by the jukebox. While choosing a Louis Armstrong medley, he turned to me and sang some, smiling, as if it were the first time he'd heard old Satchmo. Obviously born and bred in New Orleans (this guy was so laid-back he was almost horizontal), I found it a little difficult explaining to him that, having been up all day, all I wanted was to set a tee time for tomorrow, listen to him sing and hit the hay. He agreed to talk by his truck outside, which also just happened to have a barbecue on the back. 'Cos that's what Kermit does. He sings, plays trumpet, wipes his brow, runs outside to check on the steaks while his fellow member does a trombone solo, then makes it back in time to hit the final note.

Now, tell me *that's* not cool.

Although his immediate family wasn't at all musical, Kermit (whose favourite American is Martin Luther King Jr), used to love it when his uncle came around with a trumpet. By the age of 15, Kermit had his own. By the age of 17 (having found new heroes in Louis Armstrong, Cab Calloway and Dizzy Gillespie), he decided he just had to play jazz. And it was paying off; just this week he'd featured in *People* magazine.

From a sports point of view, knowing Kermit had four kids was encour-aging. Knowing he wouldn't finish his gig till four in the morning was not, however, conducive to an early-morning round of golf. Not that it would matter.

'I don't play golf,' he said.

'You sure, you've never played?'
'I play putt-putt with the kids, I'm pretty good at that. But real golf, no.'
'Right.'
It was midnight. Kermit sang. I watched for as long as I could, eventually having to walk out on one of the very reasons I had come to New Orleans.

DAY 18: BEAUMONT, TEXAS

'WHERE'S THE TRAIN STATION?' I asked, as we rumbled into Beaumont, six hours late.

'It's gone,' said the weary-looking lady next to me.

'What do you mean, *gone*?'

'It used to be there,' she said, pointing to concrete rubble.

Not only was Beaumont absent from any guidebook, its station looked like a stray asteroid had just slammed into it. I was half expecting CNN to pop up from around the corner and ask us if we'd seen anything untoward.

With a population of 120,000, Beaumont wasn't exactly small. I hardly think I was expecting too much hoping to find a phone box or a cab rank. It was, however, 1 am and I had failed to book a hotel room. As the train rolled off behind us, I helped the woman beside me carry her bags across the tracks (one thing, luckily, the station *did* have) and wondered why I ever thought flying on the seat of my pants was a good move in the first place. *You should learn to plan your trips better, son.*

It was quiet. Our old home, now chugging off into the distance, would be showing *Chicago* on its way to Houston, a place I was starting to wish I was going to. I was stuck. Everywhere I looked was pitch black: not one streetlight, not one car. I was in the middle of Texas in the middle of the night in the middle of shit creek. In the history of wrong turns I was beginning to be right up there with Bill Clinton in 1997. Broken glass crackled away under my feet. I walked in slow circles, weighing up my options, which looked a little like this:

Rob woman next to me.

Ask woman next to me for directions.

Ask woman if she's seen Chicago.

Promise I won't rob woman if she gives me a ride.

I chose the last option, electing for a less aggressive-style robbery:

'I don't suppose you're . . . I was just wondering if . . . please, you gotta help me!'

It appeared that half her family tree was waiting in the 4x4 in the ex-car park. Her grandmother, her mother and her three-year-old daughter had all turned up at one in the morning to make sure she got home safely. For that, I am eternally grateful — otherwise I'd still be there, sitting on that rubble, seven iron in hand, fending off stray dogs and builders. I piled my clubs in the back and sat with Mum and Grandma.

'Thank you so much,' I said. 'I don't know what I would have done if you guys hadn't helped me out.' I really did feel lucky; there was absolutely no reason these ladies had to help, especially at that time of night.

'You'd better be careful, Justin,' said the daughter, while driving. 'My husband would kill me if he knew I'd picked you up.'

'Come on,' I said. 'There's four of you and only one of me — you could *all* beat me up.'

'I could beat you up by myself!' said the daughter.

'So, why did you help me out?'

'You gotta trust someone, otherwise you'd never meet new people,' said the mother.

The elderly woman next to me, a great-grandmother as well as grandma to 13 kids, poked me in the ribs, adding, 'We're only like this 'cos we're from Louisiana.'

'So what are you doing in Beaumont?' the mother asked, disbelief in her voice.

'It wasn't in the guidebook so I thought I'd give it a go.'

Worryingly, they all laughed. Having once again warned me to plan my trip a little better, we pulled into a Motel 6, whereby the mother made sure I knew when the next train was due in Beaumont.

'The next train comes through on *Monday*,' she told me, as I climbed out. An Indian man, chewing on a toothpick, was sitting in a security cage in the motel's entrance, waiting to take down my details and no doubt clear out my wallet.

'No,' I said. 'I've checked, it's Sunday.'

'I think you'll find it's Monday.'

'Trust me, it's Sunday.' I knew this for a fact, having checked and re-checked it 10 or 20 times on the train. When you're six hours late and sitting in cattle class, reading timetables can be a real highlight.

'Well, you better go over there tomorrow and check.' She was looking a little more concerned. 'Check it's *Sunday* and not Monday; you'd better get that right.'

'No worries,' I reassured her. Having also studied a map of Texas for those six hours, I discovered the coastal town of Port Arthur, about 30 miles south of Beaumont, was another place I wanted to get to.

'Two quick questions,' I asked the ladies. 'Buses — do they go to Port Arthur?'

'Port Arthur?' They laughed in unison, loudly.

'*Right,* I'll take that as a no.' The Indian man now appeared to be sleeping with his eyes open, staring at nothing in particular. 'One more thing, have you seen *Chicago*?'

'Yeah, it's a dumb film,' said the daughter.

'No it's not!' retorted the mother. 'It's wonderful. The way they can sing and dance is just brilliant, and I never thought I'd say this but I thought Richard Gere was . . .'

I thanked them and left them to it.

Pleased I had at least given my Indian friend something to do, he showed me to my room, which funnily enough sat right next to a highway. It was as if I had indirectly asked for the noisiest, mustiest-smelling den that could disguise itself as one big cigarette burn. I could hardly complain. I was just glad to have successfully negotiated an escape route from where the asteroid had struck.

I couldn't sleep. Trucks roared past and late arrivals unpacked cars, slammed doors and set off alarms right outside my room. I lay there and thought about the train trip. Due to the heat, the driver had been advised not to go over 50 miles an hour, for fear of the old wooden tracks buckling and tipping the lot of us. At one stage, passengers were informed that the

142

reason we were crawling was because a town hundreds of miles away was experiencing a storm that could be heading our way. Call me old-fashioned, but surely the answer would have been to hit the gas and go like stink, right through the guts of it. That's what I would have done.

Then again, that's probably the reason I was in cattle class and reading my map for the sixteenth time, not up front wearing one of those funny hats.

Having said that, for all the stops and starts, the ride through Louisiana and into Texas was surprisingly relaxing. As we drifted through swamps and bayous, people lazed about on their front porches, sipping lemonade and playing guitar. I passed the time listening to Pastor Chuck and his 'Word of the Day' (to begin a relationship with Jesus, call 1800 778 3345) and, sadly, eating. Having been thoroughly spoiled in New Orleans when it came to cuisine, I quickly threw away any hint of culture when I put away two hot dogs, a cheesy pizza, a Snickers bar and two cheeseburgers on my trip to Texas. And to keep those among us who smoked sane, at Lafayette, Louisiana, the desperate were given the opportunity to light up and suck, as long as they did so before new passengers found their seats.

TYPICALLY, JUST AS I finally managed some shuteye at Motel 6, it was time to check out. A pounding at the door confirmed, to my surprise, that someone *did* in fact clean the rooms. Or maybe it was only on Fridays. I asked for a 20-minute extension, only to be faced with a blank stare.

With the prospect of not knowing how or even why I was going to Port Arthur, I found my way to reception where the very same Indian man was sitting at the front desk. Seriously lacking energy, I downed a few coffees and found some newspapers. Unfortunately, none were exclusive to Beaumont. Not really needing a second cup of coffee, but not knowing when I'd next be eating, I thought it only appropriate I find out a little about the city beyond those automatic doors:

> Beaumont's first permanent settlers included mainly French and Spanish fur trappers and explorers who started arriving in the late 1820s. Before the turn of the century, lumber and rice production were the major industries.
> But the new century would change Beaumont forever. At

10.30 am on January 10, 1901, the Lucas well at Spindletop blew in from a depth of 1020 feet with oil gushing 200 feet into the air. Before Spindletop, Beaumont had been a quiet town of 9000 people. By the summer of 1901, it was trying to house more than 50,000 people. Oilmen, saloon keepers, gamblers and others seeking their fortunes gave Beaumont much of the flavour of the California gold rush days.

All transactions were in cash, and money came into Beaumont from all over the country.

Tents and clapboard shanties went up quickly to house the people flowing into the city. In 1925, a second oil boom took place at Spindletop, thanks to modern technology, and the field remained active until the 1950s.

Having still not located a newspaper carrying Beaumont stories, I found a copy of the *Port Arthur News*. On the front page, Red Garrison, a local sunflower grower, was proudly showing off 10-foot-tall flowers. I must

In Full Bloom

Red Garrison, owner of Garrison's Florist, walks along side his greenhouse at the Port Arthur business where his daughter has planted some giant sunflowers. Some of the sunflowers have grown over ten-feet tall.

Port Arthur News, *Port Arthur, Texas*

admit, my first thought was, I'm sure, similar to yours: 'Sunflower grower? Front-page news? Hello, slow news week in Port Arthur!'

This may have been the case, but at least I had a potential partner to abduct and bash balls with. The man in question, Red (haven't you always wanted to meet a Red?), while not exactly young-looking, did appear to be fit and healthy. I would even go as far as to say, to the untrained eye, he *looked* like a golfer.

And I should know, I can spot them a mile off.

A big black lady turned up in a rusty, shell-shocked-looking Cordoba. She was so huge the passenger's side of the vehicle didn't even appear to be touching the ground. The car's angle was akin to the unevenness caused by wearing out the soles on your favourite trainers. Just as a pair of shoes can tell a story of how you walk, this woman's car told me how much she was in *need* of one.

I was making the most of the cool air in the foyer, thinking that when a taxi *did* arrive, the driver would no doubt politely let the front desk know. Any thought of a quiet toot to acknowledge her presence was quickly discarded, however, when The Leaning Tower of Taxi pulled into the hotel's entrance. Our impatient friend slammed her fist repeatedly on the resonating old horn, much like Marge at the beginning of an episode of *The Simpsons*.

And it didn't end there. The woman in question knew it was I who had ordered the cab, as no one else was frequenting either the foyer or indeed the entrance. Still, this didn't seem to stop her trigger-happy horn hands. Every step I took, there echoed another honk. Step, honk. Step step, honk honk. Unfortunately, in an effort to get to the automatic doors quickly, and hence save Beaumont's noise control a Saturday morning call, I forgot my bag, which happened to be lying on the couch. I went back to retrieve it. Big mistake. HOOONNNKKK! HOOONNNKKK!

This woman was in one hell of a hurry. I jumped in the passenger side, feeling sorry for tyres that had never been given the opportunity to do what they were made for. Surely my driver had a wafer-thin husband who drove every second week, when she would join him, sit on the passenger side, even up the car and save the life of an already desperately sick suspension.

She had a smile a mile wide and she was going to be driving me 30.

'Do you have the money up front?' she asked.

'Why, do you think I'm gonna do a runner?' I asked, struggling to get my wallet out of my back pocket. Sweat poured from my brow, even though I'd been outside only for the time it took me to put my clubs in the trunk. I looked at the dashboard: no air conditioning. My driver, named Daphne according to a bunch of business cards sitting on the glove box, still hadn't answered my question.

'It's too damn hot to run,' I continued. 'You really think I'd do a runner?'

'No, but a lot do.' She picked up her CB and called back to base. ''Bout to leave for Port Arthur.'

'Got the money up front?' came the reply.

'I got the money okay.'

The engine started and we were off to a place where I hoped I would meet a sunflower grower with an open mind. Still a tad miffed at having to pay up front, I asked the obvious question regarding crime.

'Yes, we get lots of crime,' Daphne said. 'Lots of bad crime. The latest thing is mothers putting their newborns in dumpsters.'

'You're joking.'

'No, they leave them there to die. Some of them *do*, some are found.'

'Does that happen a lot?'

'It has in the last year, mostly 13- and 14-year-old girls. They think their mum don't know they're pregnant, then they go and put the baby in a dumpster. One woman did it twice.'

'Twice?' I was now feeling sick, and not because of lack of air-con.

'They found a baby in a dumpster just this week and found some DNA that matched one from five years ago. The only reason they knew the last one was hers was because of that DNA.'

Contrary to my earlier reservations about her manners and general misuse of a car horn, Daphne turned out to be great company. We had a grand old time driving to Port Arthur. When asked about her favourite American, her eyes lit up. She responded quickly, as if she'd been waiting all year to tell someone:

'My daughter, my baby!' she glowed. 'She's 17, but she's still my baby. She's worked since she was 14, she's a good girl and as far as I know, still a virgin. As for my son, he's a hopeless case. He steals, smokes weed and can't read. He's *trouble*.'

146

Much like the members of the black family who were so charitable to me the night previous, I had absolutely no idea of Daphne's age. In saying that, I'm not normally the best judge; when asked how old I think a kid is, I normally say 'I don't know, somewhere between one and nine? Maybe five?' How am *I* supposed to know what a nine-year-old looks like anyway? Babies are easy — they're normally smaller, generally crawl, crap their pants a lot and suck breasts. Let's be honest, if you're still doing *that* on your 10th birthday, you've got more than a few problems. If you're still doing it on your 21st, you're probably a legend.

'How old do you think I am?' Daphne asked.

'Um, twenty . . . five?'

'Oh, you gonna get a discount! I'm 38.'

Good genes, just like the family last night. Correction: in Daphne's case, *huge* jeans.

'And what do you do in your spare time,' I asked, 'when you're not keeping your son under control?'

'I watch wrestling! I *love* wrestling. Oh, and I forgot, Jim Carrey is my other favourite American. *Dumb and Dumber* and *Ace Ventura* — best movies ever.'

I hopped out into the Texas heat thinking: isn't he Canadian?

Daphne had dropped me outside Garrison's, Port Arthur's plant and flower shop. Other than having called earlier to make sure Red was going to be there, I had made no other plans. This stunned Daphne. Try as she might, she just couldn't get her head around the fact I was going to a town in the middle of Texas to meet strangers and, of all things, play golf with them. The questions she asked on the way were the very ones I often asked myself: Where will you stay? How will you get back to Beaumont? Are you mad?

With a touch of apprehension, I walked into Garrison's, where I found myself amid soft toys, get-well cards, balloons and flowers fit for any occasion. I looked outside. Daphne, my lifeline and only friend in Texas, waved from the car. I watched as she drove further and further away, down streets I knew nothing about, past people I had never seen. My ride, gone. Where will I stay? How will I get back to Beaumont?

Am I mad?

A woman named Julie welcomed me at the counter. She was the daughter of Red and Irene Garrison, who had owned the shop for a staggering 57 years. Irene's mother had also lived in Port Arthur her whole life and was born a block from the shop. Needless to say, if the Garrisons couldn't help me find my way around this town, nobody could.

'Is Red around?' I asked. 'I called earlier.'

'Dad's out the back — he'll be here shortly,' Julie replied, staring at the golf clubs I was trying to rest where they wouldn't get in anyone's way. I could see Red and Irene in the storeroom. She was cutting and arranging flowers, he was walking around, talking on a portable phone. I placed the newspaper on the counter and remarked that, as her famous father was in the business of growing sunflowers, he should actually be called Yellow. My joke was met with the all-too-frequent response of silence.

Julie wasn't backward in coming forward when it came to talking about her family, however. With four generations working in the store (the youngest, Hannah, aged three, is often asked for by customers), this was obviously a tight-knit family. Even though her parents were 'workaholics', they were still in great nick, both aged 83. (Remind me to work in a small town for 57 years — obviously good for the ticker.)

'But isn't it hard working with your family, all day, every day?' I asked.

'We disagree, but it always seems to work out.'

Hmm, workaholics. I decided to chance my arm before I met the man himself.

'So, your father, you say he works a lot?'

'Never stops.'

'Looks like a golfer,' I said, almost too confidently.

'Golfer? No way, he gets no *time* for golf. It's work, work, work with him.'

'No one in the family plays golf?'

'Nope.'

'Not one person, not even a distant aunt?'

'Nope.'

This was incredible. Had I single-handedly managed to find every *non-golfer* there was in this country? To feature on the front page in the United States did you have to do everything *but* play the game? More to the point, how many miles away was Daphne?

'What about this guy?' I asked, clutching at straws, pointing to a picture next the cash register. 'Is he in the family?'

'That's my son, Shelby,' she said proudly.

'Does he play golf?'

'No, he plays guitar.'

'You sure he doesn't play golf?'

'I'm sure.'

The guitar Shelby was playing in the picture was of great significance to the Garrisons. It used to be owned by Julie's younger brother, who died in a car crash 22 years ago.

'We lost him,' Julie said, solemnly. 'He had just bought that guitar and I always kept it. When my son turned 14 he asked if he could play it. He's been playing for 10 years now.'

'Is he in a band?' I asked, hoping he may be playing tonight, meaning I could meet him and a few other Port Arthur locals and hence refrain from having to watch *M.A.S.H.* reruns or *Who Wants to Marry My Dad?*

'No, although he used to be in a couple. Let me see, what were their names? He was in The County Jews for a while and then Smack Down Junction. They used to just do Metallica covers.'

How cool — a middle-aged woman, working in a flower shop, who listened to Metallica. 'He loves Zakk Wylde,' she continued. 'So much so, that when he was in Detroit, Zakk autographed Shelby's arm. Shelby came home and had it tattooed on.'

Okay, practising Metallica in the lounge, that's fine. We can live with that. Tattooing some dude's name on your arm? That's a little obsessive.

Julie's love of music didn't stop at The County Jews either; she had graduated in Texas with Janis Joplin's brother, Mike (the less famous Joplin, probably now teaching woodwork in Idaho).

'I respected her for being herself,' Julie said.

'And your son . . . you sure he doesn't play golf?'

'Course I'm sure. I should know — I'm his mother!'

Red had finished his phone call and joined us. I liked him instantly. A solidly built man, it didn't surprise me to find he spent much of his youth as a tank officer in the Second World War. He spoke loudly, like he was still in the army. Every sentence was concise, to the point and ended with an

Red Garrison and his amazing sunflowers, Port Arthur, Texas

exclamation mark. He reminded me of the soldier calling the radio station in *Good Morning Vietnam*.

'Hello, what's your name?'

'MY NAME IS BOB RIVERS!'

'Where are you stationed, Bob?'

'I'M IN ARTILLERY!'

'Well, can we play something for you?'

'ANYTHING! JUST PLAY IT LOUD, OKAY!'

The 10-foot-tall celebrity sunflowers were basking in the Texas sunshine.

Some had started to wilt, others had lost their heads. The remaining few posed for a picture with Red and myself. Afterwards, he introduced me to Irene, who offered to give me a coffee-table-book-sized, hardcover history of Port Arthur. I politely declined, motioning to my already full bags, which lay on the floor.

I looked on as a proud parent, hoping my toys, Charleston, Beaker and Mo, were all getting along underneath closed zips.

'Well, Justin, if it's okay with you,' Red said, 'I'm going to drive you around Port Arthur. If you don't mind, I'd like to show you a few things about the area!'

'That would be great, Red, but don't you have work to do?' I asked.

'It's Saturday! Let's go!'

You know that feeling when you're driving through a new town with your long-lost aunt or uncle, and they're driving and driving and driving, and you're trying your absolute best to stay awake, even though all the buildings look the same and the conversation is stilted and the motion of the car makes you pine for a bed, any bed, anywhere?

That's exactly how I felt with Red. And it was embarrassing, because he was such good company and such a gracious host. But the fact is, the more he drove, the sleepier I got. It didn't help that Port Arthur looked like a town that had seen its best days. Admittedly, it was Saturday afternoon but its streets appeared empty, lifeless, carless. None of this mattered to Red, a man staunchly proud of his home town, and rightly so.

'Let me take you across to Pleasure Island. My buddy lives over there, and he plays golf!'

Sadly, Red's buddy wasn't home. This didn't stop him, however, driving to the new golf course, getting out of the car into the stifling heat and asking a couple of young greenkeepers a bunch of questions. He seemed to be out there forever, returning to the car only when he appeared to have the appropriate information.

'Well, Justin, I spoke to a couple of young guys out there, and they seem to have no idea where my buddy is! They know *of* him, they just don't know where he is. So what we're gonna do now is, I'm gonna drive you back to the house where we're gonna have a quick drink, then we'll figure out a new plan of attack. Then what we're gonna do is, we're gonna find you somewhere to stay!'

How could you not like this guy?

Red got a little emotional when I asked who his favourite American was.

'Well, I do love George Bush Senior,' he said, tears in his eyes, 'and you know what? As the days go by, I think I'm liking his son even better! As for least favourite? Well, hell, that's easy — Bill Clinton. He's a tramp, he's a thief, a liar and an immoral man. I truly believe what he did to that girl was horrible. He ruined her character for life. And as the days go by, I'm starting to realise his wife is a pretty polished liar herself!'

Red was still rattling his brain as to how he could get me a game of golf with one of his buddies in town. Unfortunately, every suggestion led to a dead end.

I was just looking forward to that drink he'd promised. Today was extremely hot; standing outside the car for more than 30 seconds was a challenge in itself. People never left the safety of their air-conditioned cars and no one, I mean *no one*, was outside.

'Got a friend who's Korean,' Red said, as we drove past the obligatory Arby's, Super 8 Motel and Mr Waffle. 'He can fix any computer in the world! Yu was his name, but he said he always wanted an American name, so he started calling himself Frank.'

'Frank Yu!' I said.

'What's that?' Red asked.

'I said, Frank Yu. Frank Yu veely much!'

Red didn't like the joke I was so proud of.

I remember a guy I used to work with in England named Mark Cockram. He used to boast that, much like the word racecar, his name was the same spelt *backwards* as it was forwards.

'Where you off to next, Justin?' Red asked. 'After Port Arthur?'

'El Paso.' The very words leaving my lips made me think of bad toilets and *Chicago*. This is one trip I had been dreading: on a train for over 24 hours, cattle class, no sleeper. I hated to think what sort of mood I would be in when I finally *did* arrive.

'El Paso? Hell, that's over 800 miles!'

'Don't remind me, Red.'

The lawns were beautifully mown and the house was cool, thankfully.

An American Tale

Port Arthur business woman Phuong Tai poses with her son Johnathan Tai in front of their newest endeavor Tai Plaza, a business plaza on the corner of Gulfway Drive and Ninth Avenue.

Vietnamese family finds success in PA

By MARILYN TENNISSEN
Port Arthur News Staff Writer

In 1978, Phuong Tai knew she had two choices, escape from Vietnam with her small son and try to make it in America, or face a life under the Communist regime.

So the single mother took her 11-year-old son Johnathan and crammed onto a refugee boat with 3,300 other Vietnamese. She knew it was going to be difficult and even dangerous, but she also believed she had what it takes to be successful in America: an entrepreneurial spirit and a willingness to work hard.

Twenty-five years later, the Tais are both successful Americans. And Friday at 10 a.m. they will see their American dream fulfilled at the ribbon cutting of Tai Plaza, a business center on Gulfway Drive and Ninth Avenue.

"We didn't expect much, we just wanted freedom. In Vietnam the Communists tried to kill my parents because they were rich. They confiscated their business (a grocery store), their money and their home and my parents fled to the mountains. So I had to leave, even though I knew it was very risky. I knew it was dangerous on the boats and sometimes the Communists would kill you for trying to escape," Phuong said.

So the Tais, who are of Chinese descent, set out for what they thought would be five days on the boat sailing from Vietnam to Hong Kong.

"On the boat it was very crowded and everybody was sick," Johnathan said. Although he was only 11 at the time, Johnathan said he remembers the boat very well.

"When someone died, they would just get thrown into the ocean," Phuong said. "One woman had a baby on the boat."

When they arrived in Hong Kong, the boat had to stay in the harbor with everyone on board for 27 days, while immigration officials tried to find a place for all the refugees.

"It was horrible, there was no shower and very little food. A helicopter would drop sardine cans and crackers for us to eat," Phuong said.

When they were finally allowed to dock in Hong Kong, they were sent to a refugee camp for the next 10 months, while they waited for an American sponsor.

"We almost went to England, because we could get in right away," Johnathan said. "But we waited because we wanted to come to America. In the refugee camps, everybody was always talking about America as the place to go. And growing up, I knew that America was the best place in the world."

Phuong's nephew eventually sponsored them and they went to California, but left in less than a year and headed to Port Arthur where she had friends.

"Los Angeles was too big, I wanted to do business and it is too hard in a big city," Phuong said. "In my hometown in Vietnam I was in business, selling jewelry and running a beauty shop."

After taking a typing class, Phuong began work as a cashier at Howard's Grocery Store in Port Arthur, and Johnathan got his first job as a bag boy soon after.

See TAI, page 4A

Port Arthur News, *Port Arthur, Texas*

Irene was bouncing about the place, calling out from the fridge, 'Anyone for drinks?'

'An orange would be great,' I said, knowing my glass wouldn't even have the chance to hit the table before it'd be thrown down a parched throat.

153

Irene peered around from the fridge door and winked. 'You wanna shot of vodka with that?'

It was 11.20 am. Irene had already poured herself one. 'Um, sure.'

'Just call me waiter number nine,' she said, dancing around the kitchen.

'Justin, I've just had a great idea!' Red said, coming in from the lounge. 'Irene, where's that *Port Arthur News* from yesterday?'

Along with a stiff Screwdriver she handed him the paper. 'This lady here,' he said, pointing to the front page, 'is Phuong Tat. She's from Vietnam and owns the local Texaco. She's a very good friend of mine! Maybe we could see if *she* plays golf!'

Red made a few calls and within minutes we were standing at Texaco. He took great delight in introducing me to this inspirational woman, who in 1978 spent 27 ghastly days on a boat (along with her 11-year-old son Jonathon, brother Xay and 3300 other refugees), fleeing Vietnam. Twenty-five years later, the Tats are successful Americans.

Tat told me to help myself to a hot chocolate which, given the sweltering temperature, was a rather strange choice, but I happily obliged and joined her behind the counter. Having leased the Texaco station since 1984, she was now the proud owner. She worked alongside her brother, who almost died on that boat all those years ago.

'He was very weak,' Tat said of Xay, who was presently serving customers and smiling the whole time. 'It was a terrible trip, very crowded and everyone was sick. A helicopter would drop sardine cans and crackers for us to eat. When someone died, they would just get thrown in the ocean. In Vietnam, the Communists had tried to kill my parents because they were rich. They confiscated their grocery store, their money and their home. My parents fled to the mountains. I had to leave, even though I knew it was very risky.'

'What did you expect from America?' I asked, burning my tongue, but choosing not to make a fuss. Now probably wasn't the best time to complain.

'We didn't expect much,' she said. 'We just wanted freedom.'

'And why Port Arthur?'

'We lived in California for a month, but we didn't like the big city. I wanted to do business but it's too hard in a big city. I came to Port Arthur because I had friends here.'

From Vietnam to Port Arthur – entrepreneur Phuong Tat

The boat ride had obviously paid off. Today, Tat owns the successful service station in which I was recovering from hot chocolate-related burns, she rents out 45 houses and, ironically, owns the Immigration and US Customs Building.

'When do you take a day off?' I asked. (You can see where I was going with this.)

'I don't,' she said. 'I work seven days a week from 4.30 in the morning to 7.30 at night.'

Oh no, not again. Do I have a sign on my head, 'Only interested in meeting non-golfing, American workaholics?'

'I've worked 15-hour days since 1984,' Tat continued. 'The only vacation I have is when I am lying down in hospital!'

A woman at the counter, who introduced herself as Tat's nurse, confirmed this:

'We put her to sleep for a while — it's the only time she stops talking!'

'I'm always getting tests done,' said Tat, laughing. 'Ulcer, gall bladder, colon — I've had everything.'

In New Zealand, a lot of Asians play golf. The wide-open spaces and cheap green fees are an incentive to do something that would be near impossible in their homeland. Even though Tat was obviously a busy lady, she didn't appear to be unfit, so it was with a fair degree of confidence that I asked the obvious. 'So, Tat, when you're not working or lying in hospital, do you by any chance play golf?'

'Golf? No, but my son plays tennis.'

I SAT IN A MR WAFFLE miles out of town and ate greasy pork chops and fried eggs. Red had dropped me off at the Super 8 Motel and made me promise that I'd call him should I need anything else. What a guy! Maybe I should hire him for the remainder of the trip? After all, he'd contributed to finding Tat, my 12th Front Pager, in surely the quickest possible time.

As I was so far out of town (and obviously carless), my only option was to grab a few newspapers, drink bad coffee and stalk, I mean *find*, new friends I hadn't yet met.

Rather foolishly, before I had a chance to muse through the *Mid County Chronicle*, I burnt the roof of my mouth with my first bite of bacon, which in turn ruined the entire meal.

My work would really be cut out for me should I need to get in touch with the news-maker on the front page, a man who'd set fire to a petrol pump at a service station, killing the owner. On the same page was a story about a blind man who worked at a local prison cafeteria (was it just me, or were there a lot of blind people in the news lately?) and a photo of the treasurer of the Southeast Texas Stamp Club, explaining why he collected these 'tiny pieces of art'.

This definitely was a slow news week in Port Arthur.

Although, as luck would have it, I remembered I had actually *brought* some stamps with me, as gifts. Before you say, 'Stamps, gifts? You cheapskate!' I should explain they were limited edition *Lord of the Rings* stamps, with scenery from back home. Upon returning to my room, I rummaged through dirty washing and threw my newly adopted family aside. In a quietly triumphant moment, I found the 40c stamps that could turn out to be an absolute trump card should I wish to meet the treasurer of the Southeast Texas Stamp Club. Stamps from New Zealand? He wouldn't be able to control himself!

A knock at the door next morning revealed a maid who took one look at my room and split. Unlike her, I was quite proud of my effort; not everyone has the ability to make such a mess in such a short amount of time. Socks, underpants and T-shirts hung from every available hook, door knob and window latch. Golf balls, toys and newspapers littered the floor. I answered the door wearing only a towel, attempting to air-dry my one and only collared shirt.

The night before, while eating inedible fried shrimps, I had the most incredible revelation that *golf courses* are actually as good a place as any to find golfers. So I set my alarm for six (turning it off three or four times in the interim), then headed for the Babe Zaharias Memorial Course, which was, conveniently, just a 10-minute walk away. My plan to tee off before seven, i.e. before the sun decided to really swing into action, was hampered only by the fact that when I stepped outside it was already very muggy.

As luck would have it, as soon as I'd left the cool of the hotel reception, a local golfer drove past, flung open the passenger door and said, 'My name's Orlando, as in Florida. You wanna ride?'

I'd like to make it clear at this stage that I don't normally just jump into cars with strangers.

Unless, of course, it's very hot.

Or they've got loads of money and want to use me for experiments.

I paid my $25 green fee, put a ball in the tray on the first tee and waited. Unfortunately, Orlando was already part of a regular foursome and my front-page friends, Red and Tat, were no doubt working. Instead, Chris and Mark joined me, two mates who never normally played here but thought today they'd give it a shot.

'You sure have found the armpit of the world,' Chris reassured me.

Meanwhile Mark, sporting a baseball cap, earring and goatee, was having a little trouble comprehending the way his Sunday morning was shaping up. 'Man, I never play this course,' he mused. 'I decide to give it a go and when I do, I end up playing with someone from *New Zealand*?'

His morning was about to get a whole lot stranger. As it turned out, Mark was going to be in Vegas, on business, at exactly the time I was planning on being there the following week.

'This is too weird,' he said, spraying his ball into the lake.

'You guys ever been on the front page?' I was getting desperate now.

'Nope, why?' Mark asked.

'You don't want to rob a bank or donate some money to a kid's hospital so we can make this round official?'

'What are you talking about?'

'Long story.'

Chris' favourite American was not a golfer, but Johnny Knoxville from *Jackass*. 'Man, those guys deserve their money, they do some crazy shit. They're dating superstars now.'

'So, who's Babe Zaharias, then?' I asked, looking at the scorecard that bore her name.

'Perhaps the greatest all-round athlete of all time,' Mark said, practising a swing. 'She was born in Beaumont and grew up right here in Port Arthur. She was nicknamed Babe because she once hit five home runs in one baseball game.'

It was clear Babe wasn't *just* an athlete. She won 17 amateur golf tournaments in a row in 1946 and 1947; she also won the 1946 US Women's Amateur and the 1947 British Amateur. Furthermore, she was the first American to capture the British title since it was first played in 1893.

From what I could muster, Babe was the kid you hated at school — good at everything. Along with being great at golf, she also gained world fame in track and field and all-American status in basketball. She also mastered tennis, was an expert diver, roller skater and bowler. In the 1932 Olympics, she won two gold medals and one silver for track and field. Sadly, in 1956, Babe died of cancer at the age of 42.

One thing was for sure — I could have done with Babe today. I was playing like an absolute nun. It was embarrassing. My back was killing me (probably those damn train seats), though by the back nine I didn't hit one dud shot.

'You just needed the front nine to warm up!' Chris said, lining up a ball bound for a merciless end. 'This sucker eats me for lunch every time I play it,' he said, convincing himself he would spew his Hot Dot out of bounds. Which he did.

Walking up the green, Chris quizzed me about guns in New Zealand.

'Not many people own them,' I said.

'Really? Everyone's got one in Texas. We got a whole lot of groups trying to save the world and have them banned, but you can't go back. You can never go back.'

'So, do you own a gun?' I asked.

'Hell yeah, I own five; Mark's got over 30.'

Speaking of shooting, I shot an 82, which I was pretty happy about.

Having finished 18 holes before the heat of the sun took full effect, we scrambled into Mark's air-conditioned 4x4. He gave me his card and told me he'd be staying at Treasure Island in Las Vegas. 'Come and join me for a drink,' he said. 'I stay there for free 'cos I gamble a lot. As long as I stay on the tables for more than three hours a night.'

No worries, I thought, just leave your guns at home.

Meanwhile, Chris was quietly racking his brain, convincing me of what I'd already read and heard: Texan hospitality really *was* second to none.

'I've got to work tomorrow,' he said to me, 'but I'm just trying to figure out a way I can get you back to Beaumont, so you don't have to pay for a cab.'

As luck would have it, he needn't have worried. I wouldn't even have to call Daphne. Tomorrow's ride to the train station would be spent in the company of a Jesus Christ lookalike, a man named Otis and a chihuahua with no sense of direction.

DAY 18/19: GROVES, TEXAS

Stamp Club members collect for different reasons

People may collect stamps for a variety of reasons such as the designs or because they come from different countries. . . . Otis Barnes of Groves and treasurer for the stamp club said he began collecting stamps as a boy, but became a serious collector about 20 years ago.

'I enjoy looking at the different pictures and designs that stamps have and the history they portray.'

THE FRONT PAGE OF the *Mid County Chronicle* lay on the bed in my hotel. Otis Barnes would be my next victim — I mean, potential golfing partner. But how was I to get hold of him? And would he be a golfer? Next to my bed lay a Gideon Bible; next to that, a phone book. No, surely I hadn't stooped that low? Surely I wasn't about to call every Barnes in the book and ask if any of them had collected stamps for two decades?

The answer, sadly, was yes.

There was another man pictured in the photo with Otis, by the name of Bill (another Bill — I tell you!) Windle, who was president of the club. I decided to try the Windles first, purely because down a phone line, Windle is easier to understand in New Zealandish than Barnes. (Don't make me go into the reasons why, it's a rolling your Rs kind of thing.)

'Hello, is there a Mr Windle living there?' I asked the first lucky recipient.

Tiny bits of art

Bill Windle and Otis Barnes look over the many stamps collected over the past 20 years.

Stamp Club members collect for different reasons

By DENNIS KUTAC
Staff Writer

People may collect stamps for a variety of reasons such as the designs or, because they come from different countries.

Bill Windle of Port Arthur and president of the Southeast Texas Stamp Club said he's not sure what it is that draws people to stamp collecting, but said it's a fascinating hobby to have because a collection is almost never complete.

Windle said he got interested in stamp collecting when he was 11 years old after his mother bought home a two-tone stamp from the Union of South Africa.

"From then on I kept saving stamps," he said. "And now I save most anything that comes along including fruit and produce stickers."

Otis Barnes of Groves and treasurer for the stamp club said he began collecting stamps as a boy, but became a serious collector about 20 years ago.

"I enjoy looking at the different pictures and designs that stamps have and the history they portray," he said.

Windle said because there are so many different stamps just in the United States alone, some collectors are topical meaning they specialize in certain types of stamps. For example, a person may collect only stamps that portray ships, planes or famous people such as U.S. presidents.

"You can pick any topic you like,"Windle said. "I like everything."

He also said there are people who collect wine sticker stamps as well as cigarette and cigar stamps.

"Some people want a good price for some of these stamps," Windle said. "It's a case of supply and demand."

Both of them said trying to collect all type of stamps can be a much more challenging task than one may think.

"You almost have to specialize in a specific topic these days because there are so many stamps being issued per year," Barnes said.

Windle said there is a large number of stamp collectors and even renowned people such as Franklin Delano Roosevelt and Queen Elizabeth II have collected stamps.

This stamp features a portrait of Edna St. Vincent Millay, an American poet.

He also said there are a lot of stamps being printed today, not so much for postal use, but rather for collectors. Sometimes, however, a used stamp is what a collector may be looking for.

"There are times when a used stamp is worth more than a brand new one,"Windle said.

The Southeast Texas Stamp

STAMP, page 2A

'What?'

'A Mr Windle?'

Click.

'Hello, can I speak to Mr Windle, please?'

'Who?'

'Mr Windle?'

'I'm sorry, I can't understand what you're saying!'

Click.

Maybe it was time to start rolling those Rs.

'Hello, is Mr Barnes there please?'

'Palms?'

'No, Barnes. Does Mr Barnes live there?'

'Bonns?'

'No, Barnes, Mr Barrrrrrnes?'

'Borrins?'

'No, Barrrrnes, as in the thing where you keep horses!'

'Houses?'

'Oh, forget it.'

It had been a long day and I was starting to get agitated. Having exhausted all avenues of how to pronounce names in Texan, I flopped onto my bed. This was ridiculous; all I was trying to do was find two guys from the Texas Stamp Club, for God's sake! With a golf course only 10 minutes away, this was a prime opportunity to play golf with someone other than that damn duck.

Just as I was about to launch into the 59-channel flick I had a brainwave.

'Red, I'm wondering if you can help me. I'm trying to get hold of an Otis Barnes.'

'Bruce Barnes?'

'No, Otis.'

'Leroy?'

'No, Otis.'

'Joe Barnes?'

'No, Red. Let me spell it.'

I spelt it.

'Justin, let me look in my Criss-Cross Directory, they have names and numbers for everyone. One second.' Red put the phone down. I could hear him walk into the other room. 'Irene . . . Irene!' A muffled '*What?*'

'Do you know anyone who's into stamp collecting?'

'*What?*'

'Stamp collecting!' A pause.

'*Stamp collecting?*'

'Yeah, collecting stamps!'

Honestly, the situations I end up in.

'Justin's looking for some guys by the name of Otis Barnes and Bill Windle!'

Red picked up the receiver. 'Justin?'

'Yeah, I'm here, Red.'

'I can't find my Criss-Cross anywhere but I'll have a look for it. Otherwise, I'll ask around and give you a call back. 'Cos, you know, sometimes people say, my husband knows such and such, and he loves his stamps.'

I didn't even have the chance to shower before Red was back on the phone. He gave me numbers for both Bill Windle and Otis Barnes, neither of which were in the phone book. This man was a godsend. I'm so glad I came to southeast Texas.

Red finished off by saying, 'You have a good evening Justin and call me if there's anything you need, okay man!'

Those numbers were like gold. I clung to the piece of paper they were scribbled on and called Bill Windle. Unfortunately, he was on vacation in Wisconsin. Otis Barnes, however, was more than happy to accommodate a desperate Kiwi. This I found unbelievable. After all, here was a man in his sixties or seventies, who didn't know me from a bar of soap, offering to pick me up from a hotel he'd never heard of and asking if I'd care to join him and his wife Mary for a drink. The only bribe I'd used were the *Lord of the Rings* stamps, but something told me I wouldn't even need them. Otis just sounded like the kind of guy who was open to new experiences.

Be interesting, give a little bit of something.

'You want me to come and pick you up and bring you back to the house?' he asked.

'Well sure! That would be great.'

'You look out for me. I've got a brown pick-up truck.'

Texas, you've been good to me.

True to his word, 20 minutes later Otis pulled into the hotel's reception. I was still in shock: one minute, a bizarre call from a New Zealander; the next, 'Darling, just popping down the road to meet some axe-wielding homicidal maniac who's after a game of golf.'

I jumped in the front seat with my putter and Otis shook my hand. Then we were driving through Texas in a pick-up truck. *And* I had someone to talk to.

'I really appreciate you coming to pick me up, Otis.'

'No problems, we enjoy having people over. We had a Norwegian girl stay with us a coupla weeks back. Although, I will warn ya, I hope you like dogs.'

'I love dogs,' I said, 'but I couldn't eat a whole one.'

He laughed at my joke. Good start.

'Mr Nut, Tiny Goober, Buddy Lee, Eyeball, Chester — get inside!'

'WOOF, WOOF! YELP! WOOF! BARK!'

'I said, Mr Nut, Tiny Goober, Buddy Lee, Eyeball, Chester — inside, now!'

The screen door swung open and Otis' wife Mary ran through it to collect five canines who bolted past us like Hurricane Claudette. Otis did his best to yell above the dogs.

'JUSTIN, THIS IS MY WIFE MARY!'

'HI, MARY, LOVELY TO MEET YOU!'

'WOOF, WOOF! YELP! WOOF! BARK!'

'LET ME JUST CONTROL THESE DOGS AND WE CAN GO INSIDE!' she yelled.

Once inside, it was quiet — that was, until the dogs discovered *this* is where we were. One by one, they barged through a door that only narrowly missed closing on the last in the pack, Buddy Lee the chihuahua. These guys were excited and there was no stopping them. We just had to accept that conversation was not going to be a happening thing in the next five minutes.

'WOOF, WOOF! YELP! WOOF! BARK!'

'Tiny Goober, sit down! Buddy Lee, get off him! Eyeball, Chester, get off there!'

Within the Barnes household, Groves, Texas

No doubt about it, this was *my* kind of house.

Within minutes, the dogs were lying in various positions on various pieces of furniture around the lounge. Having just screamed their lungs out, woken babies and scared off burglars, they now collectively lay there as if nothing had happened, smug, proud and content with their latest performance. A cacophony of yelps and uncontained excitement, followed by absolute peace and quiet. Well, almost. Typically, as was the case in this room, there's always *one* who takes it too far. While four of the dogs *had* decided to stop, Chester decided to chance his arm.

'WOOF!'

'I said, shoosh!' said Mary.

'*Woof?*'

'Shoosh, I said!'

Whimper.

I was to learn that most of the pack, along with many others not seen in the room, belonged to Otis and Mary's son David who 'picks them up from the beach and befriends them. He must have 10 or 11 all up.'

Eyeball was so called because he had two different-coloured eyes (although I preferred to call him David Bowie for the very same reason); Chester was a real daddy's boy, never leaving Otis' lap; Mr Nut was just a madman; Tiny Goober was a mutt from the wrong side of the tracks; and Buddy Lee, no bigger than a large rat, was, as I was to find out later, not too confident when it came to riding shotgun in a Corvette convertible.

As I surveyed the room, I noticed all five had their eyes closed. Chaos over. For *now*.

One thing was for sure — I bet Otis didn't get his stamps out with *this* lot around.

Mary had lived in the greater Port Arthur area her whole life, and she and Otis had lived in the tree-shaded community of Groves for 53 years. They met on a blind date, and even though Otis, at 77, was only a year younger than his wife she still took great pleasure in telling me he was her 'toy boy'. When I asked Mary how many years she and Otis had been married she replied, 'Five happy ones.'

The Barnes' house was modest but well lived in; the lounge was airy, homely and filled with knick-knacks and crafts, mostly made by David. Much like my Mum and Dad's house, most digital clocks — on the microwave, the video and oven — flashed 00.00. Obviously there'd been a power cut in the last 10 years and no one had bothered to reset them.

I really don't how people can tolerate the flashing 00.00s. Firstly, you can never find the correct time, and secondly, when you've turned all the lights off and are ready for bed the house resembles a Blue Light Disco.

On the wall in the dining room was an old saying: *I know that you believe you understand what you think I said but I am not sure you realise that what you heard is not what I meant.* Outside the front door, a sizeable Texan flag flapped about in the wind. Mary, dressed in the equivalent of a daytime nightie, sat in a La-Z-Boy by the window, feet up, playing solitaire on a computer that sat on a cardboard box.

'Do you get the Internet on there, Mary?' I asked.

'I don't know, all I know is my daughter set it up so I can play cards. This is the only thing I know how to do on it.' She rocked back and forth, content.

Otis was on drinks and came out with lemonade and root beers. I took a seat and started patting Mr Nut — happy, just so happy I had company this evening. It's the little things.

Meanwhile, the greeting ritual was again under way.

'WOOF, WOOF! YELP! WOOF! BARK!'

David had arrived.

'OKAY, OKAY, OKAY!' he said, trying his best to squeeze through the door.

'WOOF, WOOF! YELP! WOOF! BARK!'

David, long hair tied back and a beard, looked a little like Jesus Christ. He shook my hand on arrival and told the room he'd be taking a quick shower. Of course, we had to wait five minutes before we actually *had* this conversation, as the dogs had come back for one final encore. As predicted, one of them pushed his luck, just as silence resumed.

'WOOF!'

'EYEBALL, SHUT UP!'

Feeling as if I'd known them for years and completely comfortable in their company, I wandered around outside after Mary demanded I check out her garden. It was a balmy evening, the best time of day. I felt so lucky to have found this little corner of the world. With Otis and Mary, I didn't even have to try. Within half an hour of arriving, I lay on the couch, shoes off, slurped root beer and changed TV channels at will.

I wasn't missing Mr Waffle, not one little bit.

We all watched the local news, including an item involving some residents of Vidor, Texas, unbelievably dressed in KKK outfits, trying to explain to the news crew that 'living in the same town as blacks *still* just wasn't right'. The leader held up signs, asking drivers-by to honk if they agreed. 'We can't live with them,' he spat, an ugly, ugly man. 'It was never meant to be like this. They should live in their *own* part of town, lead their *own* lives and we'll do the same.'

Deciding the best history lesson was actually sitting on the couch opposite, I asked Mary about growing up in southeast Texas.

'The biggest change in this part of the town has been the growth,' she said, eyes not leaving her game of solitaire. 'There were only 12 houses when I moved here, now there are over 18,000 people. I find that sort of change mind-boggling. Then again, I've only lived in four houses my whole life.'

'You seem to be the sort of person that doesn't get wound up anyway.'

'We don't sweat the small stuff too much,' she said, rocking. 'A lot of stress is unnecessary. What will be will be.'

She didn't look 78.

David had reappeared, washed, wearing jeans with bare feet, wet hair draping over his shoulders. The dogs failed to wake from their slumber upon his return. Obviously their raucous greeting was only initiated when someone came through the *front* door; it wasn't to be used frivolously when someone just came from the bathroom.

'Let me fix you two some supper,' said Mary.

'But I've already eaten,' David said, audible only to Otis, who replied, 'Your Mom's fixed you something.'

Resigned to the fact he'd *have* to eat, he said, 'Okay then.'

For someone who wasn't hungry, he did pretty well. We both polished off two courses in record time. Mary made us a lovely meal with real, fresh — did I say *real*, did I mention *fresh* — salad. A home-cooked dinner, Texan style, complemented by sweet tea.

'If I had known you were coming over,' Mary said, offering me more but not waiting for a response before refilling my plate, 'I would have fixed you something nice.'

I had a hard time convincing her I couldn't have been happier with what was in front of me. David, on the other hand, understood. He could sympathise, having eaten where *I* had.

'Mr Waffle?' he asked, incredulously. 'Man, I go to that place sometimes, but I gotta have a few drinks in me first.'

Couldn't have said it better myself.

'I hear you've got a few dogs?' I said to David, who was now patting Mr Nut.

'Eleven altogether. Just last week I gave away six little spitzes.'

'Who comes up with all the names?'

'We all do! Once we had a mutt with one leg shorter than the other. We called her Eileen.' Mary laughed.

'We had a cat coupla years back, called her Mr Frog. Problem was, she was so fine every other cat was measured by her.'

'Oh, she was *mighty* fine,' said Mary. Otis nodded, Chester slept.

'Craziest pet I ever owned was a coon.'

'A coon?'

'*Rac*coon. Had him for two years. I found him one day, abandoned, so I took him home and raised him. We did everything together. We'd watch TV together. Coon would sit on the couch and cross his legs. One day I was taking a piss and Coon came in and did exactly the same thing, in the bath! He was copying me.'

'Did you get rid of him after two years?'

'Had to. We were both single and as long as we were living together it was gonna stay that way. Plus he started scratching me some, real bad.' He showed me scars on his arms and legs. 'Deep ones sometimes, he'd really have a go at me. One day he really ripped into my arm. I was sitting there, bleeding, and he'd be sitting by my feet, ready for a scratch. He wasn't trying to hurt me, he just didn't know he'd done nothing wrong.'

Mr Nut was now on his back, legs in the air, tongue hanging out, getting a friendly whack on the stomach. 'After two years I released him back into the wild, which was a shame 'cos him and Mr Nut were great friends.'

David was obviously a rough-cut diamond. A jack of all trades, he built boats, crafted children's wooden trikes (one of which was in the lounge), and came up with ingenious ways to scare kids at Halloween. It was obvious he wasn't a golfer, though it was about time I found out whether his *father* was.

It had been suggested to me (mainly from mates back home who were monitoring a very unsuccessful golfing odyssey taking place) that I should find a golfer, *then* put him on the front page. As it turns out, Otis had actually been on the front page numerous times. Having served as a volunteer fireman for 50 years, he showed me his scrapbook, which featured many shots of him and his buddies.

'Nobody was seriously hurt in all that time,' he said. 'We had one guy who broke his wrist and one guy who broke his arm, but no one died. Well, a few people in their homes did.'

I was a little puzzled as to how Otis could have supported a family on a volunteer fireman's wages. 'I also worked in a shipping outfit for 36 years,' he said.

'So tell us about this stamp club,' I said, knowing I still had a trump card up my sleeve, provided my *Lord of the Rings* stamps were still in my back pocket (though I daren't check, in case they fell out and spoiled the surprise).

'We've got 15 members. I'm the treasurer, Bill's the president,' he said, scratching Chester, who still hadn't left his lap. 'We meet once a month.'

'How many stamps do you think you have?'

A pause. The only sound came from the ceiling fan: clunk, clunk, clunk.

'Um, let me see.' He spoke slowly. 'Let me see.'

Mary, still playing solitaire with her feet crossed on the chair, was stroking Mr Nut (who definitely seemed to get a disproportionate number of pats compared to the rest of the room — makes you wonder whether the others noticed this unfair ratio) and moving her playing cards from one side of the computer screen to the other.

'Well, he's not gonna say when his wife's around, is he?' she quipped.

'I've got all 36 presidents and, um, I've got . . . let me go get them,' he said, getting up, much to Chester's dismay. I must admit, I *had* actually wondered where he kept all these stamps; it's not as if they were plastered all over the walls or sprayed across the coffee table. Maybe they were just too valuable to leave lying around, especially with the serial greeters pouncing and slobbering on any available surface.

Speaking of which, Chester jumped back on Otis' lap before he even had the chance to sit down. This was akin to one of those selfish tourists at the beach who hogs the deck chair all day, believing it's theirs for life should they decide to leave a towel on it while they depart for a three-course meal.

Otis had produced five or so albums from a room down the hall. They were chocker with stamps, with impeccable labelling. Here was a man who took his hobby seriously. You've *gotta* have a passion, that's what I was always told. We've all met people who keep an old shoe box full of stamps under their bed — the same friend who would rip apart letters from Japan and try to convince you that the 40-yen stamps would be 'worth something one day'.

Otis, on the other hand, wasn't a fair-weather stamp collector. He was the real deal. And I was intrigued. I loved them. I really did. They were fascinating, beautiful.

'Some people keep a record of their stamps on a computer,' he said, showing me a JFK, a Martin Luther King and a Gandhi. 'I keep mine all in a notebook. And the best thing about stamps, unlike golf or any *other* sport,' he said, pointing to my putter, which rested on my knee, 'is you can do it any time, anywhere. For a few minutes or a few hours. It doesn't matter what the weather or the season is. You can learn history, geography, all sorts of things, just by looking at stamps.'

'So, I take it . . . you don't *play* golf, Otis?'

'No, sir.'

'So I'm not going to be able to drag you out tomorrow?'

'No, sir.'

Maybe next time I should challenge Front Pagers to a 'stamp off'?

'Oh, it's such a shame you're leaving tomorrow,' Mary said, when the sun had gone down. 'I tell ya what, why don't you come over tomorrow before your train leaves for El Paso? I'll fix you a roast.'

When I got to the door to say goodbye, Otis offered also to pick me up in the morning (after I'd checked out) and show me around Groves. I gratefully accepted, watching him carefully place his latest addition — *Lord of the Rings* — into his top pocket. What he said next proved what humble people I'd had the good fortune to meet:

'How much do I owe you for the stamps?'

Our next challenge was getting two fully grown men and three dogs into David's Corvette convertible. With a bum in my face (Tiny Goober) and a water rat (Buddy Lee) leaning on the window, I waved goodbye to Otis and Mary. They were laughing. Chester, next to his master at the front door, was panicking, no doubt wondering, 'Well, I can hardly sit on his lap if he's *standing*, now can I?'

'You've got great parents,' I said to David, as we drove off and out of Groves.

'I have, and I know that. I'm really lucky. They're the best people in the world.'

Watching Buddy Lee, merely the size of a soft toy, stick his head (and virtually his whole body) out the window like one of the big dogs, made me worry that it would be only a matter of time before he flew out like a discarded piece of rubbish. David assured me he'd be fine, flooring it just to prove his point.

Meanwhile, Mr Nut was trying to find somewhere to lie down in a car with only two seats, hence no back one. Just as I was about to tell him he was dreaming, he somehow managed to find a possie between David and me, wedging his body on top of the handbrake and, amazingly, grabbing a nap.

Tiny Goober, on the other hand (who isn't that tiny at all, just for the record!), continued to stick his arse in my face and bark at anything that moved. Worse still, he had the incredible knack of knowing when you weren't looking. Just when I was finally comfortable, and finally free of anything with four legs, he would jump from David's crotch onto mine. Had it not been for my seatbelt, I may have gone sky high *before* Buddy Lee.

'This is a piece of America right here,' David yelled. We were now creaming down the motorway. Hot summer wind blew through his hair, making him look like some sort of mad scientist. Meanwhile, Tiny Goober and Buddy Lee acted as if everything on David's daily route was brand new and *incredibly* exciting. (A road, a road, a road! Did you see the sign? The sign, the sign, you idiot, the sign, back there on the road! Holy shit, here's another one! Oh boy, oh boy, oh boy! What a ride this is! You keep an eye on that side, I've got this one covered! Oh, look, a vacant crotch . . .)

'Where do you live?' David asked. 'What city I mean?'

'I live in Auckland — it's only about a million people.'

'A million? That's far too many. Anywhere you can't take a piss outside your front door is too big.'

'Well, we *can* still take a piss outside the front door.'

'It's just that people look at you funny, right?'

'Right.'

Ten minutes later, we pulled into my hotel with a couple of dogs who were still acting like it was two sleeps till Christmas, and one we couldn't wake up. I was disappointed my ride had ended; it had been a blast hooning through Texas in a convertible. I felt like a 16-year-old being dropped off after a date. Hope Mum and Dad aren't waiting up! David told me he looked forward to catching up tomorrow, held back the dogs and drove off into the distance, with seemingly not a worry in the world.

Once in the hotel reception, I checked my emails. One had arrived from *New Calliope*, a magazine specialising in clowns and clown issues. The editor had read the newspaper article about the wedding in Richmond and wanted further details on what the big day was like. How exciting: my first interview about the golfing odyssey. (Not counting the write-up in the Charleston *Post and Courier*, which, let's be honest, was really about the duck.) Sadly, it wasn't until I got to the bottom of the email that I noticed that *I* wouldn't be featuring in the article at all, just the clowns. Charming!

Just as I was logging off and entertaining the thought of 12 hours' sleep (no reason to get up early when you've got the friendliest family in Texas planning your day), a small dog scurried under the desk and through to the other side of reception. The concerned-looking Indian manager followed the dog at pace, grabbing him just before he peed in the office. What a cute dog, I thought, and vaguely familiar.

'It's hard to fathom,' said the disgusted manager, who was now scurrying past me, holding a panicky-looking canine in his arms. It was only then the penny dropped. Just as the dog was about to be thrown into oncoming highway traffic, I yelled out, my voice echoing around the hollow foyer. *'Buddy Lee!'* The automatic doors opened. It was the first time I'd seen Buddy Lee *not* excited. He was shaking, alarmed and anxious.

'Is this *your* dog?' the manager asked, flicking at his chest as if dog hair were on it.

'Buddy Lee, what the hell are you doing here? How did you get here? Where's your dad?' Within a couple of minutes the Corvette was back, containing two anxious-looking dogs and a worried-looking David. 'Buddy Lee, get back in the car!' They then headed back to the country, 20 miles away, to take a piss outside the front door.

NEXT MORNING I checked out, smugly aware that Otis would be picking me up after breakfast. Amazing what a good sleep can do — I felt alive and ready to see the sights. After nearly three weeks of running around like a madman, I was really starting to get into a groove. How would I ever be able to go back to work after this? How would I ever handle reality? Sure, I missed my mates, I was lonely, and I had to talk real slow, smile a lot and try to impress the whole time, but it was fun.

I grabbed a newspaper from reception, soon realising accuracy was *not* one of the local editor's fortes; the date at the top read Sunday, 19 July. It was actually the 20th. Still, don't let the truth get in the way of a good story.

A few more magazines found their way into my bag; it was a long way to El Paso and I was sick of reading safety manuals. This trip was going to be hell.

A brown pick-up truck was idling outside, Otis and Chester sitting inside. I threw my clubs in the back and Otis leaned over and opened the door. The front seat was cooking. I hopped in and threw Chester on the handbrake. Otis then drove me around town and told me stories about his family.

The Port Arthur Veterans Memorial Park was where we decided to take the gamble of leaving the safety of an air-conditioned cabin. Names of those who served from Orange County, Beaumont and Port Arthur in the First and Second World Wars, Vietnam and Korea were to be found next to dormant fighter jets, helicopters and tanks. Otis was incredibly proud of this newly renovated place to remember. He had a tear in his eye when he showed me his name: 'I was lucky,' he said, 'never had to fire a rifle and, better yet, never had one fired at me.'

Root beer and dogs awaited us back in Groves. Mary wasn't home, so Otis and I sat with the mutts and rehydrated ourselves. It really was a hot day. When David arrived (with his sister Kay) we all sat round telling jokes. A mammoth session ensued, a round robin of the lamest gags and one-liners we could collectively muster. Typically, though, the problem with such a session is you can't concentrate on *listening* to one joke because you're too busy trying to remember the punch line for the next one.

Mary, back from her time at the shops, had prepared a good old Southern roast, the meat so tender it fell away from the bone. This was washed down with jugs of sweet tea, a drink that had really grown on me. Mary was the first to notice my empty plate (obviously I hadn't told a joke for a while).

'Come on, Justin, you know where the kitchen is.'

'Thanks, Mary.'

'Long way to El Paso,' she said when I sat back down.

'I forgot to ask, who would be your favourite American of all time?'

'He's sitting right over there,' Mary said, pointing to Otis at the head of the table.

'What about you, Otis?'

'Yeah, she's sitting right over there,' he said shyly.

Just as your parents would do, Otis and Mary made me call the station every half hour to make sure the train was on time. It wasn't. And never had been for that matter. It probably hadn't even left New York. This bothered no one — just gave us more time to eat, drink and tell jokes. Against my better judgement (but to Mary's delight), I was now on to my third helping.

'Long way to El Paso,' she repeated.

'Don't remind me, Mary.'

When the time *did* come to leave, I was expecting David to take me to Beaumont, with dogs in tow. I couldn't have been more wrong. Otis, Kay and Buddy Lee all joined us for the 30-mile drive.

These were the best people in the world.

Mary waved from the doorstep and Mr Nut barked from the windowsill, making sure he got a prime seat in front of all the others, no doubt to Chester's disdain. We were all glad the trip was at least half an hour; unbelievably, we *still* had crap jokes to get rid of. We passed the infamous Gladys City Boom Town Museum, which boasts a full-scale replica of the Spindletop boom town, and counted the Mr Waffles and Arby's I had 'eaten' at before I'd discovered Mary's roasts.

Seeing Beaumont railway station (or lack of it) in broad daylight was even more shocking than in the middle of the night. My adopted family, staunchly proud of southeast Texas, could hardly believe their eyes. Three passengers stood under the shade of a sycamore tree, suitcases by their sides. Buddy Lee ran over the rubble and headed straight for the train tracks. The thought of stopping him crossed our minds, but we agreed that even if he *did* get hit by a surprise piece of public transport, it wouldn't be going fast enough to do any damage.

Meanwhile, David had sauntered to the other end of the platform and had introduced himself to complete strangers. I liked this guy; he had gall. Five minutes later, raucous laughter. David obviously still had jokes to dispense of. Or was he starting to tell *ours*?

Before we knew it he was back, with a middle-aged man dressed in a white suit and safari hat, with an unlit cigar in his hand. His wife stood by his side.

'Look what I found!' said David.

'I heard you're a stamp collector,' David's new friend said to Otis, out-stretching an open hand.

'Sure am. What's *your* name?' Otis asked, removing his ever-present pen and paper from his top pocket. On our tour of Port Arthur the day previous, Otis had told me this had been a lifelong habit. 'Don't need a computer when you got this,' he'd said.

'My name's Lee,' said the man in the white suit, lighting his cigar. 'Been collecting since I was 11.'

While Otis jotted down his details David asked, 'So why you going to *El Paso*?'

'Got a house out there,' Lee replied.

'What, are you going to burn it down?'

I needed a quiet word with David. There was a question I was dying to ask. I dragged him aside, pulling Buddy Lee away from the tracks at the same time.

'So, these people, you've only just met them, right?'

'That's right,' he said.

'And . . . you've been speaking for what, five minutes?'

''Bout that, I guess.'

'How did you get on to *stamp collecting*?'

He paused, smiling a crooked smile. 'Hell, *I* dunno!'

The blue summer sky was now starting to fade with dusk approaching. I followed Kay's lead and looked up. Thousands of martens were circling, swooping and darting about directly above us. 'Catching mozzies,' confirmed Kay. Amazing — from where we were standing, the birds *themselves* looked the size of mozzies. I looked up again. 'Word of advice,' she said with the confidence of a local. 'Keep your mouth shut.'

The worst thing about travel is leaving people. Much like Miss Iva, the chances of seeing any of the Barneses again was about as likely as me playing a round of golf with someone from the front page. But there was always hope. Maybe Otis and Mary would bring the dogs down to New Zealand for their 'sixth' happiest year. Maybe David and Kay would bring Buddy Lee, Mr Nut and Eyeball over on a working holiday.

We waited an hour in the heat. It was the only time on the whole trip I was glad the train was late. And the Barneses were hardly in a hurry. Otis had found a new stamp club member, Kay had discovered Beaumont *didn't* have a train station and Buddy Lee recognised that napping in front of a large train is not the best of ideas. I think he just wanted to come to El Paso.

I had that warm-fuzzy 'I've met some wonderful people on my travels' feeling when I boarded the train. This would keep me going for a couple of hours. Well, to Houston at least. Meantime, the Barneses waved from the platform, Buddy Lee held tightly in David's arms, squinting his eyes, grimacing at the roar of the engine.

'So *this* is Beaumont?' a smoking woman mumbled depressingly, the tone of her voice the same as I would have used just a few days ago to describe the 'city with no station'.

'Sure is!' I said, waving to my new family.

The trip from hell was under way. To say I'd been dreading this part of the journey would be an understatement. If life had a fast-forward button, this is where I would have reached for the remote and skipped a chapter. Sure, I'd be docked 24 hours but I would gladly sacrifice that to be sitting in an El Paso hotel enjoying a beer and burrito. If all went to plan we would reach our destination in just under 24 hours.

That's a long time, especially when the old man next to you has Tourette syndrome.

The swearing started as soon as we hit Houston. For a while there, all I heard were incoherent mumbles. I thought he may have been on a cellphone or humming along with a Walkman. But no, he was swearing, cursing and hissing obscenities at nothing in particular. Constantly. Whatever he could see from that window sure was getting its fair share of abuse. 'Jesus H. Christ!' he spat. 'Oh shit, oh fuck, fuck, FUCK!'

In between he took medication — probably too much. Meantime, I was trying my darndest to find one, just *one* position where my back wasn't wedged into a window ledge, or an armrest resembling a cattle prod wasn't poking me in the butt.

It was going to be a long night. When I finally *did* find the position sent from God, it didn't last for long. It was reminiscent of finding that warm spot in a cold ocean, then finding out the *real* reason it's warm. It didn't help that I was sleeping by the stairs, right under an exit sign that was the equivalent of a motorway off-ramp. Sadly, the sign couldn't decide whether it wanted to be a mirror ball or a strobe light; either way it was not conducive to a good night's sleep.

Miraculously, after two hours of trying, I managed a comfortable position. I was in that wonderful, twitchy, 'I'm just about to nod off at any minute' state when out of nowhere came an almighty, 'JESUS H. CHRIST! SSHHHIIIIIITTTTTTT!'

Take some more medication, old boy.

Either that, or pass it round.

When it was finally his stop (which didn't come a f%$@ing minute too soon, just quietly) he didn't move. Only when the doors were finally about to close did he make a beeline for the stairs and, ultimately, the exit.

'Shit, Jesus H. Christ,' he yelled. 'No one told me this was my stop! Jesus H. Christ! Shit. Shit, shit!'

I looked at my watch: 18 and a half hours to go.

Where was Mr Nut when I needed him?

DAY 20: EL PASO, TEXAS

'LADIES AND GENTLEMEN, this is the conductor speaking. I thought I should let you know, it's 9.30 pm. Do *you* know where your kids are at?'

As far as I knew, *my* only child was with the rest of the suitcases down in cargo. Charleston and I had had a run-in just before we hit Houston; I thought it was for the best he had some quiet time. 'America and Popejoy to the dining cart please,' the conductor continued. 'America and Popejoy to the dining cart.'

Poor kids.

For much of the trip, as we ambled through sprawling Texas, I strapped on my radio and listened to local stations. On one, I heard that the latest trend in Las Vegas was to pay some promoter ten grand to arm you with a paintball gun. You then drive into the desert and search for naked women. You spend days trying to find them and shoot them. This story seemed to be a news leader on most stations I tuned in to (not surprising really) although I was later disappointed to discover the whole thing was a hoax and the guy involved was fined.

It was now 10 in the morning and I hadn't slept, even after the old potty-mouth had left. I had been on the train 12 hours and it felt like it. Apart from listening to dud news reports, the only other thing to do was to attempt that rather dangerous game of assumption.

A bearded man opposite had just embarked with someone who appeared to be his daughter. He piled the seats high with toys. Obviously his sermon before leaving the house, i.e. 'You can take one toy and one toy only', hadn't cut the mustard. How father and child were both going to fit in seats with Buzz Lightyear, Garfield, some sort of plastic parrot and an inflatable shark was anyone's guess.

Assumption: this man, the father, had broken up with his wife, who was waving to her daughter from the platform. He *did* have custody of his daughter, but he still found it hard taking her away from the mother (hence the toys).

'She can't see you through the glass, honey,' he repeated over and over to his daughter, who then cried, wondering why on earth her mother wasn't doing the same.

'Is it okay to cry, Daddy?' she asked.

'Yes, it's okay to cry, honey,' he replied.

Divorce is the hardest thing in the world and this family had obviously seen it first-hand in recent times.

Reality: the bearded chap opposite was taking his daughter on holiday to study sea slugs.

Within half an hour, Anna (the 11-year-old daughter with the mobile toy shop) was sitting on top of me, pulling my hair, hassling me about my accent and farting on my lap. I'm not joking. I took this as a compliment — to think she felt *that* comfortable after such a short time was either incredibly flattering or entirely offensive.

I'm an optimist; I'll take the first one.

'Anna!' Greg, her father, said after she belted out another one. 'You apologise to the man.'

'Sorry,' she said, doing it again.

'So, what's this about you and slugs?' I asked Greg, just pleased I had someone to talk to. Well, someone that wasn't *letting off* on my leg, that is.

'I study them,' he offered. 'They are simultaneous hermaphrodites, you know. I study their reactions and nervous systems — kind of like the reaction you get when you drop a can of beer on your foot.'

'So you go around dropping beer cans on slugs for a living?'

'Yep.'

'Cool! Where do you get them all from?'

'Once a week, 30 of them arrive from California.'

'How do you know they're from California — do they have nose jobs and plastic tits?'

Greg did his best to explain that aplysia (actually sea hares) exhibit two simple types of learning and memory. If you touch an aplysia lightly on the tail, the animal will contract it away from the direction of the touch, because the animal perceives this touch as a possible threat to its safety. If you continue to touch the animal lightly in the same spot without harming it, eventually the aplysia will stop contracting its tail.

'Do you play golf, Greg?'

'No.'

Worth a go, seeing as this is what the trip was about and all.

'And these slugs, do they have blood?' I continued.

'They just have this purple goo inside them.'

'Do they have a mouth?'

'They have a mouth; they even have genitals.'

'If you slice one in half, does it die?' (Come on, the question had to be asked.)

'Yes.'

'And do you ever get attached to them, give them names? You know, "Sheila, meet Bryan"?'

'No, but a lot of scientists do, mostly with rats and mice.'

'And you've *never* picked up a golf club?'

'No, why do you ask?'

'Just wondering. So tell me, how can what you're doing with slugs help, say, humans? I mean, how can going round giving slugs dead arms possibly help humankind in any way?'

'Good question. Let me explain. When you first get dressed in the morning you notice how clothes feel on your skin. However, as the day goes on, seldom do you notice the sensation of your clothes *touching* your skin.'

'Unless you're wearing a G-string.'

'Correct. But the fact you haven't *noticed* is because you have become *habituated* to the stimulus of your clothes. Think about it: you're sitting quietly at home and the heater turns on. You notice the noise immediately, but with time you barely notice the repetitive noise. You have become *habituated* to the sound of the heater.'

'So, like I said, you spend your life dropping beer cans on slugs?

'Pretty much, yeah.'

The fact that slugs neither wore clothes nor purchased small home appliances didn't seem to affect Greg's way of thinking.

And my tiredness seemed to only add to the confusion.

As a bit of a change from *Chicago*, I was pleased to see some volunteers from the Amistad National Recreation Reserve doing a bit of 'show and tell' in the dining car. For the uncultured like myself, Amistad is an international recreation area on the United States–Mexico border. It contains a reservoir created by the six-mile-long Amistad dam on the Rio Grande, a river that always makes me think of Johnny Cash songs.

The volunteers let us know if anyone were game enough to jump off the train into the reserve they'd have a chance to see armadillos, jack rabbits, quail, tarantulas, scorpions and my favourite — roadrunners. (One of the wonders of the world, that cartoon; a dog chases a bird every episode for 20 years, and we not only *watch* it, but wonder what'll happen next!)

The reservoir, which boasts 890 miles of coastline, also offers great fishing for bass and, unbelievably, 40-pound catfish. Scare the hell outta me, those things — ugliest goddamn fish I ever saw.

It had been an educational wee half hour but once the 'Spot the Texas Persimmon Tree' game started, I knew it was time to head back to cattle class. While Greg read Anna a book, I introduced myself to another neighbour, Terese, who had been writing furiously since sunrise. Terese was originally from New York and was the author of 16 romance novels, none in print. Having read as much as I could about George Patton, she passed me over her children's story omnibus, which featured such classics as *Why Stars Close Their Eyes*, *Clouds Have Feelings Too* and *Henry Hippo Wants to Wear Designer Jeans*.

What a strange little ride this was turning out to be — Tourette syndrome, bruised slugs and books written while under the influence . . . of *something*.

A Mexican guard searched my bags at El Paso railway station, asking a barrage of questions pertaining to my reason for being in his part of the world. I responded as best I could: 'Holiday . . . New Zealand . . . two days . . . cheap booze . . . women . . . border hopping.'

'*Gracias,*' he said.

'Not at all.'

El Paso seemed more a large town than a city, its streets quiet, clean, somehow empty. Small boys kicked a ball around what was probably once a busy street. High-rise buildings craved business. I liked the laid-back feel and felt comfortable, but for the heat. It was five in the afternoon and still well over 100 degrees. Experiencing a wicked cross between a serious hangover and jet lag, I dribbled out what limited Spanish I knew to the bloke driving the cab, even though he probably spoke better English than me.

Still, I don't mind making a tit of myself in another language; you've gotta have a go.

Jim, looking like the typical British colonial, complete with handlebar moustache, ran a local backpackers' hostel I'd heard very good things about. He told me I looked like shit. I told him he was pretty much on the money. The good news was accommodation prices had finally plummeted to my budgetary requirements. A single room: $23.

'Air-con?' More a plea than a question.

'No.'

I was to wake up later that night feeling as if I was being fried alive, in a room with sweat-covered walls that appeared to be closing in by the second. The only solace came from a hallway fan, *outside* my room. Of course, you could always stay cool by leaving the door open all night. Then again, you could also wake up with no golf clubs and a ransom note for your plastic duck.

Jim directed me to a local tapas bar for dinner. I dragged my weary heels for a feed that would make my next morning an extremely painful experience. I never seem to learn. I just love hot food, and there's no shortage in El Paso. I'm surprised everyone's not walking around that city with boogie boards holding their butt-cheeks apart. Sorry to be so graphic, but when it happens and you're not used to it, you just wish someone from the fire department would follow you around for the day. I suppose, though, much like the experimental slug, you *do* get habituated to eating copious amounts of hot peppers. One suspects you'd be a social outcast if you *didn't* in a place like El Paso.

Just wish I hadn't been so goddamn *social*.

For fear of falling asleep at the bar, I ordered a beer. Again, I tried in

Spanish but judging by the waitress's response, i.e. telling me the time, showing me where the bathrooms were and giving me a bus timetable, I didn't feel it was entirely successful. Disastrous in fact. Luckily, a suave-looking gentleman to my left saved the day, ordering two beers and paying for them himself. (Maybe I should speak Spanish more often.)

He introduced himself as Sal. 'As in Salvador,' he smiled. 'Just got back from California,' he said pointing to his bag. 'I have a house here, a house in California. Oh, and one in Atlanta,' he added, almost as an afterthought.

Outside, El Pasoans, businessmen, factory workers and shop assistants, waited for public transport in the searing heat. Every now and again I had to remind myself I was in El Paso. How did I ever get *here*?

Sal's favourite American was JFK: 'He was the first president to give the Mexicans some recognition, the first one to say we as Mexicans had an impact on what America was doing. If you go to Mexico, across the border, and walk into a typical Mexican's house, it's not uncommon to see a JFK picture next to Jesus Christ. I've been away, just got back from California,' he said again, tapping his bag with his cowboy boot. 'Oi, two more cervezas!' He clicked his fingers at the waitress, who was necking her boyfriend at the other end of the bar. 'You wanna 'nother?' he asked me. 'Course you wanna 'nother.'

It didn't take much convincing to stay in a bar with Artic-like air conditioning and free drinks, even if I hadn't slept since Beaumont. Having not really eaten since Mary's roast either, I asked for a menu (initially I got a bus timetable) and was more than pleased to see food prices matched that of the accommodation in town. Consequently, I ordered two burritos.

'No, no two, you only eat one,' the kitchen hand, a dark-haired, smiling young lady told me.

'No, seriously, very hungry,' I said patting my stomach.

'No, you only have one.'

I wanted two and I got two, managing to finish the second only in a bid to prove a point, rather than satisfy a hunger that was no longer there. Honestly, those burritos were the size of watermelons and cheap as chips. My credit card and I could come to like this town.

Meanwhile, Sal had bought another round of beers. I started to wonder why he was being so generous. 'Got to go to court on August 1st, in California,' he slurped.

'You got a house out there, right?'

'That's right! How did you know?' he asked, overcome with excitement. I pointed to his bags. 'I wish you all the best, I really do,' he said over and over.

'So, why do you have to go to court?'

'Getting into fights, that sorta stuff. I drink too much and then someone says something, and I can't hold back. I been to jail before.'

Gosh, is that the time?

'But I wish you all the best, I really do. Life's for living, make the most of it. My mother, she died in my arms.' He kissed his fingertips and put his hand on his heart. 'I've made a lot of money in business, retired at 48. Feel this,' he said, punching his stomach. 'Come on, feel it!' I hesitantly prodded his abs — very quickly, I hasten to add.

'Hard as a rock! I'm 58, can you believe that?' He slapped the bar. 'Just got back from California.'

A middle-aged woman and her companion had been drinking to my right. Blonde and dressed in skimpy white clothing, she had done a pretty good job of disguising her age; good enough to fool Sal at least, who had been eyeing her for some time.

'And one for her,' he said to the waitress, when ordering two more cervezas for us. This must have been the fourth or fifth. I was beginning to worry I'd forgotten the name of the backpackers' hostel. *(Jim, it's Room 214, I'm at the pub, can you pick me up?)*

'Oh, thank you,' said Barbie Girl, when the beer was placed on a mat in front of her.

'You're gorgeous,' Sal said.

She wasn't. My friend, who owned two houses, sorry, three, wasn't seeing too well just now.

'Thank you,' she said.

'No, you really *are* gorgeous,' he repeated.

Really, she wasn't.

'Are you off *West Wing*?'

'No.'

'You're off the TV though, right?'

'No.'

'You're gorgeous, man.'

'Thank you.'

Bob, an El Pasoan ex-politician, also received a free beer from Sal. He puffed out his chest at the first available moment to talk about himself, later informing anyone who'd listen that he was currently writing a memoir, which was to be printed in New York.

'So, you know some pretty important people then?' Sal asked.

'I know Clinton, I know Bush, I know them all. I've worked with them all.'

When Bob went to the bathroom, Sal bought Barbie Girl another drink.

'That your boyfriend?' he asked her.

'Yes,' she replied.

'Nice guy. A little uninteresting, a little unexciting, but a nice guy. You want some excitement, give me a call. I'm sure you're happy. Another beer?' He reached for his wallet and put a 20 on the counter. 'Just got back from California.'

Sal called a taxi — his daughter — and waited outside. I thanked him for his generosity and wished him luck for his court visit. It was time I also made tracks, Bob insisting he drive me to my sauna. 'There's so much history in this place,' he said, acknowledging famous landmarks on the way.

'Don't give him a *free* tour,' his girlfriend commented, rather bizarrely. I ignored her and asked Bob about his favourite American: 'Ulysses Simpson Grant,' he said without a pause. 'American Civil War general and 18th president of the United States. He hated his job but knew he had to do it.'

Barbie Girl seemed to have a problem with anyone who wasn't Bob so I was glad to reach our destination safely. Once inside I found Jim, who'd been rummaging through the daily papers on my behalf (I was really starting to get the hang of this now) and asked him about the over-inflated ego I'd been drinking with.

'Him? He's the biggest wannabe politician you could ever meet!'

THE FAN OUTSIDE my room was the proverbial dangling carrot and knowing cooler air lay just metres away did not make the night pass smoothly. Couple that with the cacophony of a garbage truck emptying half of El Paso into a bin right outside the hostel window, and you've got one grumpy Kiwi. Thankfully, come morning, I received an email from Zabe, a good friend back home, who wanted to know the number of the hostel so he could call me. I knew when he *did* we'd have the obligatory echo that seems to accompany long-distance calls. Or maybe we'd get lucky.

'Come on, Brown,' he coaxed, once niceties had been exchanged. 'This is getting ridiculous. Are you serious — *none* of these Americans you've met play golf?'

'I'm serious, none of them do . . . *of them do* . . .

. . . or maybe not.

'Look, why don't you just make it easy on yourself, come home and find someone on the front page here. You're bound to find a New Zealander who plays golf.'

'Okay then,' I said, entertaining the thought myself, even though I only had a week of the odyssey to go. 'Who's on the front page today? . . . *page today? . . .*'

Silence. 'Well?' I asked. 'Who's on the front page, who would I have to play golf with?'

'Actually, maybe that's not such a good idea,' Zabe muttered.

'Why? . . . *Why? . . .*'

'The top story here is about how farmers are going to be charged the equivalent of "fart tax". Cows are emitting too much methane into the atmosphere.'

'Tell me about it, I'm in El Paso. Today I can barely walk.'

Even though Zabe hadn't offered a solution, he had got me thinking. Maybe I should have been working in advance? Maybe, much like the clown wedding in Richmond, I needed to turn up to towns the day *before* news actually hit the papers.

What a ridiculous notion, I told myself. For, short of having a hotline through to God who, for a small fee (plus tax), could tell me exactly where car crashes, murders and demonstrations would be taking place (time and state), how was I ever supposed to know? All *I* wanted was a game of golf.

Still, I did call John, a part-time golf reporter for the *Tucson Citizen*, whose response was an emphatic and excitable: 'Yeah, I suppose you could give us a call when you get into town, although I do want to get a haircut this week.' I also had an inspiring result from the editor of a small Las Vegas rag: 'Well, I just had eye surgery, so I can't play.'

A copy of the *El Paso Times* lay on the counter at reception. Rather excitedly, I rang the bell, ready to ask Jim my first question of the morning.

'This guy,' I said, tapping my forefinger on the front page, 'the creator of *Star Trek*, was he really from El Paso?'

'Sure was,' Jim said, refilling the coffee pot.

'This is fantastic! Maybe I should play golf with *him*.'

'I suppose you could . . . if he weren't dead.'

A *Star Trek* convention was to be held later in the year to honour Gene Roddenberry, whose early roots were, as Jim said, in El Paso. Rather surprisingly (I thought, anyway), Gene wrote *Star Trek* while in the Los Angeles Police Force. You'd think *CHiPs* would have been more up his alley.

Less exciting was the horrendous headline — *Five Die in Crushed Cars On I-10*. The dead, including two children, were killed when a tractor-trailer slammed into a car near a Border Patrol checkpoint.

Thankfully, two *light*-hearted stories were also to be found on the cover: one involved a young El Pasoan entrepreneur; the other a local horse player who, after 33 years of gambling, continued to beat the odds.

I like a bit of a flutter myself so was keen to meet up with Mr Art Canales who, according to the paper, spent most of his working (?) day at Sunland Park Racetrack & Casino. As soon as I'd downed a few coffees, I put on my stalking hat and hit the phones.

Failing to get hold of Mr Canales at the casino, I started ringing every Canales in the phone book, no mean feat considering in El Paso Canales is probably akin to Schultz in Germany. Rather predictably, most members of the Canales family had never heard of their gambling uncle so I moved on to stalking a Mr Robert 'Beto' O'Rourke. In an article titled *Saving the city from 'brain drain'*, Robert was featured as a young man who'd moved back to his native El Paso from New York in 1998. He'd since started up a successful company, Stanton Street Technology Group.

A quick look at the map Jim had given me confirmed that Robert's office lay just three buildings away. Thank God, as in my current (burrito-induced) state I couldn't walk more than 50 metres without wishing I had packed frozen toilet paper.

El Paso works to draw large businesses

Residents want incentive to stay

By David Peregrino
El Paso Times

Ending the city's exodus of talented men and women will take time and will require a variety of solutions, say local experts who are tackling the challenge of El Paso's so-called brain drain.

In fact, several efforts to reverse the drain are under way, triggered by the city's experience during the last decade, when a booming economy lured thousands of working El Pasoans to cities such as Austin, Dallas, Phoenix and Denver for better wages and career opportunities.

"There's no one stroke that is going to solve it all," said Alan Landry, a retired Army colonel appointed three months ago to be the city's economic development director.

Landry describes the approach as "holistic," combining improvements in the city's quality of life, educational opportunities, and — most important — an availability of high-skill, high-wage jobs to attract and retain young, dynamic minds.

Under former Mayor Ray Caballero's administration, the city introduced a public-private partnership with the Greater El Paso Chamber of Commerce to aggressively pursue new businesses.

The partnership's promotional material lays out the advantages of relocating to El Paso for large employers such as call centers, manufacturers and company regional headquarters.

The city and chamber also recently collaborated on a bid to lure a Boeing airplane plant to El Paso, Boeing, wooed by several Texas and other U.S. cities, is expected to select a location for its factory later this year.

For El Paso to be a contender in the high-stakes game of attracting big business, the city must demonstrate its commitment to quality-of-life projects and higher education, Landry said.

"Professionals don't want to live in communities that don't value

Please see Businesses 2A

Robert "Beto" O'Rourke moved back to El Paso from New York in 1998 and started Stan- ton Street Technology Group in the O.T. Bassett Tower, at left, in Downtown El Paso.

BRAIN DRAIN

·THE SERIES
▶ Sunday: Roots of the problem and how brain drain has developed.
▶ Monday: Outlooks

of professionals who have stayed and left.
▶ Today: Ability of industry to keep El Paso's best and brightest.

INSIDE
▶ Business development needed 2A
▶ Chamber lends a hand 2A

El Paso Times, *El Paso, Texas*

Robert had been very cordial on the phone and he was no different in person. When I arrived at his office, he was to be found checking out my website, www.golfswingusa.com, sifting through the reports I had been compiling over the past three weeks.

'My dad did something very similar to what you're doing, a few years back,' he said, shaking my hand. 'He toured the States on a bike, one side to the other.'

'On a push-bike?'

189

'Yeah, took him two months.'

'Thanks for the compliment, but that sounds a lot harder than anything I'm doing.'

Robert took me to a small burrito/taco bar for lunch (AAAGGGH-HHH!!!) and it wasn't long before regulars made him aware of his newfound fame.

'Hey Beto, nice piece in the paper.'

'Robert, saw you in the paper, looking good.'

'Thanks, everyone gets their 15 minutes,' Robert said bashfully.

Robert was born in El Paso in '72 but had spent seven years in New York.

'I went to college there,' he said, tucking in to something that was far too gastronomically challenging for me to look at, let alone eat.

'I also spent a lot of time humping,' he added.

My Dr Pepper went down the wrong way. 'I'm sorry, did you say *humping*?'

'Yeah, I was a humper,' he smiled.

'Are . . . are you sure you want to talk about this?'

'A humper means I shifted furniture, art, pianos, that sort of thing. We had some semi-famous customers: Bjorn Borg, my friend went to Sylvester Stallone's house. It was a good job, you never had to think.'

Occupation — Professional Humper. Interesting.

Robert was also a muso. He and some mates had started up a band called Foss and achieved the ultimate: touring the States and Canada.

'We drove around in this shitty old station wagon. We produced a seven-inch but that was about it. Although, *one* of the guys from the band has become famous: our drummer, Cedric Bixler, is in a band called At the Drive-In. He now lives in Long Beach; he's currently touring with the Red Hot Chili Peppers.'

'Okay, so New York, nightlife, rock-star lifestyle and humping. Why come back to El Paso?'

'I suppose I realised I wasn't a New Yorker. It was never my city. I had this crystal moment one morning, I was on the subway travelling an hour and a half to the Bronx, which is something I did every morning. Then one day I thought, I don't have to do this any more. I had this vision of driving

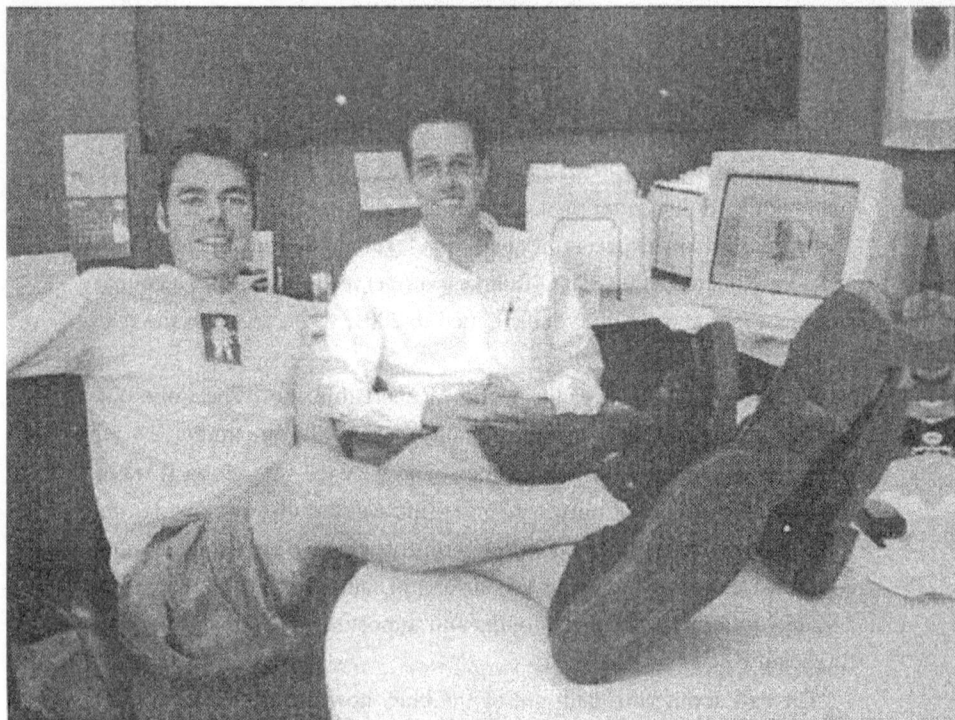

Hey, he's the boss, we can do what we want!

around El Paso in my pick-up truck, air-con going, listening to the radio, seeing my family and eating Mexican food.'

Okay, you had me till you mentioned food.

Robert refused to let me pay, instead letting me grab a few Cokes for the road. We then lived the Texan dream, scouring the streets of Sun City in a pick-up truck.

'El Paso was recently voted the third safest city in the US,' Robert said, turning on his phone to check his messages. 'It's also the most illiterate in America.'

'To be honest, most people looked at me sideways when I said I was coming down here.'

'It's true, to a lot of people El Paso is a dump. A lot of locals are very self-conscious about their city. Most are always thinking of ideas about how to make the city better. It's always a hot topic when you're out drinking with your friends. But I see a lot of opportunity here. When I decided to return, I knew there weren't a lot of businesses starting up. This was in the height of the dotcom era, but not down here, so I started up Stanton Street

Technology from my apartment. The only loan I had was 20 grand from my father. That was in 1999; there are 18 of us now.'

'So you're doing better than you ever thought?'

'I surpassed any expectations, but I don't want to do this forever.'

Sadly, Robert's father, Pat O'Rourke (who served in El Paso as a county commissioner and a county judge), died in 2001, when a car hit the bike he was riding.

'He had ridden all over the world,' Robert told me. 'Then one day he got hit. He was 58. It made me realise, when it's your time, it's your time. He was a big part of our business, and we were very close. It was a long-standing dream of ours to go into print; we started a weekly mag six months after his death. It did well in terms of what we published, 15,000 copies a week. We had achieved our dream, but after a while it wasn't a viable option. It lasted six months and almost sank us, physically and financially.'

'The call about your dad, out of the blue, how did it change you?' I asked.

'It's funny, I remember thinking at the time, all bets are off. I was going to live life differently from now on, do everything I wanted. And then you don't really at all. Life is still life.'

'I'd like to one day', 'It takes up too much time' and 'Only old people play it' were not the responses I sought when I asked Robert if he ever hit the fairways. However, like most people on this trip, this didn't seem to stop him trying to help me find someone who *did*.

My tour of El Paso would have to take a slight detour in the form of Sunland Park Racetrack & Casino.

'Mr Canales, we hope you're in town and we hope you play golf,' said Robert.

Unsurprisingly, the casino, a stark and barren building, overlooked a racetrack. No doubt its car park, big enough to house thousands of repossessed vehicles, had kindly (although *unknowingly*) been paid for by the many losers inside. With Texan temperatures soaring, one got the feeling that most people playing pokies or milling around inside were doing so just to escape the stifling heat. Robert dropped me at the front door and told me to be home before dark.

'I don't know who you're talking about,' said the security guard at the front desk.

'Are you sure? He gambles here every day.'

'Nope, never heard of him.'

'I don't suppose you could page him? It's really important.'

'No.'

The manager on duty (who supplied me with a free bottle of water while I watched old ladies attach themselves to slot machines via credit cards) knew exactly who 'Mr VIP' was, and saw it as his mission to find him. My confidence grew. Then sank.

'Sir,' he said upon return, 'I have good news and bad news. The good news is we've managed to track down your friend. The bad news is he's in Colorado.'

As he pointed me in the direction of the toilets (for the second time) I heard him finish off: 'I can't believe your luck, I really can't. He's *always* here.'

Robert, meantime, was not going to let me dine alone. He and a co-worker, Grace, picked me up from the casino and took me out for a drink at a trendy new vodka bar. Seeing his friends in there made me realise I missed mine. We sat around, drank vodka and soda and scoffed gourmet pizza (unfortunately riddled with peppers).

No one let me pay for anything. Texan hospitality!

Like Robert, most others here tonight had moved back to El Paso, either to start up businesses or just lead a cruisier, less rushed lifestyle.

'It's a good place,' they agreed, 'but it's frustrating dealing with people who, along with the city, haven't changed for hundreds of years.'

Thankfully, they all showed a particular interest in my *non*-golfing adventures and cursed Robert for never having played the game. As well as that, they sympathised with my Delhi belly, adding, 'Around here, life is *not* like a box of chocolates, it's like a jar of jalapeños — you never know when it's gonna burn your ass.' They also collectively wondered how on earth I'd ended up drinking with ex-politician (and soon to be bestselling author if he had anything to do with it) Bobby Vale.

'You drank with him last night?' they shrieked.

'I think it was him, yeah,' I said.

'Short guy?'

'Yep.'

'Comb-over?'

'Yep.'

'That's him. Oh that guy's the biggest wannabe! Even spent a few years in prison.'

If that were true (and I'm in no way saying it *was* for fear of being sued), then I'd spent last night drinking between two convicts.

Unlike myself, Robert had work in the morning so he gave me a lift back to my hostel. Judging by his demeanour, ambition and conviviality, I was convinced he would have certain American mentors.

'My favourite American? I have two. Firstly, Abraham Lincoln: I love his story, from humble beginnings. I admire his honesty, his brilliance at holding the country together at a precarious time, his sense of honour, his oddness, his big ears. He was so unique and had some of the best qualities of America.

'My other one would have to be Bob Dylan. He decided who he wanted to be and became it. An upper middle-class Jewish refugee who became a dustbowl hobo refugee. He'll go down in history like Shakespeare.'

The last place I wanted to go once inside the hostel was up to my room (for fear of fainting in the heat), so instead I decided to check my emails in the foyer. Antonio, a short, bearded man with thick-rimmed glasses, was on reception. An open, friendly kind of guy who required no effort to start a conversation, he was engaged in one with a guest who was after some local knowledge. 'I want to go across the border,' he told Antonio. 'Can you recommend any good places?'

'For drinking or dancing or what?'

'Um, yeah, maybe. Maybe meet some girls?'

'What sort of girls?'

'You know, maybe see some shows?'

'So you wanna strip bar?'

'Yeah . . . sort of, I suppose,' the guest said, leaning closer into the counter, now almost whispering.

Antonio suggested a bar.

'What do they do there?' the guest asked, nervously stroking his beard.

'Just strip, no touching,' Antonio said.

'Can you recommend anywhere else?'

Antonio recommended another. 'What do they do there?' the guest asked.

'Almost everything, *some* of them everything. But be careful.'

'If I'm not back by two, send out a search party,' the guest finished, tying back his Santa Claus grey hair into a ponytail. He then tucked his T-shirt into his shorts and headed off to Mexico. 'We accommodate everyone here,' Antonio winked at me as soon as he'd left.

'Looks like it,' I said. 'Try getting that service in the Hilton.'

An hour passed and I still didn't have the nerve to go up to my room. Antonio knew all about my frivolous search for Texan golfers. Shuffling through today's paper, which featured the car crash, Robert and Mr Canales, I let out a small, dissatisfied moan.

'There must be another newspaper in town, Antonio. Even a small local one would do.'

'No, that's the only one in town.'

'Until when?'

'Tomorrow.'

So, there I sat in an El Paso backpackers' hostel, fondling my underused and barely marked golf clubs. Antonio had obviously had enough of my moping.

'You really wanna play?' he asked.

'Would love to.'

'When?'

'Tomorrow.'

'What time?'

'Early, when it's not hot.'

'How 'bout six?'

'Done.'

I hardly slept a wink; I was going to play golf, in public, with a real person! Okay, so he wasn't off the front page but he *had* been an attorney in Kansas a number of years ago and *had* once been on TV defending crooks.

Tenuous I know, but cut me some slack here.

'You wanna cart or you wanna walk?' we were asked upon arriving at Lone Star Golf Course.

'Let me tell you,' Antonio said while practising his putting in the pro shop. 'I love to walk when I play golf; I always seem to play better.'

Sadly, what Antonio *didn't* know was that I had eaten enough jalapeños to sink a ship in the last few days, and every time I took a step I thought I was going into labour.

'I think we'll take a cart,' I grimaced at the assistant.

We got around in under three hours. Mind you, it *was* 6 am and we were the only ones mad enough to get up at that time. The greens were fast and the company was great. Antonio (who's got a girl across the border himself) told me his favourite American was his father, 'even though he was Mexican'. I managed 85, Antonio 108. The poor guy must have hit every tree on that course, bar none. I called him Tiger Woods as he spent most of his time *in* them.

Chalk it up: proud moment, third game of golf in America.

DAY 23: TUCSON, ARIZONA

WE NEVER DID SEE WINSLOW, Arizona that the Eagles sang about in 'Take it Easy', hence I never had the chance to stand on a corner *in* it. Instead, I relished the fact this was my very last ride on the Amtrak network.

That the train was two hours late didn't even dampen my spirits.

To make things even better, I'd had a call from a mate in Canada who was going to be in Tucson at the same time as me — the only difference being, I was there to find a golfing partner, he was there to sell conveyer belts. Being the organised type, he had accommodation sorted (thank God!) and a rental car. Because of this we even toyed with the idea of him driving from Tucson to El Paso to pick me up, potentially saving me from one last screening of *Chicago*.

He'd called on my mobile the night previous. Lying on my bed wearing only boxer shorts (in a bid to combat the heat), I sprinted downstairs with the phone ready to pick Antonio's brain regarding how many hours the journey might take — and more to the point, whether it would be feasible.

Unfortunately though, a strange man I'd never encountered was attending the desk.

'Excuse me,' I said, 'I don't suppose you could tell me how many miles —'

'You can't come down here with no shirt and bare feet!' he yelled.

'But, I was just wondering if you —'

'Get back to your room and put some clothes on!'

The result of that particular call was that we found the trip would have been entirely *un*feasible — unless of course you enjoyed driving 20 hours

197

nonstop. Besides, had we driven to Tucson, I would never have met my new friend, a Vietnam War vet from California, a man who despite having a son in the military about to leave for North Korea had a refreshingly healthy view of the world: 'A lot of guys from my era blamed things. Many of them came back from war and expected sympathy. Some even relished it. You've got to remember, a lot of those guys would have been losers had they *not* gone to war. So we went to war? Big deal, get over it.'

Countless towns in southwestern Texas and Arizona were now of the ghost variety. With major highways dictating where people would shop and eat, many old main streets lay dormant, with empty shops, faded paint and smashed windows. 'It's sad,' said my neighbour, later adding as the train passed through miles and miles of open, barren, useless, parched land, 'And we *fought* for this? We should have just moved the border up to Missouri and given the rest to Mexico.'

Within five hours we'd arrived in Tucson: no breakdowns, no hold-ups, no delays. It was the trip Amtrak should surely have bottled and sold everywhere. Adding to the already perfect evening was the fact that during the trip the time zone had changed twice, many a thankful person realising that by the time they got off they were actually two hours younger.

Rob and I successfully met up in Arizona's second largest city and, as an added bonus, *remembered* each other, something some people take for granted when they agree to meet up with old friends. I always take old photos — that seems to do the trick.

Hotel Congress, a funky hotel, café and bar dating back to the 1920s, couldn't have been more convenient, located right opposite the train station. Rob and I sat at the bar drinking locally brewed beer served by a Daisy Duke lookalike and took in some live jazz. A two-man band was doing its version of 'Baby Elephant Walk' as well as a few Louis Armstrong numbers. As agreeable as it was, halfway through the second drink we decided to hit the sack, finding the temptation of a double bed each, a ceiling fan and a room to ourselves too hard to ignore.

Next morning, while I drank coffee and scoured a virgin newspaper, Rob had some stern words to offer:

'As your agent, I want to make it clear that you are no longer allowed to call people from the paper. It's getting ridiculous.'

'What do you mean?' I said, knowing exactly what he meant. 'Just one more . . .'

'No. Look, I've been following your progress on the web; it's not working, there are no golfers in America. We'll have to think of something else.' He glanced at the page I was reading. 'I mean, who are you trying to get hold of today?'

'Well, there's this homeless guy on the front page who's got a job with a new recycling firm. But he's not your typical bum. He was once a journalist; he even used to own a house. He's just decided that having no possessions is the way to go.'

'So he has no possessions?'

'No.'

'How are you going to get hold of him?'

'What do you mean?'

'You think he'll have a cellphone?'

'Good point. How 'bout this one?' I continued. 'A local Tucson dude who's been let of jail for good behaviour?'

'Brown, you are forbidden from calling these people; it's not good for your health. You've discovered something very important — there are *no* golfers in America.'

It appeared Rob was my new agent and my trip, as I knew it, was over.

Despite this, when Rob disappeared to his room, confiscated newspaper tucked firmly into his day-pack, I bought another one from the hotel reception. In doing so I felt I had broken the law, but I couldn't help it. I was addicted. Stalking news-makers had become an obsession. While other tourists strolled past Tucson's 19th-century buildings and hiked the Sonoran Desert valley, a New Zealander set about harassing the dodgy and weeding out the extraordinary.

Which could be a tad difficult given today's headlines:

Priest Will Serve 8.5 Years For Sex Abuse

Korean War Vets Honored

Man Opens Fire At NY City Hall

Gunfire Leaves One Dead, One Hurt

14-year-old Twins Robbed Bank To Save House

'Hey, come on, put those down!' Rob said, piling down the stairs, clean-shaven and spruced up. 'What did I say?' Again, he took the paper from me. 'No more!'

'Look,' he said, noting my disconsolate mood and sensing my abject feeling of failure. 'How 'bout we try something different? I'm looking to buy an old Porsche while I'm down here — why don't we just go through the classifieds and find someone that way?'

Hence we met an Arizonian Porsche dealer called Dave who bought Porches, fixed Porches and basically slept with Porches. For most people, lying under a roasting second-hand car on the hottest day of the year would be hell on earth. For Dave, it was all in a day's work.

Just as Rob had given me grief that *my* trip was a waste of time, so should I have given *him* advice when it came to buying second-hand vehicles. In other words, every car on this yard was a piece of shit. Ten or so 914s (I only know the model number because I asked my agent) sat parked under the blistering sun. Dave informed Rob that most needed a little bit of work.

'Little bit of *work*?' I nudged Rob. 'This is like a scene from *Mad Max*.'

'You heard the man,' he replied. 'They just need a little bit of work.'

'Rob, even if you put bay windows, a veranda and another floor on, they're all still rusty old pieces of shit. Come on, let's play golf.'

Unfortunately it was too late — Rob had fallen in love. He was running his fingers up and down the side of an extremely rusty, extremely yellow two-seater.

'Just needs a bit of work, that's all,' he said dreamily, opening the boot, scorching his hands at the same time.

'Oh God, are they scorpions?' I shrieked.

'Don't worry, they're dead.'

'Even so, they're *scorpions.*'

'Gives it character.'

I think the heat was getting to him.

For the next half hour I felt like I was a kid again, waiting for Dad at the hardware store.

'Just five more minutes,' he'd say. 'Go and play on the motorway or something.'

To make matters worse, Dad (Rob) decided to speak 'Porschen' with Dave.

'Introduced in '69, wasn't it?'

'Yeah, you can tell by the Targa top and four-cylinder Boxster engine.'

'You know where the idea came from for the 914, don't you?'

'No.'

'The presidents of VW and Porsche collaborated to produce a new sports car for each of their companies. Volkswagen wanted a new, sportier model to replace the Karmann Ghia and Porsche would also use the car, but with all the components coming from the 911 series.'

'Oh, okay.'

'VW would take 914 bodies and finish them as 914/4s, and Porsche would take their portion of the body shells and build 914/6s. When sold in North America, however, all 914s would be considered Porsches.'

Dad, can we go now?

Dan, Dave's offsider, at least seemed semi-normal. He was working on another 914 inside the workshop. Thankfully, unlike Dave, Dan could (and did) talk about other things — that is, until the other two arrived.

'Dan,' said Dave, 'this is Rob. He's looking at the yellow model outside.'

'Hey, cool man, that is a *nice* car. Did you notice when you're looking at a 914 you don't see the likeness of other Porsches? Like the pop-up lamps and the vertical windshield . . .'

Oh, for God's sake.

I pulled Rob aside, but not before he called his best mate in Canada to see whether he should purchase the yellow piece of shit. We were standing in 110 degrees, frying.

I asked Rob whether he'd made any progress regarding the real reason we were here.

'No, I haven't asked Dave yet. Oh look, this one's a 914-6 GT!'

'Rob!'

Dave and Dan were eating lunch when we went back inside. A ceiling fan did its best to cool an otherwise baking office filled with a plethora of scraps, tools and thingumabobs that *may* just come in useful one day. Dave, among other things, was obviously a hoarder.

First I asked Dan about joining us for 18 holes.

He responded staunchly: 'I don't associate myself with any ball sports:

baseball, football or golf, nothing. Cars are my thing.'

None from one; let's try Dave.

'I played a couple of times in my life, that's all.'

'Really? You wanna play tomorrow?'

'Nope, gotta work on my baby. It's the only chance I get to work on my own car.'

'Is this your one over here?' Rob asked, patting the bonnet of another piece of shit.

'That's her, Rob. You'll notice that the transmission is like the 928s with first down and to the left. The steering is pretty tight, and the suspension is hard . . .'

Dad, I'm leaving, find your own way home.

'Well that was a complete fucking waste of time,' I said to my agent once back in the air-conditioned rental. 'Now can I get back to my paper?'

'No. Not the cold calling, bad for your health. Okay, how 'bout this idea? We go out and find people who have *been* in the paper, not necessarily today's. Just any paper, any time. We track them down, *then* take them to golf.'

I didn't like this, not one little bit. The rules were changing. Rob had just burst on to the scene and changed a . . . I was going to say 'winning formula', but, well, he'd just changed things. Surely springing upon someone who had *been* in a paper, any paper, any time was just too easy. I mean, *everyone's* been in the paper. Where's the challenge in that?

Rob tried out his new strategy at our hotel bar that afternoon. While the barman (who had a ring poking out of every orifice) served us a cold beer — and, thankfully, not his own concoction of the day (Free Kitten — $3.50) — Rob asked him the million-dollar question.

'Ever been in the paper?'

'I used to be a cartoonist,' he gleamed, two teeth missing.

'That count?' Rob asked, looking at me.

'No.'

Gene Pitney's 'Who Shot Liberty Valance' sounded from the jukebox. The barman continued to convince customers they *really* needed a Free Kitten in their lives ('Come on, you gotta have one, it's my own drink!') while Rob took a wander outside. He returned with an Australian and his

Canadian girlfriend. Nick (who we would later dub Nick Dundee) and Claire were on their way down to Mexico — but not just yet, not before my agent had asked his questions.

'Sit down, sit down,' he said to his guinea pigs. 'Can I get you a drink?'

'No, thanks,' Nick said, pulling out a chair for Claire, a look of apprehension on his face.

'Let me ask you a question,' he said, edging toward them at the table. 'I don't suppose by any chance . . . either of you have ever been in the paper?'

'What sort of paper?' Nick asked. Claire looked nervous.

'You guys wanna try a Free Kitten?'

Rob ignored the yell from the bar. 'A paper, any paper, a newspaper,' he continued. 'You know, like maybe you won a trophy at school, or saved some dude from a burning building, or discovered Blu-Tack.'

'No,' Claire said coldly.

'Never?'

'Never,' they said in unison.

I nudged Rob. 'Can we just go back to my —'

'No.' He stared at the couple again, waiting for the answer he needed. 'Are you *sure*?'

'Oh no, wait, I have!' said Claire. 'But it was years ago.'

'That's fine.'

'And it's pretty embarrassing.'

'Even better,' Rob said, rubbing his hands together.

'I . . . oh God, this is embarrassing. I don't know if I should say it.'

'What?' Rob squealed. It was now Nick who looked worried, though he needn't have been.

'When I was 13,' Claire confessed, 'I won the Greenwoods Beauty Pageant.'

'A princess!' my agent hollered. '*Wow!*'

Nick Dundee, not to be outdone, had suddenly remembered his *own* 15 minutes of fame.

'Our family grew up in the outback and when I was two I went out to get the mail.'

With Nick Dundee on the Quail Canyon Golf Course, Tucson, Arizona

'You got the mail at *two*?' I asked.

'Yeah well, what else is there to do in the outback?'

'Fair call.'

'Anyway, so I was getting the mail and Mum came out to see how I was doing. Which, as it turned out, was not so good. A massive snake was right behind me and about to strike. Mum yelled like mad and the neighbour turned up with a spade and bashed the hell out of it. That was on the front page of the *Riverine Herald* in 1980.'

'1980!' I said. 'Surely that's too long ago —'

'That's fine, that's fine,' said Rob. 'You play golf, Nick?'

'Yep.'

'You *wanna* play?'

'Sure.'

Rob poked me in the ribs, tapping his nose with his forefinger.

Nine holes were booked for three people at Quail Canyon Golf Course. Unfortunately, we forgot to consult the princess. Later that afternoon Nick

Dundee joined us in the foyer and informed us that Claire wanted to do something else.

'What else does she want to do?' Rob asked.

'Something, anything — just not golf.'

This wasn't going to halt our progress. After countless miles and endless rejections this was merely a flat tyre; we weren't going to let an ice queen get in the way of hitting the fairway with an Aussie snake charmer. So we kidnapped Nick and took him to golf.

In an afternoon that sounded like the start of a joke ('an Aussie, a Kiwi and a Canadian walk on to a golf course . . .') Rob got us lost more times than we cared to count, and drove down more one-way streets than I care to admit. To add to our woes it was rush hour. I started to panic that the golf course with the funny name wouldn't even be open. When at last we arrived, no one else was there and, by the looks of it, never had been. An old man in the pro shop took our money and told us to be careful of snakes.

'Yeah, right,' we said.

'No, be *careful* of snakes.'

Yet by the time we hit the first tee it was rabbits I was more concerned about. They were everywhere! Cute little entrée-sized rabbits. If there really *were* snakes, as the old guy had suggested, they weren't exactly doing a good job of keeping the buck-toothed little blighters at bay. In fact, I was beginning to wonder whether this was in fact a golf course *at all*. Situated in an old riverbed, this strange little piece of Arizona offered no fairways, just clumps of dirt in between greens, which coincidentally were hairier than a chimp's armpit. And just so our dinner didn't get lonely, the rabbits had company in the form of chattering geese, ducks, ground squirrels, geckos and lizards.

It was decided very early on that due to some very average golf, we would dedicate the remainder of the afternoon to throwing golf balls at rabbits. We didn't keep score after that.

Nick was good company and an open-minded sort of bloke. Having worked in Canada with the princess, he thought they should at least try out the States before they headed to Mexico. 'I didn't think I'd enjoy America at all,' he told us as we drove back to the Congress to drop him off and pick up our belongings. 'I didn't even want to come but I'm glad I did; I just had no idea Americans would be as kind as they are.'

'RIGHT,' ROB SAID, once we'd packed our bags into the trunk of the rental. 'As your agent I demand that we go and stay in a nice place and play a *proper* course.'

The Tucson sun had ensured we couldn't actually touch any part of the car without suffering serious burns. The steering wheel was on fire and the seats ablaze. It's always a trying time: jumping into a moving sauna, but having the fortitude to resist putting the window down, thereby allowing the air-con to kick in. I can never do it.

'Put your window up, we've got air-con!' my agent said.

'I'm frying here, I can barely think!' I opened the glove box to try to find a map. 'Aagghh!'

'What'd I tell ya — just don't touch anything, not until it kicks in.'

Rob was right — after 10 minutes the inside of the sedan was so cold you could have hung meat in there.

Nestled in the Catalina Mountain foothills on 93 acres of ancient Sonoran desert is the Ventana Canyon Resort. When Rob mentioned he wanted to stay in a nice place, never in a month of Sundays did I think he'd be talking about a 400-room retreat with two swimming pools, eight tennis courts, and five restaurants and lounges. He must have sold a few conveyer belts in the last few days. An hour later we found ourselves ordering cocktails and burritos by the pool, having handstand competitions *in* it and drying ourselves with hotel towels. (Some things you never grow out of.)

'Dad, what day are we leaving?' asked a six-year-old next to us.

'Tomorrow morning,' his father replied, throwing his son from his shoulders into the water.

'I've had 21 swims!'

The nonstop splashing, shenanigans and general excitement exhibited by the youngster next to us reminded me of our family holidays.

'You guys want to play a game?' Dad would ask.

'Yeah! Yeah! Yeah!'

'See how quickly you can run down the road and get me some cigarettes. I'll time ya.'

'Okay!'

When we returned he would say, 'Right, who wants to play another game?'

'Yeah! Yeah! Yeah!' we'd reply, almost too excited to control ourselves.

'How about we play a game called hopscotch?'

'Okay! Okay! How do you play it?'

'*Well*, how it works is, you hop around . . . while I drink Scotch.'

'Yay!'

Of course, one good thing about being an adult is you can do your own packing. From my experience this is one thing that fathers could be a *little* bit more relaxed about. Etched forever in my memory is Dad packing the car before we'd leave for the family holiday. Something must be written in stone that when one becomes a father, the boot of a car, much like the barbecue, is *your* domain. If you interrupted his routine, it would be at your own risk. The car was packed *specifically* and one had to act accordingly.

Whatever you do, don't arrive late on the scene (i.e. just before you're about to leave) and say, 'Dad, I need the Game Boy, it's just under the sleeping bag under the toilet bag under the tent under the pillow under the basket of fruit under the tennis racquets.'

As was the case in our family, we'd finally hit the road and have travelled only 10 kilometres before Mum would say, 'Wait, wait, wait, we have to go back, I've forgotten my make-up bag.'

Dad would turn around, drive home and we'd get the make-up bag.

'*Now* have you got everything?' he'd ask Mum once she'd retrieved her cosmetics.

'Of course I have,' Mum would say. 'I can't leave without my face on.'

Twenty kilometres down the road.

'No, no, no, sorry, turn the car around. We've forgotten the flowers.'

Dad would turn around, drive home and we'd get the flowers.

'Now, are you *sure* we've got everything?'

'Don't give *me* a hard time, would *you* have remembered the flowers?'

'Let's just start our holiday.'

Thirty kilometres down the road. Dad stops the car.

Mum asks, 'Why have we stopped the car?'

'I just want to be absolutely sure that we've got everything.'

'Of course we have. Now can we go, we're late.'

'No.'

'Why?'

'I think I've left the directions at home.'

Our room overlooked two magnificent golf courses surrounded by saguaro cactus forests. Men and women wearing matching plus fours and polo shirts were putting on the 18th green. They looked loaded, and suitably dressed. I looked at my dirty backpack lying on a beautifully made bed. Not a clean article of clothing to be seen.

'We're teeing off at 7.50 tomorrow,' said my agent, setting up his MP3 player.

'On . . . that course?'

'Yep.'

I felt like I was on the set of the movie *Tin Cup*. I'd seen these courses only on TV. The course was stunning, almost unreal, perfect. All I could think about was how much damage we'd soon be doing on those otherwise pristine fairways, and how many balls we'd lose. I just hoped like hell we wouldn't be teeing off with a couple of PGA pros.

Which is exactly how my agent and I acted for the next few hours. For us, this was the night before the US Masters. Rob got out his best shorts and ironed a shirt. I washed my one and only collared shirt in the bath, giving my clubs a quick wipe down at the same time (once a backpacker, always a backpacker). We then dined at the hotel restaurant overlooking the 18th hole, had a few drinks (lemonade) and talked strategy:

'So how many balls you taking out?'

'Heaps.'

'Take a few more.'

Then we said our golf prayers and went to bed.

Most pros get up early and do their exercises. *These* pros got up late and worried about embarrassing themselves on a world-class course. *Most* pros then have muesli and tea. *These* pros scoffed bacon and eggs and read the paper on the dunny. *Most* pros then go and hit a few balls on the driving range. *These* pros couldn't afford to.

It would be fair to say, the odds were firmly stacked against us right from the word go.

As we lined up in the pro shop to pay our fees we found ourselves surrounded by walking money boxes — men who, unlike us, weren't scared of the cost of green fees or playing a course you normally saw only on TV.

There were two tee times — 7.50 am or 12.50 pm. If you teed off at 7.50 you'd pay full price but not die of heatstroke. Alternatively, if you teed off at 12.50, it would be half the price but you may as well write out your will before you hit your first ball.

We were warned by numerous locals to drink *plenty* of water.

For 72 golfers to be able to tee off at the same time (7.50) we all had to start on different holes — a shotgun start. My agent and I were nervous. They were good; we were shit. Please God, let us hit the first ball okay.

Michael, a big burly hulk of a man and David, a dweeby little investment banker, were to be our partners for the day. We followed them in our cart to the fifth hole, which was to be our first tee.

Already it was hot, damn hot. Funnily enough, the ball which was going to do the most damage today wasn't a white one sitting at the bottom of my bag, but a bloody great big yellow one above, ready to punish fools for playing such a dumb game in such a dumb place.

We were now on the first tee. From what I could see (that is, when I wasn't wiping sweat from my eyebrows) there was a *lot* of rough and a *lot* of cacti. Unfortunately, most tees had a big dirt patch right in front that you had to hit over if you wanted to land on the fairway. This well-planned decoy was littered with various forms of desert flora and fauna. Throughout the day, my agent would manage to find this undesirable real estate with alarming regularity. And I would normally piss myself laughing.

'How many balls do you think we'll need out here?' I asked Michael, who seemed the more approachable of the two.

'Lots,' came the reply.

It was time to walk the walk. Michael did the honours, smashing his ball down the middle of the lush, carpet-like fairway. David then drove a spear through our hearts by doing the same. Two balls down the middle.

Enter the weekend hackers.

I didn't want to be last so walked up to my ball, closed my eyes and watched it veer into the woods. My agent, looking ever the pro in his crease-free, freshly ironed shirt, sliced his straight into the lake. It skimmed like a perfectly thrown stone, six or seven times, before it sank.

Our partners were on the green for two. Rob and I hoped our balls were still in Arizona. Michael was helping me find mine which, although not visible, had been spotted flying into some rather dense bush off the fairway.

'Do you really find rattlesnakes around here?' I asked, about to enter the undergrowth.

'Oh yeah,' said Michael.

'Really?' I could now *see* my ball, less than two metres away. 'What should I do?'

He paused.

'Just be careful.'

'Rob, put me down for a seven!'

I watched my agent tee off on the second and noted his back was already covered in sweat. Sixteen holes to go and already we were frying. Every couple of holes a medic disguised as a food lady would greet us in a golf cart and make sure we were drinking enough, filling a polystyrene cup with crushed ice while she was at it.

Michael, obviously having played here before, carried a large supply of towels with him to wipe off the sweat. Rob and I had to be content using our shirtsleeves. Of course, Rob *could* have just killed two birds with one stone by following his balls into the *water*, as that's where his second tee shot ended up as well.

I didn't laugh this time.

Because I followed him.

By the time we reached the fourth, my agent and I were playing so badly I was beginning to wish I'd never told Michael and David I was from New Zealand. A pattern had developed whereby they'd hit their balls down the middle, then spend the rest of the hole helping us find ours. We didn't have the heart to tell them we had only a few left.

You have to really hit a new low on a golf course if you have to ask your playing partner, a complete stranger up until a few hours ago, if you can use one of *his* balls. Clearly it was time to change the subject:

'Michael, I don't suppose you've ever been in the paper?'

'No, unfortunately I'm not a priest that likes little boys. That seems to be the only story around at the moment.'

I didn't feel I knew Michael well enough to ask whether he *knew* any

Saved by my agent – Ventana Canyon Resort, Tucson, Arizona

of these priests (or maybe that was a tad desperate, even for the front-page golfer). He did inform me that he'd recently been involved in a rather elaborate court case in Washington, however.

'Can you talk about it?' I asked.

'Your shot,' he said.

I'm sure if my agent and I played here again in a week's time we may have fared a little better — simple reason being that by then we may have acclimatised to the drop-dead-beautiful course. For the moment though, neither of us could concentrate. I gazed at 30-foot-high cacti (most of which had been peppered with golf ball-sized bullet holes from stray hackers like ourselves) while Rob marvelled at million-dollar homes perched precariously on rock faces overlooking the PGA-rated golf course, in a terrain that shouldn't even be possible.

The last hole of the day looked as if it were straight from one of those fictitious golfing calendars — a masterpiece that cost a million bucks to make 20 years ago. As we stood on the tee, high atop a steep overhang, we could see the flag was just a nine iron away. It was roosting on the middle of an island, surrounded by the famous Whaleback Rock with a view that stretched all the way to Mexico. How is anyone supposed to hit a ball after seeing *that*?

Unfortunately I *didn't*, overcooking mine, which ended up in the Esperero Canyon. Rob laughed; this time he was two feet from the pin.

My agent shot 120 and me, 90. We lost a lot of balls and a lot of weight. Thankfully we played a little better on the second nine, redeeming ourselves in the eyes of Michael and David.

At the conclusion of our round we soon discovered one of the problems of staying in a five-star resort: everyone thinks you're loaded.

'Can I take those bags for you, sir?'

'Here, let me open that door.'

'Can I wipe your arse?'

Of course, this would be no problem if they didn't *expect* anything for it, but they stand there afterwards with their hand out, like a child on those Feed Africa ads.

Having just made it back to the clubhouse I was having a yarn to one of the young club pros. Before I knew it his mate, who I hadn't even *seen*, had cleaned my clubs, shoes and golf bag. Now, did I *ask* for my clubs to be cleaned? No. More to the point, have they *ever* been cleaned? No. Do I have any spare change? Ask Rob.

The young club pro confirmed our reasons for not trying to retrieve our wayward balls.

'I've seen a rattler in the last week,' he told us. 'I was sweeping the steps by the pro shop with my headphones on and I felt something by my foot, so I kicked it. Turned out to be a rattler. I've seen about 50 this year. They're cold-blooded, so this is their favourite time of year.'

It may sound a very *unprofessional* thing to say, but Rob and I were very glad we hadn't made the cut. There were three reasons we wouldn't be joining the others out there chasing the US Masters:

1. We didn't have another collared shirt.

2. We couldn't afford it.

3. We couldn't have hit the bright lights of Tucson.

First, however, we would sit by the pool, sip lager and call Nick Dundee to ask whether he and his better half would care to join us for a swim.

He declined, informing us she'd prefer to do the washing (now *that's* living).

Our room had been cleaned when we returned (don't you just love hotels?) and the thought of checking out a new city had my agent and I bouncing off the walls. Unfortunately, our room fee didn't include a babysitter or crèche service so we decided to run a bath for Charleston and leave him there for the night. I'm sure it's illegal to leave such a young child in your room (especially in the bath) but he seemed happy enough.

Leaving the Ventana Canyon in our rental we came across a sizeable tarantula crossing the road right in front us. We stepped out into the pouring rain and caught a glimpse of something *else* we'd only ever seen on TV. As I leaned down to take an even closer look, Rob (predictably) did the old, run-your-fingers-along-the-top-of-your-mate's-shoulders trick. He thought it would scare the shit out of me.

It *absolutely* scared the shit out of me.

Home to the University of Arizona, Tucson has no shortage of live music and funky second-hand clothes stores. Rob and I indulged in some typical Arizonian food (sushi) and sampled a little of the local tipple (sake). Soon after that we stumbled, rather confusingly, upon the corner of First and First Streets.

Much like New Orleans, every bar in this town seemed to have live music. I was in paradise. From jazz to country to pop to gothic, thanks largely to its youthful inhabitants, Tucson could hardly be described as conventional. The night was to end on a rather raucous note with one student figuring if he smacked a bouncer over the head with a beer bottle, he'd get a free ride in a police car. He was right.

(Note: I have to say I could never live in Tucson, not because of the heat or because of stray beer bottles, but mainly because I can never *spell* it. I've been writing this chapter for over a week now and still, every time I punch out that bloody word, the spellchecker tells me I've stuffed up again. Go ahead, try it and spell it — I bet you get it wrong.

From now on I'm just going to spell it fenetically.

Not in Dictionary — suggestions:

phonetically

frenetically

fanatically
genetically
Oh, bugger off . . .)

We were in for a treat on our taxi journey back to the resort. Toosonne turned on one of the best thunderstorms I've ever witnessed — even better than New Orleans. The outside temperature (which was shown on the cab's dashboard) plummeted from 102 to 75 within 10 minutes. The thunderclaps sounded far-fetched — not real, just too loud. Normally, you'd be lucky to see a tiny sliver of lightning in the corner of the sky. This storm, however, lit up the sky, the town and the surrounding hills, making it look (if only for a split second) like it was one in the afternoon.

And it went on for hours, long into the night. TV ratings must take a dive on a night like this; who'd watch crappy old *Survivor* when you can watch the real deal?

I know for a fact that *dogs* don't like thunder but, sadly, I had no idea when it came to ducks. Stumbling in the door at 2 am we found Charleston in a foul mood. He was still in the tub but facing the wall, much like a scene from *Days of Our Lives*.

It's not easy being a parent, I'm sure you'll agree.

As we rose next morning we watched all those who were playing today putt on the 18th green. It was another scorcher in the desert and we had a small problem — no car. While my agent called a taxi I sneakily flogged a paper from the foyer and browsed the front page:

Monsoon fells saguaro

A 200-year-old saguaro survived one year after being transplanted to make way for a road, only to be felled by a summer storm Friday night. The cactus was moved 150 feet west of North La Canada Drive to make way for the road's extension last year.

It took Oro Valley planners a year to figure out what to do with the saguaro.

It took one of Arizona's leading horticulturalists six months to prepare the cactus for the move. And it took one hot day in the sun for a half-dozen workers and a 240-ton crane to move the 40-foot, 40-ton cactus.

Mother Nature was far more efficient, taking one evening thunderstorm near the Tortolita Mountains to topple the giant. A small, blackened patch of desert a couple of hundred feet west of the saguaro shows nature might have needed a couple of tries to bring the cactus down.

Holy hell, a 40-foot tall, 40-ton cactus! This I gotta see!

As they say, travelling is the best geography lesson. In the last few days I had learnt more about these magnificent succulents than I had in my entire life. Very much like spiders and rattlers, saguaros are protected, and if you have one in your yard taller than three feet, you need permission to cut it down. And those funny little appendages sprouting off either side are for balance. They're normally 50 to 75 years old before they even *start* growing them.

Class dismissed.

Dalton was our new taxi driver. Born in Nigeria, raised in Louisiana, he now lives in Twosonne and wonders why everyone in this city has a fireplace.

'I just don't understand — we're in the middle of the desert. I decorate mine with plants.'

'So you call yourself a local, do you Dalton?'

'Sure do,' he replied.

'Can you spell Twosonne?' I asked.

'Course I can, who can't?'

'Oh . . . just a few people I know . . . have a bit of trouble.'

Rob and I had a bad feeling about this cab ride. For a start, the inside of the car was incredibly clean, Dalton was dressed in a suit and tie and the air-con was working. Our fears were realised when we discovered a ride that should have cost less than 20 bucks was bumped up to 40.

'I'm not a taxi,' said Dalton, smiling. 'This is a hotel car.'

My agent was not happy, especially when the bag containing his MP3 player was run over by Dalton when he backed up and sped off. A quick scour of the flattened contents confirmed that while his toilet bag, sunglasses and conveyer belt pricing information were either squashed or covered in sunscreen, his music was just fine.

Oro Valley treasure gone

The cactus, moved last year to the north side of West Tangerine Road, lies broken after Friday's storm.

Monsoon fells saguaro

**It could survive
a transplant,
but not a storm**

*By Jennifer Sterba
and Jenna L. Bravo*

A 200-year-old saguaro survived one year after being transplanted to make way for a road ... only to be felled by a monsoon storm Friday night.

The cactus — on the north side of West Tangerine Road — was moved 150 feet west of the North La Cañada Drive intersection to make way for the road's extension last year.

It sent Oro Valley planners a year to figure out what to do with the saguaro. It took two of Arizona's leading horticulturalists six months to prepare the cactus for the move. And it took one hot ...

... day in the sun for a half-dozen workers and a 200-ton crane to move the 40-foot, 49-ton cactus.

Mother Nature was far more efficient, taking one evening thunderstorm near the Tortolita Mountains to topple the giant. A small, blackened patch of desert a couple hundred feet west of the saguaro shows nature might have needed a couple bites to bring the cactus down.

SEE SAGUARO / A12

Arizona Daily Star, *Tucson, Arizona*

We rested our weary heels in a quaint little coffee shop run by a pregnant woman. Unfortunately, the old grey matter also got a once-over. In a bid to avoid 'nappy-brain', our friend behind the counter ran what she called the Question of the Week. I don't know about you, but I hate these teasers:

A man lives on the tenth floor of a building . . . etc.

A man is lying dead in a field. Next to him is an unopened package . . . etc.

A man was walking downstairs in a building when he suddenly realised that his wife had just died. How?

I don't care. I didn't know him.

Yet some people adore these things. Maybe I hate them because I can never work them out?

'What is the largest sum of money you can have in coins and not be able to make change for a dollar?' Mother-to-be asked Rob, aware that I had pulled out.

Apparently the answer is $1.19 but I still don't get it, even as I write this six months later!

As it was too hot to be outside longer than a couple of minutes, we ducked into as many shops as we could, purchasing second-hand shirts we'd never wear once home and managing to find a seat in one of Twosonne's best-known cafés — only today, it stank of fat and grease. I was, however, most impressed with the menu:

> Please do not move our furniture around, stand on our chairs, mess with our lights or plug in your laptops.
>
> We will work with you — well, let us know what you need, we might work with you.
>
> Golden rule — this should be first or have its own page or something — we do not tolerate racism, sexism, ageism or any other isms. We reserve the right etc etc, we reserve so many rights.
>
> No panhandling, don't sit with pretty girls you don't know, don't drink the condiments, and no damn table-hopping.
>
> Be aware that any food may contain harmful bacteria, and forks are dangerous; don't put them in or near your eyes.
>
> Hot coffee can burn you. Chew your food before swallowing.
>
> Don't talk with your mouth full. Don't talk to a big man's girlfriend. Don't eat off the floor.

As we were about to pay I saw 20 or so well-produced colour leaflets announcing the death of a Mr Jason Lee Crosby on the counter. I thought this to be most strange: a death announcement next to breakfast specials.

'Why do you have these here?' I asked the teenage bloke serving us.

'Dunno, some people dropped it off.'

'Did he used to work here or something?'

'No, but the chef told me he killed himself at Denny's.'

What a place to end it all!

When Rob asked how we might fill in the remainder of the afternoon (before I flew out for Vegas) I offered what I felt was the perfect solution. Thankfully, he failed to see the evil plan I was concocting at the same time — to play golf with a dead 200-year-old.

For a few days now we had passed a madman who was selling sheepskin car covers on a major intersection. It was 110 degrees and he wasn't under cover. Today he caught our attention because he was swinging a golf club.

Matt, from a place called Drain in Oregon, normally sells Christmas trees and pumpkins but this year, for a change, he decided to come to Twosonne, midsummer, to sell wool.

'How can you *do* this?' we asked from the safety of the car, fearing for our lives if we got out.

'It's a dry heat!' he yelled, chipping a ball across an empty car park.

We'd heard this a lot in Toosonne. Hot heat, dry heat, wet heat, cold heat. Whatever it was it was a *too damn hot* heat.

'Believe it or not, a lot of people buy sheepskin covers in summer.'

'I don't believe it. You obviously play golf?'

'Yep. Played since I was 15, normally shoot in the low 90s.'

'Ever been in the paper?'

'Yep, but only for business.'

Matt couldn't play today as he had sheepskin covers to cook but he did tell us his favourite American was his eight-year-old daughter and his least favourite was Bill Clinton, 'for all the obvious reasons'.

Rob and I drove to the scene of the death and jumped the fence. The cactus appeared to be on private property. The 40-foot national treasure was knocked over by the roadside part of the property; the house, however, was about 100 metres away. I nervously walked up the long drive and knocked

A hell of a lie!

on the door. No answer. Two empty cars sat outside the garage. Horses roamed the back yard. I knocked again. No answer. I was all too well aware of trespassing laws in this part of the world.

And all too well aware that they could own a gun.

And be allowed to use it.

Bugger it, I thought, walking back as fast as I could in the heat. Only then did my agent recognise my ulterior motive. I popped the boot, grabbed my seven iron and posed with this incredible piece of nature. The 200-year-old cactus plays the front-page golfer. I'm pleased to report I beat him.

He played like a prick.

SO THERE I WAS on my connecting flight from Arizona to Las Vegas.

When the flying waiters turned up I ordered a Pepsi and felt a little guilty when the youthful-looking elderly Asian chap next to me ordered a club soda. Damn, so that's the trick, you healthy bugger, I thought. That was until he sneakily pulled out the biggest bottle of duty-free rye you've ever seen and proceeded to pour himself a couple of generous nips. Not long after that he was evicted somewhere over Flagstaff for bringing alcohol onto the flight.

Tough times.

DAY 26: LAS VEGAS, NEVADA

THE MOST IMPORTANT THING when flying into Las Vegas is having an appropriate compilation CD. Hence I had gone to great lengths to make one before I left New Zealand. I figured a bit of cheesy rock as well as a bit of Ol' Blue Eyes should do the trick. As we came in to land, Steve Miller, Bob Dylan, Bruce's 'Born in the USA' and AC/DC's 'Highway to Hell' rang through my ears as well as (judging by disparaging looks and an occasional shake of the head) those of my fellow passengers.

This was my second time in Vegas and, being August, one of the only times of the year locals would see clouds in the desert sky. Knowing Charleston and I were but two of the 35 million annual visitors to this crazy place only added to the excitement. I checked into the Sahara at midnight and rather stupidly decided to hit the infamous Strip to try to find something to eat. Bad move! What food wasn't sitting collecting mould in casino buffets was cold, fried and attainable only after waiting in line with broke-looking parents and kids that should have been in bed hours ago.

Come on, this is Vegas, lighten up!

One thing you do need in Vegas is a mate to share the madness with. I'm glad to say AJ, one of my best, was there. It was by sheer fluke that he was even in town, as he normally resides a few thousand miles away in London. Unfortunately (or fortunately, depending on how one tolerates hangovers), we only had the one night to play up like second-hand lawnmowers. It's fair to say golf was the last thing on our minds. A desire to hit a small white ball around the desert was quickly overtaken by the need for glitz, guns and gambling. Not that we had a gambling *problem*, it's just that outside temperatures didn't stop climbing until after 5 pm. And we were all too aware of heatstroke, a serious condition that mustn't be taken lightly. A preventative, we discovered, can be found in the form of piña coladas, cranberry vodkas and gyrating your hips to Snoop Doggy Dogg at first light in a stretch limo.

So in a city that shouldn't even have electricity; a city where logistically you shouldn't be able to flush a toilet; a city that boasts six kilometres of wondrous, evil, marriage-ending casinos, how did AJ and I try to make our first million?

Wheel of Fortune.

Wheel of bloody Fortune, I tell you — a game where you need about as much nous as if you were playing Snakes and Ladders or Monopoly. A game so embarrassingly simple it wouldn't be out of place in your local pub with a free meat pack hanging off the end of it.

But we loved it. And we won, dollars and dollars.

It all started in the older part of Vegas, Downtown, where a middle-aged Chinese croupier named Ming had us in the palm of her hand (well, she had free *drinks* in the palm of her hand anyway). Sadly, we spoke about as much Mandarin as Ming spoke English. This made explaining Wheel of Fortune very difficult. Fortunately, I'd won a few meat packs in my time.

As you should well know, the wheel sports the numbers 1, 2, 5, 10, 20 and 40. AJ and I quickly discovered (no help from Ming) that if I put $1 on 1 and 2, he could put $1 on 5 and 10. This would cover all bases (apart from 20 and 40, which never came up) and, most importantly, would make us look like big-time gamblers. And big-time gamblers equals free drinks.

Earlier in the evening we had discovered that taking a 'non-tipping stance' in Vegas was a very stupid thing to do. In New Zealand, nobody tips. You order your meal, you eat your meal, the waitress clears your plate, you pay for your meal and we all get on with our lives.

I personally hate tipping: it's the proverbial encore. You *know* the band is going to do one more song — they always do — but given the state of the audience, i.e. most have left and those that haven't aren't clapping, do they really deserve another? What incentive is there to work harder if you know you're going to get a tip anyway?

As you can probably guess, this kind of attitude made us no friends in a place like Vegas. In Bellagio (the Italian-influenced hotel featured in *Ocean's Eleven* and sporting $300 million worth of Cézanne and Picasso paintings) we found leather recliner chairs with our names written all over them, in front of massive TV screens showing baseball and horse racing. Making a $1 bet every half hour (what'd I tell ya, big-time rollers!) ensured us free drinks — in our case, very strong piña coladas. We didn't tip.

And we weren't served again at Bellagio.

We may not have been the smartest boys on the planet but by the time we got downtown we realised there must be some relationship between our empty pockets and our empty stomachs. Our waitress at Ming's place, an 85-year-old walking corpse (this is not being rude — she really was the living dead), similarly only came back if we tipped her.

So, Ming continued to spin the wheel and we continued to place bets on 1, 2, 5 and 10. Via pieces of paper with hand-drawn maps, we tried to explain to Ming where New Zealand lay on the globe. Talking to Ming — I should say *communicating* with Ming — was still difficult despite many vodkas. What took us completely by surprise was when she asked us, 'Do you speak English?' Poor lass. I'm sure she meant, 'Do you speak English in *New Zealand*', but the way it came out and her own atrocious, albeit humorous, attempt at the mother language in the previous half hour resulted in AJ and me losing it.

Despite our 'South Pacific, Wheel of Fortune, we have no idea when it comes to gambling' upbringing, we now moved up with the big boys. We were joined at a roulette table by an LA lesbian, a Virginian builder and Mario the Italian. We were a very friendly table, applauding when someone won and shouting drinks when someone lost (drinks were still free, via the walking corpse).

What happened between 3 and 7.30 am is a little hazy but I do know at 8 am, when we stepped out into the Nevada sunshine, there sat a gleaming white limo waiting for someone important. Luckily, they never turned up. We knocked the guy down from $50 to $15, jumped around in the back seat like a couple of five-year-olds, gyrated our hips to the sounds of Nelly and sipped imaginary champagne from empty glasses. We must have looked like a couple of prize fools.

Unfortunately, when we got back to our hotel, AJ now had a gambling problem. He needed one more roll before bed. Along with a short-term loan (one of many in this town I'm sure) he provided me with a Jim Beam for breakfast, which I would nurse for the next hour, managing to fish out and stomach only the accompanying ice cubes. When I wasn't nodding off, dribbling, or doing that embarrassing pre-slumber jolt, I was literally *handing over* AJ's hard-earned money to a croupier who was, by my standards anyway, far too savvy and alert to be robbing two pissed Kiwis.

Basically, I missed Ming.

The next morning we discovered that guns — big, semi-automatic, straight-from-the-extras-cupboard-in-*Miami-Vice* guns — are the perfect hangover cure. If you've ever been to Vegas, you'll know that hawkers take over the Strip and throw 'specials' and 'two for one' deals in your face all day long. However, among the usual 'Girls, Girls, Girls' and 'Margaritas by the Yard' brochures was an offer AJ and I could not refuse, even if it *did* make us both a little nervous. The brochure read, 'Fire an M-16, 50 rounds for 50 bucks.'

Now kids, let me just say here, you do have to be in a sound state of mind to handle such a dangerous weapon. It's not a toy and bad things can happen. This was a big decision. Collectively, though, we could not think of a better time to do it — after all, what *better* state of mind than the ones we currently possessed: AJ couldn't put his pants on and I wanted to throw up every time I opened my eyes. So, in the city that never sleeps, we had a far too short one and then went to blow shit up.

First, though, it was time to be tourists. Time to strap on our purple leisure suits, step out of reality and travel the world without a passport. New York, New York with its rollercoaster ripping right through the middle of it; The Mirage with its trademark volcano erupting every 20 minutes (and costing as much as the average family car each time); The Venetian with its 6000 rooms and gondolas gliding past Prada and Banana Republic stores, passengers being serenaded 'Volare' as they go. Popping off to Paris and looking up at a replica of the Eiffel Tower and believing, if just for a minute, that you really were next to the Seine, only to be deafened by the ding, ding, ding of slot machines as soon as you hit the foyer.

One couldn't help but wonder, with hotels like The Sahara (camels, rooms decorated in Moroccan motifs), The Luxor (pyramids, more camels), Bella-gio (Italian luxury and elegance), Excalibur (English castle, swords, knights), Paris (obvious), Venetian (same), Monte Carlo (European elegance), Alad-din (the mystical allure of 1001 Arabian Nights) and Caesar's Palace (ancient Rome), the only place or theme missing from this lot seemed to be that of Australia or New Zealand. However, I hasten to add, a hotel featuring flies, barbecues, some sheep and a game of rugby may not do much for the average American.

It may have been nerves, it may have been the fact that neither of us could string a sentence together; whatever the reason, without a feed of some description, arming ourselves with an M-16 was not the wisest thing to do. Hence, we discovered a casino whose only theme seemed to be destitute people scouring a cigarette-stained carpet in a bid to find quarters and, for just 99c, we piled our plates high with eggs, toast, hash browns, sausages and unlimited coffee. Unfortunately, we found out just how these places made their money when we tried to leave. Failing to find an exit (they really do hide them well and they are never signposted) we quickly became discouraged, exhausted and desperate.

Then spent $30 on a craps table.

THE GUN STORE was run by a fat redneck who had a pistol hanging off one side of his belt and ammo on the other. He looked like the kind of kid who was always getting beaten up at school, only now he could do something about it.

We stood at the glass counter and viewed guns as if they were candy. I needed a drink. I was parched and nervous, kind of like when you were a kid going on go-carts for the first time — only these so-called go-carts blew people's heads off and ruined societies. For a laugh, AJ said to the redneck (in his best Forrest Gump accent), 'Guns don't kill people. *People kill people.*' Rather worryingly the redneck not only agreed, he finished off the sentence for him.

The hangover was now spreading to my hands. They were shaking. I couldn't choose a gun. I wanted this to be over. Why had we come to this place? I wanted to shoot a gun, sure; I *wanted* to join my mates on the race-track and say I did it. I really did. I just didn't want to crash or mistake the brake for the accelerator or, worse still, get *beaten*.

'Do you always wear that?' I asked the redneck, pointing to the gun on his belt.

'Ask me if I've ever been mugged.'

'Have you ever been mugged?'

He shook his head. I think that was a rhetorical question.

After much discussion, AJ and I opted for the *Miami Vice*-inspired semi-automatic 9-millimetre Beretta handgun. The prospect of firing an M-16 rifle was tempting, though when we thought about it, and its value for money, i.e. throwing away 50 bucks in 10 seconds, we decided we may as well have been playing blackjack.

The redneck took our passport numbers, cracked a few in-jokes with his co-workers and took us through to the firing range. As we entered the range (which looked exactly like a golf driving range: no cages, no barriers, just a few Las Vegans popping in at lunchtime to let off a bit of steam), the redneck gave us the only instructions we were to be given that day: 'Keep the gun pointing to the ground at all times.'

'Even when we're shooting?' I was dying to ask.

Didn't. He had a gun.

AJ and I stood in our designated cubicles. The redneck had left. He was now sitting at his desk, behind a glass wall, feet up on the desk, smiling. My gun sat on the ledge. I didn't want to pick it up. It was a real gun. And it was sitting right there. We had been given 50 bullets in a cigarette packet-sized box. Fifty bullets. For a real gun. Which was sitting right there. AJ was white. These were big go-carts.

I knocked on the window and motioned for the redneck's assistance; he'd be working for his money today.

'Can you . . . ah . . . give us a hand loading these?' I asked him, very politely.

He loaded the bullets as if he were changing batteries in a TV remote, grunted, wiped his nose with his sleeve and made way for a smartly dressed man in a suit to take his own M-16 into a cubicle.

RAT-A-TAT-A-TAT-A-TAT-A-TAT!

Jesus Christ! In less than 10 seconds it was over. It was as if he'd come down to hit a couple of golf balls at lunch time. He wished us good day and left. Meanwhile, we stood there like the complete bunnies we were: two pacifists holding deadly weapons.

It was AJ who fired first.

BANG!

Fuck, that was loud.

BANG!

The redneck was smiling through the glass. My first empty shell hit AJ in the head.

BANG!

When my confidence rose I started quoting *Pulp Fiction* and *Dirty Harry* scenes.

'Go ahead, make my day.'

BANG!

'The path of the righteous man is beset on all sides with the iniquities of the selfish and the tyranny of evil men. And you will know my name is the Lord when I lay my vengeance upon thee.'

BANG! BANG! BANG!

It's a big buzz firing a gun, no doubt about that. You really have no idea how powerful they are until you hold one. Scary how they're carried around in glove boxes in these parts. I prefer maps and tissues myself.

CLEARLY, THE SOONER AJ returned to London the better. I had work to do and nutcases to find. Once he had left, I found a copy of *The Dallas Morning News* lying around the hotel. Although it was obvious this wasn't a local paper, it did feature an incredibly eccentric man I wanted to meet; luckily he didn't live in Dallas, but California.

David Ford was born in Stillwater, Oklahoma in 1968, grew up in Michigan and got his BFA in sculpture at Grand Valley State University. When he moved to New York he started working as a freelance artist and installer with a trucking firm.

And this is where he came up with the idea of Truck Drawings. Bored with long hauls driving across the country, David decided to get 99 water-filled plastic bottles with pencils attached to their tops, and hang them from a web of straps in the back of an empty truck. As the truck travels, the pendulums draw on paper mounted on the floor. In other words, you leave

New York with a bunch of bottles hanging from the ceiling, arrive in LA a couple of days later (after bumps, winds and turns), open the back door and voilà, you have a Jackson Pollock-esque piece of art.

Brilliant — give that man a Nobel Prize!

I was later to find out David had also done door- and window-generated drawings. A pencil strapped to the top of a door in his apartment added to the picture each time the door was opened. (Sure makes life more interesting, don't you think?) When asked in the *Dallas Morning News* article, 'What next?' David replied, 'I don't want to give anything away, but I'm thinking . . . escalator. I've also been doing drawings on the subway. Initially I was dangling a small pendulum from the ceiling of the train down to a small piece of paper on the floor, but this seemed to make people uneasy [*you think!*], especially when I used a bottle that I had partially filled with anti-freeze. I'm not sure if it was the attachment to the ceiling or the milky green liquid-filled bottle, but I really freaked a guy out on the C Train at 125th Street. So now I use a long tall cardboard box to hide it.'

I'd had enough difficulty tracking down *local* people from the front page — I'd be pushing shit uphill should I need to get hold of a Californian, who featured in a Dallas paper, for 18 holes in Las Vegas. But try I did. And failed. Dave Ford's wife, Lisa, although very amiable on the phone, thought the chances of him joining me in Vegas were slim, even if I did offer him a bed for the night. Besides, he didn't play golf. Which was a shame — I was kind of looking forward to doing some Golf Cart Drawings.

That evening I went back to Bellagio, ate healthily, drank healthily and reflected on the day (and trip) I'd had thus far. Suddenly it dawned on me that I had only a few days left. Before I knew it I'd be back in New Zealand, lying to friends and family about famous people I'd met and great courses I'd played. I'd been in the USA for 26 days and not found one front-page golfer. It was time to make amends. Finding a newspaper at all in this town was quite a struggle, though when you think about it, why would you come here and *read*? Thankfully, I found two at the front of the restaurant and went to work.

The *Las Vegas Sun* bore the sad news of Bob Hope's death. Its pages were filled with tributes, obituaries and memorable quotes. I'd like to think

228

Bob, of all people, would have appreciated the absurdity of my non-golfing odyssey. I hear he liked his golf. Rest in peace, old boy.

The family next to me, Mum, Dad and three kids, were squabbling. An old man, no doubt the grandfather, sat in silence at the head of the table. He had that rather strange bald patch old men get on their ankles from having worn socks their whole life. I don't know exactly when men acquire that hairless region, but much like the rings on a tree, you can normally tell a bloke has been around a while if he has it.

With arguments erupting over leftovers and who should pay for what, it was quite clear no one was enjoying themselves. Bed, no doubt, would be the best place for all involved. Unfortunately, the waiter saw a camera on the table and asked if the family would care to have their picture taken. The family smiled falsely. They put their arms around each other, hammed it up for the camera, resuming their barney only once the waiter had left. 'This is us in Vegas. Yeah, we had a wonderful time.'

Walking around Las Vegas at the hottest time of the year is not for the faint of heart. How families managed to do it (and there were no shortage of those) for hours on end made my head spin. Pounding the Strip from one end to the other had left me feeling like an injured footballer. Luckily an Iranian taxi driver came to my aid.

'So you moved from Iran to Vegas — that's quite a change,' I said to him once inside the cab. We were on our way to the Gold Coast casino to *hopefully* meet someone who, rather bizarrely, went by the name of Bobby, Jackie, Johnny, Marvin, Richard and Stevie.

'Hmmph, Las Vegas?' he replied. 'Work, sleep, work, sleep, it's all I do. Where you from?'

'New Zealand.'

'*I* want to move to New Zealand. You have a lot of sheeps, yes?'

'Forty-five million.'

'Hmmph, that's a lot of sheeps.'

'Fifteen for each person,' I said cheerfully. He didn't answer. Maybe it was my accent again. Admittedly, the longer I'd spent in this country and the slower I spoke, the more I achieved. However, that didn't seem to stop the odd hotel clerk checking me in as 'Destin' or 'Jeffrey'.

'Who's your favourite American?' I asked my Iranian friend, who was dodging pedestrians, going through red lights and waving his fist at anything that moved.

Again, no answer, then: 'Hmmph, I want to move to quiet place.'

BOBBY BROOKE, a man who was in the navy for 12 years, was often told he looked like Jackie Wilson. Bobby thought nothing of this until one day he was spotted singing in a karaoke bar. The producer in question urged him to quit his day job and concentrate on his craft. Now, some 10 years later, Bobby is a regular at the Gold Coast casino.

It was his face I saw on the front page, a face cleverly disguised with dark glasses, long beaded hair and a big grin, a face resembling none other than Mr Stevie Wonder.

'Hello, I'm looking for Stevie Wonder,' I said to the lady in the ticket booth once safely ensconced at Gold Coast. The respite from the heat was badly needed.

'You mean Bobby?' she said. 'He won't be here till tomorrow night.'

'Are you sure? If I come back tomorrow will he be performing?'

'Should be. Sometimes he plays two gigs in a day, but be warned, he's always late.'

The lady serving me was in her late forties. At the moment her hair colour of choice was purple, though it was plain to see she had once opted for blonde, red and, perhaps most naturally, grey. When I asked her the show times she produced a programme and licked her fingers to turn the page. She told me to be back at 7.45 the next evening.

She laughed at my lack of success in America. The newspaper article that featured Bobby also had other tragic lookalikes — namely Bette Midler, Frankie Valli and Cher.

'If there's anyone you should meet out of this lot, it's Bobby,' she reassured me. 'He's great, a wonderful man. You'll want to meet him.'

'Yes, but does he play *golf*?'

'I'm not quite sure — I think his wife might.'

Come morning I felt I deserved a swim. After all, I had nothing else to do all day. What newspapers I *had* managed to find in town were still flowing with Bob Hope tributes. It appeared a Stevie Wonder impersonator was my only hope.

Conversely, I wouldn't have said no to a game with the *real* guy. Reminds me of a joke Bud told me on the golf course in Jacksonville:

Stevie Wonder meets Tiger Woods and offers to give him a game.

'You're kidding, you really wanna play me?' says Tiger.

'Sure,' replies Stevie. 'How 'bout we make it interesting — play for $100,000.'

Tiger insists he couldn't possibly play him for money because of his sight handicap. But Stevie argues until he finally gets his own way.

'Okay,' Tiger says, 'it's your money, when do you wanna play?'

'Midnight.'

So it was with a fully rested mind and a towel draped over my shoulder that I did the smug 'I'm staying in a hotel, got my own key and everything' corridor saunter and strolled to the hotel's pool entrance. There I was confronted by a black security guard who sat on a stool that seemed far too high for any human being to be comfortable on. As her short, squat legs dangled in the air, you got the feeling she didn't want to look down. I couldn't help but think if we all needed to leave the building in a hurry, e.g. if there were a fire, she'd hardly be much help; we'd all have to give this poor woman a hand *down*.

'Pool's closed for the rest of the day,' she mumbled as I reached for the door.

'Closed? Why's that?'

'I don't know, some kid probably pooped in it.'

Oh great, it's 119 degrees out there and I can't take a swim because some kid binged out on jalapeños. Charming!

One of the challenges you're confronted with in Las Vegas is finding somewhere to *sit* (that is not in front of a pokie machine). Just as there are no clocks in the casinos, there seem to be no couches either. It's like they don't want you to stop. If you stop, you won't spend money. If you stop, you can think. Then again if you wanted to *stop*, you wouldn't have chosen Vegas in the first place.

At least there was solace in my room, which is where I headed after the poop debacle. There, waiting for me like a long-lost friend was a little red light flashing on my phone. Somebody loved me.

It turned out to be a bloke. True to his word, Mark, my golfing partner from Port Arthur, was in the midst of throwing away money at Treasure

Island. He asked if I'd care to join him for a drink; last time I looked the Pope was still Catholic.

Against my better judgement I then walked around town for the next seven hours. My knees and calves argued with each other. The desert sun was in a foul mood; thank God for 99-cent sunglasses. I even seriously considered scoffing one of those watered-down, out-of-the-packet, Margaritas by the Yard. The glasses they sat in were the size of antique vases. I wisely decided against it, saving myself another future garage-sale item.

Mark the Texan, complete with baseball cap and goatee, was waiting at Treasure Island. He was a little disappointed we hadn't managed to hook up for golf that morning. I wasn't — the round had cost him $160, a figure which was petty cash compared to what he spent at his home-away-from-home:

'I get to stay here for free as long as I gamble for six hours a day. That's no problem — I lost $1500 the other night but then won two grand. It's just so damn crowded at the moment, where are all these people *from*? There are kids everywhere. Who would bring their kids to this town — they can't drink, they can't gamble.'

When he wasn't collecting guns, Mark ran a trucking business.

'It's a dog-eat-dog world, man. There's always someone breathing down your neck wanting your money. I'm only 35, I've made a bit but I'm ready to retire. I want to start working on my house.'

Displaying the typical Texan trait of hospitality, Mark provided the first couple of rounds. However, on discovering that I was soon due at a show, he informed me I should be thinking about getting my skates on. But I was nervous. This was potentially my last chance of finding a golfing partner. Tomorrow I would be leaving for LA, then home. The waiter took our glasses. Mark paid. I could no longer delay the inevitable. Two men, one from the Southern states and one from the bottom of the earth, then shook hands. One headed for the roulette table, the other to find a Stevie Wonder lookalike.

For someone who enjoys their travel (and does so at every available opportunity) I have a shocking sense of direction. And I wasn't let down tonight. If I wasn't *already* late for the show, jumping on the wrong bus and going via Barbary Coast ensured I was even more so. Although, being late was good in one regard — I missed the complimentary buffet.

I ran to the ticket office outside the theatre and passed over my stub.

'Oh, I heard about you,' said the attendant. 'My supervisor mentioned you'd be coming tonight. We've reserved a table for you down the front.'

You'd think this would have been good news. Two feet from the stage *should* have been the best seat in the house, but you've got to remember this show was filled with (not you, Stevie) very poor, very tragic, wannabe impersonators. As generous a gesture as it seemed, one couldn't help but feel the solitary, plastic table an arm's length from the performers was akin to sitting in front of the comedian who spits every time he speaks. In other words, if people *wanted* to sit there they would have.

An important-looking man clutching a clipboard was showing a retired couple to their table. I asked him whether Bobby Brooke had arrived. 'Affirmative,' he said. I followed up by asking whether I'd be able to meet with him after the gig.

'You may be able to get him, but you'd better be quick.'

Having failed to grab a drink on the way in, and simultaneously ignoring red alerts from my bladder, I sat down feeling like a sixteen-year-old who'd been stood up. To make matters worse, everyone was staring at me. Ladies with blue hair pointed and whispered to their friends. Couples my age looked at me with sympathetic eyes. Even the performers befriended me: 'See the lonesome boy down the front,' they'd say backstage, 'the one with no drink and a sad look in his eye? He needs to be serenaded.'

The next hour and a half (was it really only that long?) seemed more drawn out than a train ride to El Paso. First Cher, then Janis Joplin, then Frankie Valli and Connie Francis. I'd like to say Bette Midler brought the house down. Sadly, it was more a case of her bringing the house *down*.

The only exceptions were Little Richard, Johnny Mathis and Stevie Wonder. (A credit to Bobby's ability was the fact that most people in the audience didn't know it was the same guy!) Or was that just me?

By the time the final curtain came down I felt as though I'd been tied to a stake and made to listen to every tragic hit that had ever been recorded. Had it not been for Bobby (and an albeit *slim* chance of a round of golf) I would have left before Nancy Sinatra had the chance to transform herself into one of the Supremes. As it was, and because I was the proverbial

Bobby Brooke (aka Stevie Wonder) and friends

rabbit in the headlights, I had to pretend I *too* was having the night of my life. I smiled, clapped and clenched my teeth (as well as my fists) through a torturous and tumultuous time. This was most definitely Vegas at its worst.

A less dedicated golfer would have headed straight for the bar at the conclusion but this one had work to do. Having just finished an encore of 'We Are The World' the impersonators had split backstage (and out of the city if they knew what was good for them) so I knew I had only a small window of time in which to find Bobby. Unfortunately, before I had a chance to enter the Entertainers Only door, the old ladies with blue hair were blocking my way, glaring at me like bouncers.

'We were all trying to figure out what it is you *do*,' one said.

'Pardon?' I was desperately trying to look past their boofy hairdos to see whether Bobby was out the back. What a disaster it would be if after all this time (and having to sit through that god-awful show) I didn't even get to meet the man I'd been tracking down due to four widows with punk-coloured mops.

'We saw you taking pictures — do you work for *The New York Times*?' another asked, breathing gin all over me.

'No, no, I don't,' I said, finally spying Bobby, who was now coming down the stairs. (Honestly, the way I was behaving you'd think I was trying to track down Michael Jackson or the Prime Minister of England. I had to remember, this wasn't *the* Stevie Wonder but merely a man who dressed up as him, sang his songs and got cheap laughs by banging into things on stage. But I was too far gone to realise that. After 28 days I had finally gone mad. I had convinced myself if I didn't meet Bobby tonight I would fall off the earth. I was exhausted, hungry, thirsty and delirious. 'We Are The World' had tipped me over the edge.

The room was now empty. Cleaners were putting chairs on tables and emptying ashtrays. I noticed a very good-looking woman standing with two men in suits. They were the only others in the room. Confident they weren't here to grab a prime seat for tomorrow's show, I guessed that she was Bobby's wife. She couldn't see a problem with me talking with her hubby. The suits, however, were in a hurry and had a meeting planned with Stevie Wonder themselves.

Wearing civilian clothing, my potential golfing partner was now standing right beside us. He was wearing a grin only performers can. Obviously pleased another night was over and he hadn't died a slow death (unlike his peers), Bobby appeared light-headed, incoherent, 10-foot-tall and bulletproof.

But best of all, genuine.

I was now so parched, the temptation of finding empty glasses and sucking the remaining ice did not seem so far-fetched. I dragged Bobby to the nearest bar, ordered two Cokes and downed mine before he had a chance to ask why I was dating myself.

Bobby was a warm, humble man who was obviously happy with his new career. If it hadn't have been for that producer drinking where he was singing, he may have been looking for more work at sea.

'I remember that producer asking me, how long have you been singing? I said, I don't sing. He said, you do now. I then performed in Hawaii for a year, singing doo-wop and shedding weight. I was 75 pounds heavier then.'

I guzzled the ice cubes from the bottom of my glass, realising too late I had stuffed too many in my mouth. Just as I was about to relieve my teeth of an impromptu cryogenic experience, an all-too-efficient waiter removed my glass. Consequently, I had to grimace, frown and bounce the frozen blocks around in my mouth until the dust settled. Bobby probably just thought I was crying.

Dreams are free and Bobby's was to one day front his own one-man comedy musical revue. After his apprenticeship in Hawaii he realised he loved being on stage, but like most aspiring musos, the last thing he wanted to be was someone else.

'Someone once told me, you look just like Jackie Wilson. I said I don't want to be an impersonator. But then I changed my mind. I ended up imitating Jackie for a number of years. Then one day I was told the crowd don't want Jackie any more — if you don't try someone else you'll be fired. In the end I imitated Little Richard, Marvin Gaye and Johnny Mathis.'

Fortunately, the ice in my mouth had liquefied and I no longer had to pull strange faces.

'Surely,' I said, 'one of those guys would be your favourite American?'

'Jackie Wilson was a major influence, definitely. I love the way he performs and his voice is phenomenal. But as far as my favourite human being goes, I'd have to say Stevie Wonder.'

I was feeling good. Granted, the past 27 days had been a struggle but I'd met many new friends and seen a part of the world I wanted to visit again.

Everything (bar the golf) had worked out just fine. I didn't get shot. I

A Stevie Wonder impersonator and someone who needs a good sleep

wasn't mugged. I survived Amtrak cheeseburgers. I learnt that you could watch *Chicago* with the sound down and still know what was going on.

And that's what any trip is: a movie, a script. Just like the movies the main character (me) faces constant challenges (no golf, no sense of direction, no patience) but through this, he grows. And if any movie is to become a classic it needs a happy ending. Or a game of golf at least. That's why I was so confident sitting next to Bobby, a man who was not only fit and toned, but obviously sporty. (Are you telling me he lost 75 pounds without once hitting a golf ball?)

It was time to throw caution to the wind. This was now death or glory and Bobby, whether he knew it or not, was my happy ending.

'Bobby, I have one more day in Las Vegas. How 'bout we go and play some golf tomorrow?'

'Golf?'

'Yeah, how 'bout it? You and me.'

'I don't . . .'

Don't say it.

'I've never . . .'

Please no, it's my last night.

'I'm not . . .'

Come on!

'My wife plays.'

'Your wife, the wife I met? The wife over there?' I pointed to the table where she was sitting, drinking mineral water with two talent agents. 'How 'bout we all go out? Doesn't matter that you don't play, you could just come for a laugh.'

'Sorry, Justin, that's not possible.'

'Okay, how about I just play your wife?'

He laughed. 'We're going home tomorrow.'

'Home? Well that's no problem! Where's home — Vegas, Hoover Dam, Carson City? 'Cos you just have to name it, Bobby, I'll go there! Where's home?'

'Hawaii.'

MIDNIGHT HAD ROLLED AROUND and I hadn't turned into a pumpkin, more a squashed, worn-out melon. Bobby and I shook hands and exchanged email addresses and I jumped on the (correct) bus back to the Strip. Vegas was still pumping when I made my way back to the Sahara. As I pounded the footpath bed-bound I realised I hadn't had time to eat since breakfast. A spotty manager at Burger King informed me they didn't take Visa. You'd think I'd asked to pay with coconuts or a recently slaughtered goat.

Lying in bed with a throbbing head and a restless mind I reflected on my night. Playing golf with Stevie Wonder impersonators' wives in Hawaii — now *there* was a top idea for a TV programme. Funding, though, for such a jaunt may be an issue. It would have to be educational — or at least have lots of bikini shots.

I wasn't going to go out for lunch the next day as my flight was leaving early afternoon. I'd planned to just eat whatever was on the plane but it was my last day in Vegas and I wanted to leave in style.

Bill (another one!), looking like some sort of mad scientist with wispy hair, false teeth and bulging eyes, ran the downstairs bar at the casino. He recommended I try the margarita. It would have been rude to decline so I accepted.

Virginia, a French girl, also pulled up a pew, doubling the order.

'How can you *work* in this town?' she asked Bill.

'What do you mean?'

'I hate it here. It's crazy, everyone thinks about money all the time. I've never been so lonely as I have here. I thought I would have met lots of people but they are all in such a hurry.'

'You've got to have a sense of humour in Vegas,' I said.

'But it must be a horrible place to live.'

'*I* live here,' said Bill. 'And I raised two kids here — very well-rounded individuals.'

'How can you raise kids here?'

'Its all a state of mind. You can either gamble or never put your hand in your pocket. Las Vegas has the least amount of alcoholics in the world. Why? Because you can get a drink any time, night or day. In California the bars close at 2 am. Last call, at 1.30, everyone's chucking it down their neck as fast as they can.'

I asked Bill if he drank.

'Used to,' he said smashing a glass fresh out of the dishwasher. It was obviously one of those days. 'Used to be a very bad drunk. Used to make some bad decisions but, unlike gamblers in Vegas, I never blamed it on the fact that I was drunk. I used to drink anything I could get my hands on, even drank whisky out of the bottle as a kid. I gave up 10 years back; my wife still drinks like a fish.'

He forgot to charge me for the second margarita.

Bill had been married for 40 years. His son now lives in London and his daughter in Seattle. 'They couldn't get out of here fast enough.'

'Who's the rich bloke who built the Mirage and Bellagio, Bill?' I asked.

'Steve Wynn is the man you're thinking of. That man cost me my job when he knocked down one of the casinos I worked at, but I still admire him. He hates being outdone — he built the Mirage, then Treasure Island, then Bellagio. He's designing a new one as we speak — 6000 rooms. It's going to be the largest hotel in the world.'

'You see, in France,' Virginia whispered while Bill was pouring another margarita, 'we *look after* our people. That man would *not* have to be working at that age. I see so many people working here after the age of 65. It's sad.'

Virginia left, thanking us for changing her view of Las Vegas. When she had gone, Bill, who'd obviously heard her talk about his working life, told me, 'I've made some choices in my life, not to be a doctor or a scientist or whatever. I wanted to be a family man, live the simple life and work in a bar. I'm happy — this is me.'

DAY 28: LAX, LOS ANGELES, CALIFORNIA

BACK TO WHERE it all started.

Twenty-eight days ago I sat in this very place thanking the god of golf that I wouldn't have to chance upon André Agassi, Donald Rumsfeld or Buddy Hackett. Now I sat here wondering how on earth I was to fill in seven hours at an airport that resembled Delhi's railway station. (LAX may be one of the *so-called* hubs of the world, but that doesn't stop it from being one big toilet.)

I passed on the opportunity to buy the *LA Times*, instead opting for a small provincial music rag. That it was free may have had some bearing on it, but you just never know where you're going to find some luck.

On the front page of this otherwise nondescript weekly was an article featuring the Californian musician Beth Hart and her new album. I had interviewed Beth back home when I used to do a show on a music TV channel. I then met her a year later when she popped in to see us at Classic Hits, a radio station I work for in Auckland.

With only hours left in America, I deemed this to indeed be a very fine piece of luck. Was *this* to be my happy ending?

Would I *finally* hit a course with a Front Pager?

The next hour of my life was spent calling newspaper editors, record companies and managers. A plentiful supply of Post-it Notes with phone numbers written on them hung from any available surface in the phone booth.

'No, I have no idea how you'd get hold of her.'

'Do you have an appointment?'

'Are you an agent?'

The god of *golf* may not have given me the time of day on this trip but the god of good luck was definitely in full swing. Eventually I tracked down David, Beth's manager, and he put me in touch with the woman herself.

My memories of Beth were that she was mad as an ox but had a heart the size of Texas. When she'd come into the radio station she'd kissed and hugged everyone, sung so loud (and with such feeling) we thought she was going to burst into tears, and played guitar till her strings snapped.

Nothing, we discovered, was done in halves when it came to Miss Hart.

The fact that I'd met her didn't stop me feeling nervous when I finally had her phone number in my hand. David had told me she was currently at her home in California.

I dialled. The phone rang. I felt like I was calling to ask her out.

'Beth, it's Justin Brown speaking, I met you in New Zealand last time you came out.'

'Oh man, I was so wasted that trip I hardly remember a thing.'

Despite this rather indifferent (some would say disastrous) start to a conversation, the rest of our exchange went swimmingly and Beth was most amiable. Furthermore she offered me a string of words I'd been striving to hear all over America:

'I'd love to play golf with you —'

'Really!' I hollered, first looking at my watch, then my boarding pass.

'Yeah, but —'

There's that word again.

'— I'm about to fly out of the country and promote my new album.'

The proverbial fairway yanked from beneath my feet.

'Where are you going to promote your album?'

'I'm going back to New Zealand.'

'What?'

'New Zealand.'

'Oh my God, that's where I'm going, tonight!'

'Do you still *live* there?'

'Sure I do.'

'I thought you mentioned you were living in the States now?'

'No, I'm only here on holiday. I'm flying out this evening.'

'Well, why don't we just play *there*?' she asked in a tone suggesting we should have just thought of that in the first place.

'It's a date,' I said. 'Just out of interest, Beth, would you really have played with me today if you weren't taking off to promote your album?'

'Sure I would have, sounds like fun. I fucking *love* golf.'

What'd I tell you? She's mad, up for anything.

New Zealanders are a pretty laid-back lot. In other countries, when the ground crew announce that the plane is now free to board, people jump up from their seats, stampede over anything in their way and bowl down the ramp to the waiting ship. New Zealanders, on the other hand, as was the case with the Kiwis waiting on the day I was in the lounge, have to be told *three* times before they'll finally get off their chuffs.

I totally support this lazy approach to boarding. I mean, who really cares whether rows 28 to 65 have safely found their seats and have started the slow decline to deep vein thrombosis? Do you ever get off the flight at the other end and boast that you had 10 minutes *more* on board than the loser next to you?

So, having smugly boarded at the last second (in doing so finding no room to put my bags, upsetting an old man by needing to get to a window seat and getting a bollocking from a steward who told me I should have embarked when told), I sat down, kicked off my shoes and waved goodbye to America.

As I looked east I thought of Bobby and Otis, Mr Nut and Miss Iva. I thought about Jack and his 'gators, Bonkers and his new wife, Kermit and his deep-fried turkey necks.

I thought about New York City and the beaches of Georgia, the sunflowers of Port Arthur and the thunderstorms of Jacksonville. I thought about firing a gun and playing golf with a cactus, befriending a duck and never meeting Ernie K-Doe.

But mostly I thought about home.

And a shower.

And my own bed.

And a salad.

And not having to ask for directions.

And driving my car.

And never looking at a train again.

And calling my mates for a game of golf.

Without having to find them in the paper.

And planning another trip to America.

The smog of LA quickly disappeared once we flew over the Channel Islands — the high barren cliffs and deep blue sea reminiscent of what the coast of the City of Angels must have once looked like before ten million people (and their cars) arrived.

Unlike I am on normal flights, I was asleep within the hour. To give an indication of how totally demented, deranged and drained my quest had made me, two hours in to the flight I woke up in a cold sweat thinking I had missed my stop.

Then I remembered I was on a plane.

Twelve hours later I was at the other end of the planet, in my own bed — head spinning, mind overloaded and washing walking out the door. Summer to winter, right-hand drive to left, Texan drawl to New Zealand twang.

As I was due back at work in just three days, I called John, the music director at Classic Hits, and asked whether he knew when Beth Hart would be arriving in the country. In my excitement 12 hours previous I had forgotten to take down Miss Hart's details. Thankfully New Zealand is a small place — if a star is in town everyone knows about it.

SITTING IN THE FOYER of the Stamford Plaza in Auckland (where Bill Clinton stayed when he toured these parts; don't tell Red from Port Arthur) two days later, I ordered a coffee (didn't tip) and waited for Beth Hart and her boyfriend Scotty. It's always an anxious time waiting to meet famous people. Will they be rude? Will they take one look at you and decide they want to be somewhere — anywhere — else? Ironically, often the bigger the star the more pleasant they are. It's the upstart little boy bands you've got to be wary of. In the end, though, no matter how many albums they've sold, no matter how many movies they've been in, no matter how much money they have in their wallet, they're all just like you and me — blood and bones.

Times like this I always think of the quote about the sage who carried a piece of paper in one pocket on which was written, 'All in the world was made for my use.' In his other pocket was a note that said, 'I am only food for the worms.'

Even so, I was still nervous.

To be honest, also a little hungover. A mate I hadn't seen in years had thought it a good idea to drink and watch rugby till the wee small hours. Hence I was a little late turning up to the hotel. Thankfully Beth, being a rock star and all, was also fashionably so — although, *unlike* your quintessential celebrity, the first thing she did was apologise.

'I'm *so* sorry I'm late,' she professed.

She was five minutes overdue, if that.

Scotty, Beth's boyfriend, was with her. Built like a truck but just a gentle giant, he was an ex-roadie for the likes of Ozzy Osbourne, The Scorpions, Motley Crue and Live. He is now Beth's partner, best friend and most avid supporter.

Keeping in the New Zealand tradition, Beth and Scotty informed me that they'd bungee jumped the day before — Scotty, twice.

'Excellent,' I said, 'so a game of golf will literally be a walk in the park for you both.'

'Are you serious about this golf?' Scotty asked me, maybe concerned that Beth was going to incur some sort of bizarre injury. She was due to play a concert in Auckland the next night, as well as front an LA showcase the next week.

'Beth, you don't even *like* golf,' he said, putting his arm around her.

'I fucking *love* golf!' she said, throwing her arms around like an Italian.

'No you don't,' said Scotty.

'Yes I do, I fucking *love* golf! Can we play? Can we, can we, can we? I haven't played since I was five. And even then I only played one shot. Is there a course around here?'

'Sure, there's one just around the corner,' I said.

And I know exactly how to get there.

And I have a car.

A real car with wheels and a stereo.

And we don't need Amtrak or a taxi driver.

And I've got a map in the glove box.

But we won't be needing that.

'Anyway,' Scotty said to Beth, 'you don't have to play a *whole* round. Why don't we just go out there and see how it goes?'

'No, I want to play!' she demanded.

'Okay, okay,' he said.

I could hardly contain myself. It was really going to happen. A real game of golf with a real Front Pager.

Unfortunately, my home town could not have turned on a shittier day. This was *not* one for the travel brochures. Playing golf in this would be akin to being on the set of the movie *Blade Runner* (did you notice it never stopped raining in that flick?). Wind, rain and hail would accompany us for this historic game — in contrast to the Tucson desert.

Meanwhile we had to get Beth kitted out. Normally, for a game in such atrocious conditions at such an average golf course (hey, gimme a break, I'd spent all my money in America) I wouldn't bother with new balls or nice attire. But Beth just *had* to have the shoes.

'You don't need golf shoes, Beth,' Scotty insisted. 'Your trainers are fine.'

'I want golf shoes!' she protested.

'But you don't need them.'

'I *want* them!'

'Okay.'

'Do you have a jacket, Beth?' I asked.

'No, do you think I'll need one?'

Auckland is famous for its four seasons in one day, meaning just because it is fine *now* doesn't mean it will be in five minutes. Let's just say no jacket may mean doggy paddling back to the car park.

'No,' I said, 'you should be fine.'

Minutes later we were on the first tee. Finally. After 30 days of travel I had a game lined up with someone from the front page. If I wasn't so jet lagged I would have been ecstatic. Beth, looking more like a snowboarder than a Tiger Woods clone in her beanie, wraparound glasses and cargo pants, couldn't stop going on about her new shoes.

'These are *so* cool!' she said, admiring them from every possible angle. 'I want to wear them home.'

First tee with Beth Hart, Auckland

Scotty, on the other hand, opted for the very sensible black leather jacket with the not-so-sensible matching suede shoes.

Then it started to rain. And rain and rain. What I thought were permanent water hazards were actually puddles. The sun made a brief appearance, then split just as you took your jacket off. (What's the saying: 'If you want to make it rain, go home and put your shorts on'?) Only one other Aucklander was mad enough to be out on a day like this; he was later to give up after the second hole.

'Shouldn't we be wearing helmets?' Beth asked when I demonstrated how to place a ball on the tee.

'Helmets, why?' I asked.

'Well, a ball might hit us.'

'No, Beth, golf's not that dangerous.'

'But there's balls flying everywhere and we might get hit!'

'Trust me, Beth, there's no one out there. I think we'll be all right.'

Beth lined up her shot, swung five or six times and eventually got it off the tee — but not before she took a good slice of Auckland with it. Scotty hooked his ball into the bushes and mine rolled about 10 feet. As we strolled through the slush Scotty's black shoes soon transformed into mud-caked clogs, quickly becoming three times their original size and twice as heavy. Even the pros didn't have to put up with these conditions.

But I couldn't stop — not now, not after such a long journey trying to get a game. Besides, Beth seemed to be enjoying herself.

'So where do I go now?' she asked from the other side of the fairway.

'Go for the green flag down the end.'

Beth continued to play down the left side while Scotty and I favoured the trees to the right. Once in a while she would hit her ball over to us, maybe because she was a social creature or maybe, as I thought, because she'd never hit a golf ball in her life. To retrieve her ball she would then sprint across the fairway, hide behind her golf cart and shelter herself from oncoming white dimpled missiles (as if there really *were* any).

'Oh my God, oh my God,' she would yell, wishing for the helmet she'd left behind.

This scene, I tell you, although on a golf course, was straight from *Tour of Duty*.

Eventually Scotty and I made it to within a few metres of the first green. Just as we were lining up our approach shots Beth peered over my shoulder.

'I got 13,' she said, water dripping from her nose.

'Thirteen?' I said. 'But we're not even on the green yet, how can you have 13?'

'I finished the hole.'

'How can you have finished the hole? We're not even on the green yet.'

'You said to go for the green flag.'

'Yeah, *that* green flag,' I said pointing to the green in front of us.

Bless her, she'd been playing the wrong hole.

I was dying to know, given the conditions and given this god-awful sport, what Beth actually thought of it all so far. After all, here I was taking a rock star around a well-below-par golf course, while she was probably contracting hypothermia.

'What do you think of it so far, Beth?'

'I love it, I think it's *wonderful*. I even like the rain and hiding in the bushes.'

'What did you get on the first hole again?' I asked, scorecard at the ready.

'I got 13 but I would have gotten less if I had known that it was the *red* flag and not the *green* flag.'

'So you went for the wrong hole?'

'I went for the wrong hole, but in the hole I was *going* for I got 13.'

'Right.'

Obviously, the sound of running water (in the form of constant rain) was playing havoc with Beth's *own* plumbing. As we reached the second hole she asked, 'How come they don't have bathrooms out here?'

'They do, but they're on the eighth hole.'

'You reckon I can pee in those bushes?'

'Sure.'

'Can you tell Scotty I've just gone for a pee?'

'Okay.'

'Oh, this is so much fun!'

She ran into the shrubs while I cleaned my balls.

Beth was in New Zealand promoting her fourth album, *Leave the Light On*. Having made her first record when she was 19 that 'never did anything' and her second two years later with the company Atlantic, she finally hit the big time with 'LA Song' off *Screaming for my Supper*.

'I got off Atlantic 'cos I was a tripper,' she told me once she returned from the ladies. 'They didn't want me any more.'

'So tell us about when "LA Song" was going off. Did you know it was going to be such a big hit?'

'I thought that it had a good chance because of the way the label reacted to it, and the way audiences received it before I released it. It was a reaction I'd never received before. I just had a feeling something was going to go. It was an awesome but totally bittersweet experience. Awesome in that I opened for loads of artists: Bryan Adams, Jewel, Alanis Morissette. But it was totally hard. It was all around a pretty busy tour but I can't remember a lot of it 'cos I was taking a lot of pills.'

'Are you pissed off about that?'

'Yeah I am, 'cos I missed out on a big part of my life from drinking and using drugs. I mean, God, I've got so much to be grateful for to be clean today. And to have a *life* today. I could have easily died, you know.'

'Were you on Jay Leno?'

'Yeah, but that was not a very good experience. That was right at the end and I was really, really messed up.'

'And you met David Letterman?'

'Yeah, I was on his show. I met him and sat with him. That man has loads of charisma.'

We were now playing the second hole and the weather had become a joke. There was no solace, even if you sat under the trees, which is where Beth was to be found, huddled in a ball like a small child, beanie soaked, gloves too wet to even hold a club.

'This is great fun!' she said quite seriously. 'How many more holes after this?'

'Well, we can play nine or we can play 18,' I said, pulling up my collar, quickly tiring of excess water dripping from the pine trees above.

Meantime Scotty's leather jacket resembled a very sick, very drenched animal — and smelt like one too.

'Great!' Beth squealed. 'I love this, I'm gonna join a country club when I get home. I'm gonna get right into this game. I love it, I *love* golf. It's kinda like fishing!'

Beth's analogy had Scotty and me in fits of laughter for the entire hole. When he managed to clear the tears he noticed that his better half wasn't looking too well.

'We'd better get you inside, Beth, you don't wanna get sick. You've got a showcase on Wednesday, remember?'

'No, I'm fine,' she said bashing a ball to nowhere in particular.

That's the girl, a dedicated golfer. The rain was now just unbearable; every part of our bodies was soaked. I'm surprised the greens didn't just float away in protest. I looked up and wondered how there could *possibly* be any more rain up there.

None of this, however, seemed to bother Miss Hart in the slightest. To prove this she agonised (in the pouring rain) over a one-inch putt for two or three minutes. She was really concentrating. After all, this putt was the difference between 12 and 13.

'Come on, Beth,' Scotty yelled above the wind. 'Just putt it, we're getting wet here!'

Beth was now struggling. Her zigzag approach to utilising fairways was doing her no favours, and even though she was getting her money's worth (or mine) by using as much of the course as possible, she was wearing herself out in the process. Like most players new to the game, she just couldn't *understand* why the ball wasn't flying directly from the tee into the hole.

Plus we were all still getting drenched.

If I wasn't playing with such a superstar, I would have stopped long ago.

'Beth,' Scotty said, wiping his muddy shoes on the grass much like a dog does after it's done its business. 'Do you want me to get your jacket from the car?'

'Oh, would you?'

'Sure I will.'

'Oh, I love you, Scotty.'

Beth and I hid under the nearest tree and awaited her sweetheart's return. Despite the wet she managed to light a cigarette. 'I got another 13 there.'

'Oh, okay.' I thought we'd actually flagged the idea of scoring but Beth had other plans. Getting less than 13 was obviously one of them.

'So how long have you and Scotty been seeing each other?'

'Let me see, I've known Scotty since I was 27 and a half. I'm now 31 and a half and we've been fooling around since I was 28 and a half.'

'You're a great team.'

'He's the bomb, man, I love him . . . he is so sweet,' she giggled. 'I mean, he went to get my coat 'cos it's so cold and rainy, isn't that nice?'

'So what are you two doing after New Zealand?'

'We're gonna go home and we're gonna relax for a bit. Then Scotty's gonna go and get our dog. She's with my mum right now. I love my mum. And *I'm* gonna make him meatloaf and tomato gravy and chocolate cream pie from scratch!'

'The dog?'

'No, Scotty!' she laughed.

The meatloaf lover returned, carrying an item that would mean Beth wouldn't have to swim back to the car after all. Scotty, too, had been in the music business for a while, having been a drum tech for Motley Crue. 'That was the best job on tour,' he'd say, grinning. He also worked with Ozzy Osbourne: 'a very clever man, a lot funnier in real life than on TV'. And the Scorpions: 'They'd walk 100 metres out of their way just to say hello', and Live: 'absolute wankers'.

Meanwhile, the new and improved, *drier* Beth was again about as far off the fairway as anyone could get. In a bid to help her game she was singing one of her hit songs, a slightly adjusted version to suit the circumstances. 'LA Song', which goes 'Man I gotta get out of this town', was altered, quite fittingly, to 'Man I gotta get outta this *rough*'.

Hearing Beth sing at any available moment made me wonder whether she wanted to perform forever.

'I love music, I want to do it all my life. I just want to sing, even if it's a tiny little bar, locally. It doesn't have to be big-scale stuff. The most important thing I learned over the years is that it can't be about money. If it's about money, go get a job. It has to be about the music.'

Ironically, just 10 days before, I had visited the small town in Texas where one of Beth's biggest idols hailed from. Janis Joplin — born in Port Arthur in 1943, died in 1970, and played by Beth Hart in *Love, Janis*, a stage musical based on the late, great singer at the Village Theater in New York, 2001.

'I take it then that you're happiest on stage?'

'I wouldn't say I'm *happiest* on stage, I just have one of the best, favourite times on stage.'

'What do you do after a gig?'

'If I've had a good gig and I've done a good job everything is amazing. Food tastes better than it ever has, conversations sound better, taking a hot bath feels great. I feel like I've done a hard day's work.'

'Do you always have to go for that euphoria?'

'I don't feel like I'm *going* for the euphoria. My job, after all, is to get up and do a good show for the audience. My job is to make everyone feel good.'

'And how do you know it's *been* good?'

'You can tell when people are into it, man, you can feel it. I can tell if they're lying.'

'You're a beautiful lady, Beth.'

'I love you, man.'

Beth is one of the most down-to-earth people I've ever met. There's no bullshit, no hidden agendas. Despite living in the *Oprah* and *Jerry Springer* age, not many people can *truly* wear their heart on their sleeve and make a career out of it. Basically, Beth is honest.

And that's rare for a golfer.

We were now halfway down the fourth. Knowing that Beth was keen to keep score I asked what she'd managed on the previous hole.

'Well that last hole, I think I got a little chipped up 'cos of the rain and 'cos it was cold. It took me 17 times. So that's 13, 13 and 17 so far. This time, though, I'm going to do a little better.' She clubbed her ball into knee-length grass. '*This* time I predict 10 or less.'

Sadly, any hopes of Beth's single-figure dream were dashed 100 metres out from the fourth green. As she was about to hit her god-knows-how-many-th shot, she hollered out to Scotty, who was getting *his* money's worth in a sand trap.

'Scotty, I can't,' Beth said, desperation in her voice.

'You can't what?'

'I can't play my shot!'

'Why not?'

She pointed to the green. Four ducks were waddling across our target. Much like other animals you sometimes see on courses (sheep and goats) these little fellas couldn't have given two hoots that a Top Flite 4 had their name on it.

'Beth,' Scott yelled, *still* in the bunker, 'you haven't hit the ball further than 10 yards all day — I hardly think you're going to trouble a couple of ducks!'

Despite her willingness to take out the Masters, Beth just *had* to stop after five holes. Having had a work-out that morning (and due for another that night) she really was toast. Scotty asked if we could call it a day.

I dropped him and Beth off at their hotel.

In my own car.

In my own city.

Without the help of a map.

They waved goodbye and disappeared through the automatic doors of the Stamford Plaza, Scotty with his muddy shoes in one hand and his sweetheart holding the other. A couple that were paddling their canoes in tandem, heading off to start a new chapter in their life. And me, a chapter in mine.

Quite ironic, don't you think, that I ventured all the way across America to get that elusive game of golf when I *could* have achieved it just driving 10 minutes down the road?

But where's the fun in that?

For sales, editorial information, subsidiary rights information
or a catalog, please write or phone or e-mail
iPicturebooks
1230 Park Avenue, 9a
New York, NY 10128, US
Sales: 1-800-68-BRICK
Tel: 212-427-7139
www.BrickTowerPress.com
email: bricktower@aol.com

www.Ingram.com